10/2/13

Northeast Argentina & Uruguay

Ben Box

Credits

Footprint credits

Editor: Alan Murphy
Production and layout: Jen Haddington
Maps: Kevin Feeney

Managing Director: Andy Riddle
Content Director: Patrick Dawson
Publisher: Alan Murphy
Publishing Managers: Felicity Laughton,
Jo Williams, Nicola Gibbs
Marketing and Partnerships Director:
Liz Harper
Marketing Executive: Liz Eyles
Trade Product Manager: Diane McEntee
Account Managers: Paul Bew, Tania Ross
Trade Product Co-ordinator: Kirsty Holmes
Advertising: Renu Sibal, Elizabeth Taylor

Photography credits
Front cover: Dreamstime
Back cover: Dreamstime

Printed in Great Britain by CPI Antony Rowe,
Chippenham, Wiltshire

Every effort has been made to ensure that
the facts in this guidebook are accurate.
However, travellers should still obtain advice
from consulates, airlines, etc about travel
and visa requirements before travelling.
The authors and publishers cannot
accept responsibility for any loss, injury or
inconvenience however caused.

Publishing information
Footprint *Focus Northeast Argentina
& Uruguay*
1st edition
© Footprint Handbooks Ltd
May 2012

ISBN: 978 1 908206 66 4
CIP DATA: A catalogue record for this book is
available from the British Library

® Footprint Handbooks and the Footprint
mark are a registered trademark of Footprint
Handbooks Ltd

Published by Footprints
6 Riverside Court
Lower Bristol Road
Bath BA2 3DZ, UK
T +44 (0)1225 469141
F +44 (0)1225 469461
footprinttravelguides.com

Distributed in the USA by Globe Pequot
Press, Guilford, Connecticut

The content of Footprint *Focus
Northeast Argentina & Uruguay* has
been extracted from Footprint's
South American Handbook, which was
researched and written by Ben Box.

Titles available in the Footprint *Focus* range

Latin America	UK RRP	US RRP
Bahia & Salvador	£7.99	$11.95
Brazilian Amazon	£7.99	$11.95
Brazilian Pantanal	£6.99	$9.95
Buenos Aires & Pampas	£7.99	$11.95
Cartagena & Caribbean Coast	£7.99	$11.95
Costa Rica	£8.99	$12.95
Cuzco, La Paz & Lake Titicaca	£8.99	$12.95
El Salvador	£5.99	$8.95
Guadalajara & Pacific Coast	£6.99	$9.95
Guatemala	£8.99	$12.95
Guyana, Guyane & Suriname	£5.99	$8.95
Havana	£6.99	$9.95
Honduras	£7.99	$11.95
Nicaragua	£7.99	$11.95
Northeast Argentina & Uruguay	£8.99	$12.95
Paraguay	£5.99	$8.95
Quito & Galápagos Islands	£7.99	$11.95
Recife & Northeast Brazil	£7.99	$11.95
Rio de Janeiro	£8.99	$12.95
São Paulo	£5.99	$8.95
Uruguay	£6.99	$9.95
Venezuela	£8.99	$12.95
Yucatán Peninsula	£6.99	$9.95

Asia	UK RRP	US RRP
Angkor Wat	£5.99	$8.95
Bali & Lombok	£8.99	$12.95
Chennai & Tamil Nadu	£8.99	$12.95
Chiang Mai & Northern Thailand	£7.99	$11.95
Goa	£6.99	$9.95
Gulf of Thailand	£8.99	$12.95
Hanoi & Northern Vietnam	£8.99	$12.95
Ho Chi Minh City & Mekong Delta	£7.99	$11.95
Java	£7.99	$11.95
Kerala	£7.99	$11.95
Kolkata & West Bengal	£5.99	$8.95
Mumbai & Gujarat	£8.99	$12.95

Africa & Middle East	UK RRP	US RRP
Beirut	£6.99	$9.95
Cairo & Nile Delta	£8.99	$12.95
Damascus	£5.99	$8.95
Durban & KwaZulu Natal	£8.99	$12.95
Fès & Northern Morocco	£8.99	$12.95
Jerusalem	£8.99	$12.95
Johannesburg & Kruger National Park	£7.99	$11.95
Kenya's Beaches	£8.99	$12.95
Kilimanjaro & Northern Tanzania	£8.99	$12.95
Luxor to Aswan	£8.99	$12.95
Nairobi & Rift Valley	£7.99	$11.95
Red Sea & Sinai	£7.99	$11.95
Zanzibar & Pemba	£7.99	$11.95

Europe	UK RRP	US RRP
Bilbao & Basque Region	£6.99	$9.95
Brittany West Coast	£7.99	$11.95
Cádiz & Costa de la Luz	£6.99	$9.95
Granada & Sierra Nevada	£6.99	$9.95
Languedoc: Carcassonne to Montpellier	£7.99	$11.95
Málaga	£5.99	$8.95
Marseille & Western Provence	£7.99	$11.95
Orkney & Shetland Islands	£5.99	$8.95
Santander & Picos de Europa	£7.99	$11.95
Sardinia: Alghero & the North	£7.99	$11.95
Sardinia: Cagliari & the South	£7.99	$11.95
Seville	£5.99	$8.95
Sicily: Palermo & the Northwest	£7.99	$11.95
Sicily: Catania & the Southeast	£7.99	$11.95
Siena & Southern Tuscany	£7.99	$11.95
Sorrento, Capri & Amalfi Coast	£6.99	$9.95
Skye & Outer Hebrides	£6.99	$9.95
Verona & Lake Garda	£7.99	$11.95

North America	UK RRP	US RRP
Vancouver & Rockies	£8.99	$12.95

Australasia	UK RRP	US RRP
Brisbane & Queensland	£8.99	$12.95
Perth	£7.99	$11.95

For the latest books, e-books and a wealth of travel information, visit us at: www.footprinttravelguides.com.

 footprinttravelguides.com

 Join us on facebook for the latest travel news, product releases, offers and amazing competitions: www.facebook.com/footprintbooks

Contents

Northeast Argentina

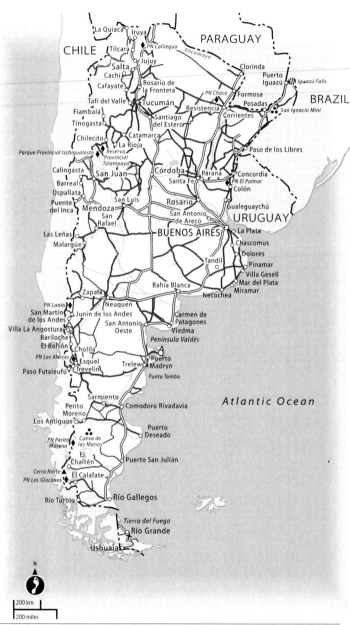

6 • Northeast Argentina

Buenos Aires is one of the world's great cities: grand baroque buildings to rival Paris, theatres and cinemas to rival London, and restaurants, shops and bars to rival New York. But the atmosphere is uniquely Argentine, from the steak sizzling on your plate in a crowded *parrilla* to the tango being danced in the romantic *milongas*. If the city's thrills become too intense, take a train up the coast to the pretty colonial suburb of San Isidro or take a boat through the lush jungly delta, where you can hide away in a cabin, or retreat to a luxury estancia until you're ready for your next round of shopping, eating and dancing.

Of all Argentina's many natural wonders, there is nothing quite as spectacular as Iguazú Falls. With a magical setting in subtropical rainforest, alive with birdsong and the constant dancing of butterflies, the colossal Garganta del Diablo waterfall at their centre is an unforgettable sight. Take a boat underneath and get drenched in the spray, or stroll along nature trails at first light. Along red earth roads through emerald green vegetation, Misiones province holds other delights: Jesuit missions unearthed from the jungle at San Ignacio, and the extraordinary Saltos de Moconá, 3000 m of falls more horizontal than vertical. The northeast's rich culture stems from its indigenous peoples, the Guaraní and Wichí, who produce beautiful art. The gently meandering rivers set the pace, giving the land its lush vegetation and generating in its people a charming laid-back warmth.

Planning your trip

Where to go

The capital, **Buenos Aires**, has a distinctly European feel, its architecture mostly 20th-century, though earlier buildings can be found in San Telmo district. The central docklands have been reclaimed as an upmarket restaurant zone and the Palermo district, with its large parks and its cobbled streets, has become increasingly sought after. Across the Río de la Plata is Uruguay; just northwest is Tigre, on the Paraná delta, a popular spot for escaping the city; to the southeast are coastal resorts which lead round to the most famous, Mar del Plata. West and south of Buenos Aires stretch the grasslands of the pampas, home of the *gaucho* (cowboy) and large estancias.

In the **Northeast**, the wetlands of Mesopotamia have some interesting wildlife zones, such as the Iberá Marshes, and in Misiones province, sandwiched between Brazil and Paraguay, are ruined Jesuit missions, principally San Ignacio Miní. The highlight of this region are the magnificent Iguazú Falls, usually included on any itinerary to the country.

Best time to visit Argentina

From mid-December to the end of February, Buenos Aires can be oppressively hot and humid, with temperatures of 27-35°C (80-95°F) and an average humidity of 70%. The city virtually shuts down in late December and early January as people escape on holiday. Autumn can be a good time to visit and spring in Buenos Aires (September-October) is often very pleasant. The Northeast is best visited in winter when it is cooler and drier.

Getting to Argentina

Air

Most South American countries have direct flights from Europe. In many cases, though, the choice of departure point is limited to Madrid and one or two other cities (Paris or Amsterdam, for instance). Argentina, Brazil and Venezuela have the most options: France, Germany, Italy, Spain and the UK (although the last named not to Venezuela). Where there are no direct flights connections can be made in the USA (Miami, or other gateways), Buenos Aires, Rio de Janeiro or São Paulo. Main US gateways are Miami, Houston, Dallas, Atlanta and New York. On the west coast, Los Angeles has flights to several South American cities. If buying airline tickets routed through the USA, check that US taxes are included in the price. Flights from Canada are mostly via the USA. Likewise, flights from Australia and New Zealand are best through Los Angeles, except for the Qantas/LAN route from Sydney and Auckland to Santiago, and Qantas' route to Buenos Aires. Within Latin America there is plenty of choice on local carriers and some connections on US or European airlines.

Prices and discounts

Most airlines offer discounted fares on scheduled flights through agencies who specialize in this type of fare. If you buy discounted air tickets always check the reservation with the airline concerned to make sure the flight still exists. Also remember the IATA airlines' schedules change in March and October each year, so if you're going to be away a long time it's best to leave return flight coupons open. Peak times are 7 December-15 January and 10 July-10September. If you intend travelling during those times, book as far ahead as possible. Between February and May and September and November special offers may be available.

Transport in Argentina

Air

Internal air services are run by **Aerolíneas Argentinas** (AR), T0810-222 86527, *www. aerolineas.com.ar*, **Austral** (part of AR), **LAN**, T0810-999 9526, within Chile 600-526 2000, www.lan.com, and the army airline **LADE** (in Patagonia, Buenos Aires, Córdoba and Paraná), T0810-810 5233, *www.lade.com.ar*. **Sol**, T0810-444 4765, flies to cities in the centre of the country and, in summer, to coastal destinations and Uruguay, *www.sol.com. ar*. **Andes**, T0810-777-26337, based in Salta, flies between Buenos Aires and Salta, Jujuy, Córdoba and Puerto Madryn, *www.andesonline.com*. Some airlines operate during the high season, or are air taxis on a semi-regular schedule. Children under three travel free. **LADE** flights are heavily booked in advance, especially for travel during December and January. Check in two hours before flight to avoid being 'bumped off' from over-booking. Meals are rarely served on internal flights.

Bus

Long-distance buses are by far the cheapest way to get around. *Coche cama* or *semi cama* buses between cities are more expensive than the *comunes*, but well worth the extra money for the comfort of reclining seats and fewer stops. Fares vary according to time of year: advance booking is essential Dec-Mar, Easter, Jul and long weekends. The biggest bus companies are: **Andesmar**, T0261-429 5095/011-6385 3031, www.andes mar. com; **Chevallier**, T011-4000 5255, www.nuevachevallier.com.ar; **Flecha Bus**, T011-4000 5200, www.flechabus.com.ar; **Vía Bariloche**, T0800-333 7575, www.viabariloche.com.ar. Long-distance tickets can be bought online or over the phone. At www.plataforma10.com you can check bus prices and times and book tickets throughout the country. Student discounts of 20% are sometimes available – always ask. Buses have strong a/c, even more so in summer; take a sweater for night journeys. On long-distance journeys, meals are included. They can vary from a sandwich to a full meal, so take your own food and drink for longer journeys. Note that luggage is handled by *maleteros*, who expect a tip (US$0.35 or less is acceptable) though many Argentines refuse to pay.

Taxi

Licensed taxis known as *Radio Taxi* can be hired on the street, or can be called in advance and are safer. *Remise* is a system common in smaller towns where there are no taxis, where car and driver are booked from an office and operate with a fixed fare (more than a regular taxi).

Maps

Several road maps are available including those of the **ACA** (best and most up-to-date), **Firestone** (also accurate and detailed), and **Automapa**, www.automapa.com.ar (regional maps, Michelin-style, high quality). Topographical maps are issued by the **Instituto Geográfico Nacional** ① *Av Cabildo 381, Buenos Aires, T011-4576 5576 (one block from Subte Ministro Carranza, Line D, or take bus 152), Mon-Fri 0800-1400, www.ign.gob.ar*. Some maps may be bought online, others only at the office. Take passport if buying maps there. For walkers, the **Sendas y Bosques** series is recommended: 1:200,000, laminated and easy to read, with good books containing English summaries; www.guiasendasybosques.com.ar.

Where to stay in Argentina

Hotels
Bills in four- and five-star hotels are normally quoted without 21% VAT. It is often cheaper to book a room at reception, rather than over the internet. If you pay in cash (pesos) you may get a discount, but more expensive hotels sometimes have more expensive rates for non-Argentines. For a selection of B&Bs see www.bedandbreakfast.com/argentina.html.

Camping
Camping is very popular in Argentina and there are many superbly situated sites, most with good services, whether municipal or private. Some are family-oriented, others are livelier and frequented by younger people (often near beaches), with partying till the small hours. Prices vary widely, from US$5 to US$10 per tent, sometimes less. Camping is almost impossible in Buenos Aires and many sites are closed off-season. Camping is allowed at the side of major highways (not recommended) and in most national parks (not at Iguazú Falls). Many ACA and YPF service stations have an area for campers (usually free) and owners are generally friendly, but ask first. Most service stations have hot showers. A list of camping sites is available from ACA (for members, but easily available) and from the national tourist office in Buenos Aires. *Guía del Acampante* is published annually, on sale at kiosks, and has a full list of campsites and discount vouchers.

If you are planning a long trip, renting a motorhome is a good idea. A recommended company is **Andean Roads Motorhome Rentals**, see www.andeanroads.com for contact details and rates (starting at US$110-195 per day for three weeks or more).

Estancias
An estancia is, generally speaking, a farm, but the term covers a wide variety of establishments. Accommodation for visitors is often pricey but most estancias are extremely comfortable and offer an insight into traditional country life. In the pampas, they tend to be cattle ranches extending for thousands of hectares; in the west they often have vineyards; northeastern estancias border swamps; those in Patagonia are sheep farms at the foot of the mountains or beside lakes. Many also offer horse riding, fishing, canoeing or birdwatching. The national tourist board website lists all estancias: www.turismo.gov.ar (rural tourism page). For some suggestions see the sites listed on www.caminodelgaucho. com.ar (for the Pampas) and www.estanciasdesantacruz.com (for Santa Cruz province).

Youth hostels
Hostelling International Argentina ① *Florida 835 pb, Buenos Aires, T011-4511 8723, www. hostels.org.ar*, offers discounts to cardholders at their 70 hostels throughout Argentina, buses and backpacker tours. An HI card in Argentina costs US$20. See www.hostelsuites. com for a chain of HI-affiliated hostels. Very few Argentine hostels have laundry facilities, which may be tricky if you have expensive trekking gear to wash carefully. HI hostels sometimes give vouchers for 10% discount on bus tickets.

Price codes

Where to stay

$$$$ over US$150   **$$$** US$66-150

$$ US$30-65   **$** under US$30

Prices include taxes and service charge, but not meals. They are based on a double room, except in the **$** range, where prices are almost always per person.

Restaurants

$$$ over US$20   **$$** US$8-20   **$** under US$8

Prices refer to the cost of a two-course meal, not including drinks.

Food and drink in Argentina

Restaurants

The cheapest option is always to have the set lunch as a main meal of the day and then find cheap, wholesome snacks for breakfast and supper. Also good value are *tenedor libre* restaurants – eat all you want for a fixed price. Most Argentines have lunch around 1300; restaurants open 1200-1500. Out of Buenos Aires, offices close for lunch and a siesta 1200-1700. Around 1700, many people go to a *confitería* for tea, sandwiches and cakes, but cafés are open all day except 0200-0600 and get busy from 2400. Dinner often begins at 2200 or 2230, and restaurants rarely open before 2100. Nightclubs open at 2400, but usually only get busy around 0200.

Food

National dishes are based upon plentiful supplies of beef. Many dishes are distinctive and excellent; the *asado*, a roast cooked on an open fire or grill; *puchero*, a stew, very good indeed; *bife a caballo*, steak topped with a fried egg; the *carbonada* (onions, tomatoes, minced beef), particularly good in Buenos Aires; *churrasco*, a thick grilled steak; *parrillada*, a mixed grill (usually enough for two or more people), mainly roast meat, offal, and sausages; *chorizos* (including *morcilla*, blood sausage), though do not confuse this with *bife de chorizo*, which is a rump steak (*bife* de lomo is fillet steak). A *choripán* is a roll with a *chorizo* inside. *Empanada* is a tasty meat pie; *empanadas de humita* are filled with a thick paste of cooked corn/maize, onions, cheese and flour *Milanesa de pollo* (breaded, boneless chicken) is usually good value. Also popular is *milanesa*, a breaded veal cutlet. *Ñoquis* (gnocchi), potato dumplings normally served with meat and tomato sauce, are tasty and often the cheapest item on the menu; they are also a good vegetarian option when served with either *al tuco* or Argentine roquefort (note that a few places only serve them on the 29th of the month, when you should put a coin under your plate for luck). *Locro* is a thick stew made of maize, white beans, beef, sausages, pumpkin and herbs. Pizzas come in all sorts of exotic flavours, both savoury and sweet. **Note** Extras such as chips, *puré* (mashed potato) are ordered and served separately, and are not cheap. Almost uniquely in Latin America, salads are quite safe. A popular sweet is *dulce de leche* (especially from Chascomús), milk and sugar evaporated to a pale, soft fudge. Other popular desserts are *almendrado* (ice cream rolled in crushed almonds), *dulce de batata* (sweet potato preserve), *dulce de* *membrillo* (quince preserve), *dulce de zapallo* (pumpkin in syrup); these *dulces* are often eaten with cheese. *Postre Balcarce*, a cream and meringue cake and *alfajores*, wheat-flour biscuits filled with *dulce de leche* or apricot jam, are very popular. Note that *al natural* in reference to fruit means canned without sugar (fresh fruit is *al fresco*) Croissants (known as *media lunas*) are in two varieties: *de grasa* (dry) and *de manteca* (rich and fluffy). For local recipes (in Spanish) *Las comidas de mi pueblo*, by Margarita Palacios, is recommended. *Food and Drink in Argentina*, by Dereck Foster and Richard Tripp (Aromas y Sabores, 2003) is a pocket guide to eating customs, food terminology, wines and all things culinary.

Drink

It is best not to drink tap water; in the main cities it is safe, but often heavily chlorinated. Never drink tap water in the northwest, where it is notoriously poor. It is usual to drink soda or mineral water at restaurants, and many Argentines mix it with cheap wine and with ice. Argentine wines (including champagnes, both charmat and champenoise) are sound in all price ranges. The ordinary *vinos de la casa*, or *comunes* are wholesome and relatively cheap; the reds are better than the whites. The local beers, mainly lager, are quite acceptable. In restaurants wines are quite expensive. Hard liquor is relatively cheap, except for imported whisky. *Clericó* is a white-wine *sangría* drunk in summer. **Vineyards** can be visited in Mendoza and San Juan provinces and Cafayate (in the south of Salta province). If invited to drink *mate* (pronounced 'mattay'), always accept; it's the essential Argentine drink, usually shared as a social ritual between friends or colleagues. *Mate* is a stimulating green tea made from the yerba mate plant, slightly bitter in taste, drunk from a cup or seasoned gourd through a silver, perforated straw.

Essentials A-Z

Accident and emergency
Police T101. If robbed or attacked, call the tourist police, **Comisaría del Turista**, Av Corrientes 436, Buenos Aires, T011-4346 5748 (24 hrs) or T0800-999 5000, turista@ policiafederal.gov.ar, English, Italian, French, Portuguese, Japanese and Ukrainian spoken. Fire department, T100. Urgent medical service T107.

Electricity
220 volts (and 110 too in some hotels), 50 cycles, AC, European Continental-type plugs in old buildings, Australian 3-pin flat-type in the new. Adaptors can be purchased locally for either type (ie from new 3-pin to old 2-pin and vice-versa).

Embassies and consulates
For all Argentine embassies and consulates abroad and for all foreign embassies and consulates in Argentina, see http:// embassy.goabroad.com.

Festivals in Argentina
No work may be done on the national holidays (1 Jan, Good Fri, 1 May, 25 May, 10 Jun, 20 Jun, 9 Jul, 17 Aug, 12 Oct and 25 Dec) except where specifically established by law. There are limited bus services on 25 and 31 Dec. On Holy Thu and 8 Dec employers decide whether their employees should work, but banks and public offices are closed. Banks are also closed on 31 Dec. There are gaucho parades in San Antonio de Areco (110 km from Buenos Aires) and throughout Argentina, with fabulous displays of horsemanship and with traditional music, on the days leading up to the Día de la Tradición, 10 Nov. On 30 Dec there is a ticker-tape tradition in downtown Buenos Aires: it snows paper and the crowds stuff passing cars and buses with long streamers.

Money → *US$1 = AR$4.43 (May 2012)*
The currency is the Argentine peso (ARS or $, we use AR$), divided into 100 centavos. Peso notes in circulation: 2, 5, 10, 20, 50 and 100. Coins in circulation: 5, 10, 25 and 50 centavos, 1 and 2 pesos. Foreigners are advised to use credit cards to withdraw cash, where possible, and for making payments. You will need to show your passport with your card. If paying in cash, do so in pesos. Dollars and euros may be accepted in some tourist centres. US dollar bills are often scanned electronically for forgeries. ATMs (known as *cajeros automáticos*) can be found in every town and city. They are usually Banelco or Link, accepting international cards, but they impose withdrawal and daily limits and a charge per transaction (limits change, check on arrival). Some international banks' machines may have fewer restrictions, but you need to check each machine, eg Citibank (www.argentina.citibank.com, changes only Citicorps TCs cheques, no commission), HSBC (www.hsbc.com.ar). Commission is usually 2-4%, but check with your card's issuing company. Changing TCs can involve lengthy bureaucracy and high commission charges, usually 10%. When crossing a land border into Argentina, make sure you have some Argentine currency as there are normally no facilities at the border. Note that fake notes circulate, mostly AR$100, 20 and 10. Check that the green numbers showing the value of the note (on the left hand top corner) shimmer; that there is a watermark; that there is a continuous line from the top of the note to the bottom about ¾ of the way along.

Credit cards
Visa, MasterCard, American Express and Diners Club cards are all widely accepted in the major cities and provincial capitals,

though less so outside these. There is a high surcharge on credit card transactions in many establishments; many hotels offer reductions for cash. For lost or stolen cards: MasterCard T0800-555 0507, Visa T0800-666 0171.

Cost of travelling

You can find comfortable accommodation with a private bathroom and breakfast for around US$50 for 2 people, while a good dinner in the average restaurant will be around US$10-15 pp. Prices are cheaper away from the main touristy areas: El Calafate, Ushuaia and Buenos Aires can be particularly pricey. For travellers on a budget, hostels usually cost between US$10-20 pp in a shared dorm. A cheap breakfast costs US$4 and set meals at lunchtime about US$7, US$8 in Buenos Aires. Fares on long-distance buses increase annually and very long journeys are quite expensive. Even so it's worth splashing out an extra 20% for coche cama service on overnight journeys. Domestic flight prices were raised by 20% in February 2012. The average cost of internet use is US$0.50-2 per hr.

Opening hours

Banks, government offices and businesses are not open on Sat. Normal office hours are 0800-1300 in summer, 1000-1500 in winter. Some businesses open again in the evening, 1700-2000. **Banks:** opening hours vary according to city and sometimes according to the season. **Post offices:** stamps on sale during working days 0800-2000 but 0900-1300 on Sat. **Shops:** 0900-1800, many close at 1300 on Sat. Outside the main cities many close for at 1300 the daily afternoon siesta, reopening at about 1700.

Post

Post offices: Correo Central, Correos Argentinos, Sarmiento y Alem, Buenos Aires, T4891 9191, www.correoargentino.

com.ar, Mon-Fri 0800-2000, Sat 1000-1300. Poste Restante (only to/from national destinations) on ground floor. Philatelic section open Mon-Fri 1000-1800, T5550 5176. **Centro Postal Internacional**, for all parcels over 2 kg for mailing abroad, at Av Comodoro Py y Antártida Argentina, near Retiro station, Buenos Aires, helpful, many languages spoken, packing materials available, Mon-Fri 1000-1700. **UPS**, www. ups.com. **DHL**, www.dhl.com.ar. **FedEx**, www.fedex.com/ar/

Safety

Argentina is generally a safe country. All travellers should, however, remain on their guard in big cities, especially Buenos Aires, where petty crime is a problem. Robbery, sometimes violent, and trickery do occur.

Tax
Airport taxes

By law airport taxes must be included in the price of your air ticket. When in transit from one international flight to another, you may be obliged to pass through immigration and customs, have your passport stamped. There is a 5% tax on the purchase of air tickets.

VAT/IVA

21%; VAT is not levied on medicines, books and some foodstuffs.

Telephone → *Country code +54.*

Ringing: equal tones with long pauses. Engaged: equal tones with equal pauses.

To call a mobile phone in Argentina, dial the city code followed by 15, then the mobile's number (eg 011-15-xxxx xxxx in Buenos Aires). To call a mobile from abroad, dial the country code, then 9, then the city code and number, omitting 15 (eg+54-9-11-xxxx xxxx). Note that area phone codes are constantly being modified.

Time
GMT -3.

Tipping

10% in restaurants and cafés. Porters and ushers are usually tipped.

Tourist information

The national office of the Secretaría de Turismo, Av Santa Fe 883, Buenos Aires, T011- 4312-2232, www.turismo.gov.ar. For free tourist information anywhere in the country T0800-555 0016 (0800-2000). For tourist information abroad, contact Argentine embassies and consulates.

Websites

www.argentina.ar Promotional website of the various bureaux and ministries covering tourism, culture, economy, education and science.

www.argentinacontact.com Travel guide and hotel directory in English and Spanish.

www.expat-connection.com Expat group in Buenos Aires which organizes events.

www.buenosairesherald.com *Buenos Aires Herald*, English language daily.

www.argentinaindependent.com Fortnightly online newspaper covering cultural, economic, social, political and environmental topics, also promoting tourism.

www.getsouth.com An excellent site for accommodation and tour recommendations, travel advice and discounts covering Argentina, Chile and Uruguay.

www.guiaypf.com.ar Site of the YPF fuel company, with travel and tourist information.

www.infobae.com An Argentine online newspaper, in Spanish.

www.smn.gov.ar Useful web site for forecasts and weather satellite images.

www.tageblatt.com.ar *Argentinisches Tageblatt*, German-language weekly, very informative.

www.welcomeargentina.com and **www. interpatagonia.com** Online travel guides to the whole country.

Visas and immigration

Passports are not required by citizens of South American countries who hold identity cards issued by their own governments. No visa is necessary for British citizens, nationals of western European countries, Central American and some Caribbean countries, plus citizens of Australia, Canada, Croatia, Hong Kong, Israel, Japan, Malaysia, New Zealand, Russia, Singapore, South Africa, Turkey and USA, who are given a tourist card ('tarjeta de entrada') on entry and may stay for 3 months, which can be renewed only once for another 3 months (fee US$70) at the Dirección Nacional de Migraciones, Av Antártida Argentina 1355 (Retiro), Buenos Aires, T4317 0234, open Mon- Fri 0800-1400, or any other delegation of the Dirección Nacional de Migraciones (www. migraciones.gov.ar). For all others there are 3 forms of visa: a tourist visa (multiple entry, valid for 3 months; onward ticket and proof of adequate funds must be provided; fees vary depending on the country of origin; can be extended 90 days), a business visa and a transit visa. If leaving Argentina on a short trip, check on re-entry that border officials look at the correct expiry date on your visa, otherwise they will give only 30 days. Carry your passport at all times; backpackers are often targets for thorough searches – just stay calm; it is illegal not to have identification to hand.

At land borders if you don't need a visa, 90 days' permission to stay is usually given without proof of transportation out of Argentina. Make sure you are given a tourist card, otherwise you will have to obtain one before leaving the country. If you need a 90-day extension for your stay then leave the country (eg at Iguazú), and 90 further days will be given on return. Visa extensions may also be obtained from the address above, ask for 'Prorrogas de Permanencia'. No renewals are given after the expiry date. To authorize an exit stamp if your visa or tourist stamp has expired, go to Dirección Nacional de Migraciones and a 10-day authorization will be given for US$70, providing a proof of transportation out of the country. If you leave the country with a tourist card or visa that has expired, you will be fined for the number of days you have overstayed (may be as much as US$200 a day).

Reciprocal fees

In 2010 Argentina introduced entry fees for citizens of countries which require Argentines to obtain a visa and pay an entry fee, namely Australia (US$100), Canada (US$75) and the US (US$140).

At the time of writing this fee was payable only at Ezeiza and Aeroparque airports, not other airports, nor land borders, and did not apply to other nationalities. Either or both of these factors may change. For Australians and US citizens, the fee is in theory for the life of the passport; Canadians must pay US$150 for multiple entry. Payment may be made in US$, pesos, by credit card or travellers' cheque.

Weights and measures
Metric.

Buenos Aires

With its elegant architecture and fashion-conscious inhabitants, Buenos Aires is often seen as more European than South American. Among its fine boulevards, neat plazas, parks, museums and theatres, there are chic shops and superb restaurants. However, the enormous steaks and passionate tango are distinctly Argentine, and to really understand the country, you have to know its capital. South and west of Buenos Aires the flat, fertile lands of the pampa húmeda stretch seemingly without end, the horizon broken only by a lonely windpump or a line of poplar trees. This is home to the gaucho, whose traditions of music and craftsmanship remain alive.

Arriving in Buenos Aires → *Phone code: 011.*

Getting there

Buenos Aires has two **airports**, Ezeiza, for international flights, and Aeroparque, for domestic flights and most services to Uruguay. Ezeiza is 35 km southwest of the centre by a good dual carriageway which links with the General Paz highway which circles the city. The safest way between airport and city is by an airport bus service run every 30 minutes by *Manuel Tienda León*, www.tiendaleon.com.ar, which has convenient offices and charges US$13.75 one way. Radio taxis charge US$45 (make sure you pay for your taxi at the booth and then wait in the queue). *Remise* taxis (booked in advance) charge US$42 (including toll for a return journey) airport to town. Aeroparque is 4 km north of the city centre on the riverside; *Manuel Tienda León* has buses between the airports, US$16, and also runs from Aeroparque to the centre for US$5.75. Remises charge US$18 and ordinary taxis US$15. As well as by air, travellers from Uruguay arrive by ferry (fast catamaran or slower vessels), docking in the port in the heart of the city, or by bus. All international and interprovincial buses use the Retiro **bus terminal** at Ramos Mejía y Antártida Argentina, which is next to the Retiro railway station. Both are served by city buses, taxis and Line C of the Subte (metro). Other train services, to the province of Buenos Aires and the suburbs use Constitución, Once and Federico Lacroze stations, all served by bus, taxi and Subte. ▶▶ *See also Transport, page 44.*

Getting around

The commercial heart of the city, from Retiro station and Plaza San Martín through Plaza de Mayo to San Telmo, east of Avenida 9 de Julio, can be explored on foot, but you'll probably want to take a couple of days to explore its museums, shops and markets. Many places of interest lie outside this zone, so you will need to use public transport. City **buses** (*colectivos*) are plentiful, see below for city guides. The fare is about US$0.30 in the city, US$0.50 to the suburbs. The **metro**, or Subte, is fast and clean. It has six lines; a single fare is US$0.60. Yellow and black **taxis** can be hailed on the street, but if at all possible, book a radio taxi by phone as it is much safer (make sure the meter is reset when you get in). *Remise* taxis, booked only through an office, are the most reliable. See Transport, below, for full details. Street numbers start from the dock side rising from east to west, but north/south streets are numbered from Avenida Rivadavia, one block north of Avenida de Mayo rising in both directions. Calle Juan D Perón used to be called Cangallo, and Scalabrini Ortiz used to be Canning (old names are still referred to). Avenida Roque Sáenz Peña and Avenida Julio A Roca are commonly referred to as Diagonal Norte and Diagonal Sur respectively. **Note** Many places' websites give details on how to get there.

Tourist offices

National office ⓘ *Av Santa Fe 883, T4312 2232, info@turismo.gov.ar, Mon-Fri 0900-1700*, maps and literature covering the whole country. There are kiosks at Aeroparque (*Aerolíneas Argentinas* section), and at **Ezeiza Airport** daily 1000-1700. **City information** ⓘ *municipal websites www.bue.gov.ar, in Spanish, English and Portuguese, and www.buenosaires.gov.ar.* There are tourist kiosks at Florida 100, T4313 0187, 0900-1800 daily; at the junction of Florida and Marcelo T de Alvear (Monday-Friday 1000-1700); in Recoleta (Avenida Quintana 596, junction with Ortiz, 1000-1700), in Puerto Madero (Dock 4, T4315 4265, 1000-1700, also has information on Montevideo), and at Retiro Bus Station (ground floor, T4313 0187, Monday-Friday 0730-1430). Free guided tours are organized by the city authorities: free leaflet from city-run offices and suggested circuits on www.bue.gov.ar. Audio guided tours in several languages are available for 13 itineraries by downloading MP3 files from www.bue.gov.ar, or by dialing *8283 from a mobile phone (look for the grey plaques on the pavement showing a code in many sites around the city). **Tango information centre** ⓘ *on the first floor of Galerías Pacífico, Sarmiento 1551, T4373 2823.*

☐ **Federal District of Buenos Aires**

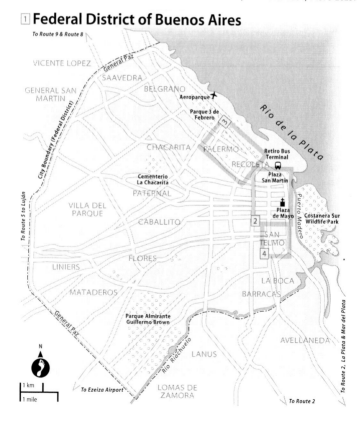

Those overcharged or cheated can go to the **Defensoría del Turista** ① *Piedras 445, p 8, T4338 5581, www.defensoriaturista.org.ar, 1000-1800*, with branches at ① *Av Pedro de Mendoza 1835 (Museo Quinquela Martín, La Boca), T4302 7816, Defensa 1250, T15-4046 9682, Florida y MT de Alvear, T15-3856 1943, and Alicia Moreau de Justo 200 (Diq 4, Puerto Madero), T15-4078 8654, all daily 1000-1800*.

South American Explorers ① Piedras 1178, San Telmo, baclub@saexplorers.org, Mon-Fri 1400-1800, is a good meeting place for travellers and source of knowledgeable advice. It has luggage storage, guidebook library, internet access and book exchange for members, weekly Spanish conversation and regular events.

Information Good guides to bus and subway routes are **Guía T, Lumi, Peuser** and **Filcar** (covering the city and Greater Buenos Aires in separate editions), US$1-9 available at news stands. Also handy is Auto Mapa's pocket-size **Plano** of the Federal Capital, or the more detailed City Map covering La Boca to Palermo, both available at news stands, US$4.50; otherwise it is easy to get free maps of the centre from tourist kiosks and most hotels. **Buenos Aires Day & Night** is one of several free bi-monthly tourist magazines with useful information and a downtown map available at tourist kiosks and hotels. *Bainsider* (www.bainsidermag.com) is a fantastic magazine for getting to know the city, US$1.50. **La Nación** (www.lanacion.com.ar) has a very informative Sunday tourism section. On Friday, the youth section of **Clarín** (*Sí*) lists free entertainment; also see www.clarin.com. **Página 12** has a youth supplement on Thursday called **NO**. The **Buenos Aires Herald** publishes **Get Out** on Friday, listing entertainments. Information on what's on at www.buenosairesherald.com and www.wipe.com.ar. See also **The Argentina Independent**, www.argentinaindependent.com, in English, and www.whatsupbuenosaires.com.

Blogs worth exploring include http://baexpats.com and www.goodmorningba.com.

Places in Buenos Aires

The capital has been virtually rebuilt since the beginning of the 20th-century and its oldest buildings mostly date from the early 1900s, with some elegant examples from the 1920s and 1930s. The centre has maintained the original layout since its foundation and so the streets are often narrow and mostly one way. Its original name, 'Santa María del Buen Ayre' was a recognition of the good winds which brought sailors across the ocean.

Around Plaza de Mayo

The heart of the city is the **Plaza de Mayo**. On the east side is the **Casa de Gobierno**. Called the *Casa Rosada* because it is pink, it contains the offices of the President of the Republic. It is notable for its statuary and the rich furnishing of its halls. The **Museo del Bicentenario** ① *Paseo Colón 100, T4344 3802, www.museobicentenario.gob.ar, Wed-Sun 1100-1900 (21 Mar-20 Sep 1000-1800), free*, in the Fuerte de Buenos Aires and Aduana Taylor, covers the period 1810-2010 with historical exhibits and art exhibitions, permanent and temporary. In the semicircular Parque Colón, is a large statue of Columbus. **Antiguo Congreso Nacional** (Old Congress Hall, 1864-1905) ① *Balcarce 139, Thu, 1500-1700, closed Jan-Feb, free*, on the south of the Plaza, is a National Monument. The **Cathedral**, on the north of Plaza, stands on the site of the first church in Buenos Aires ① *San Martín 27, T4331 2845, www.catedralbuenosaires.org.ar, Mon-Fri 0800-1900, Sat-Sun 0900-1930; guided visits to San Martín's mausoleum and Crypt, religious artefacts, and Temple and Crypt; mass is held daily, check times*. The current structure dates from 1753-1822 (its portico built in

2 **Buenos Aires centre**

1827), but the 18th-century towers were never rebuilt. The imposing tomb (1880) of the Liberator, Gen José de San Martín ① *Mon-Sat 0930-1300, 1500-1700, Sun 0900-1100, 1500-1900*, is guarded by soldiers in fancy uniforms. **Museo del Cabildo y la Revolución de Mayo** ① *Bolívar 65, T4334 1782, Tue-Fri 1030-1700, Sun 1130-1800, US$0.75*, is in the old Cabildo where the movement for independence from Spain was first planned. It's worth a visit for the paintings of old Buenos Aires, the documents and maps recording the May 1810 revolution, and memorabilia of the 1806 British attack; also Jesuit art. In the patio is a café and stalls selling handicrafts (Thursday-Friday 1100-1800). Also on the Plaza is the Palacio de Gobierno de la Ciudad (City Hall). Within a few blocks north of the Plaza are the main banks and business houses, such as the **Banco de la Nación**, opposite the Casa Rosada, with an impressively huge main hall and topped by a massive marble dome 50 m in diameter.

On the Plaza de Mayo, the **Mothers and Grandmothers of the Plaza de Mayo** march in remembrance of their children who disappeared during the 'dirty war' of the 1970s (their addresses are H Yrigoyen 1584, T4383 0377, www.madres.org, and Piedras 153, T4343 1926, www.madresfundadoras.org.ar). The Mothers march anti-clockwise round the central monument every Thursday at 1530, with photos of their disappeared loved-ones pinned to their chests.

West of Plaza de Mayo

Running west from the Plaza, the Avenida de Mayo leads 1.5 km to the **Palacio del Congreso** (Congress Hall) ① *Plaza del Congreso, Av Rivadavia 1864, T6310 7222 for guided visits, Mon, Tue, Thu, Fri 1000, 1200, 1600, 1800, www.congreso.gov.ar; passport essential*. This huge Greco-Roman building houses the seat of the legislature. Avenida de Mayo has several examples of fine architecture of the early 20th-century, such as the sumptuous La Prensa building (No 575, free guided visits at weekends), the traditional *Café Tortoni* (No 825, www.cafetortoni.com.ar), or the eclectic Palacio Barolo (No 1370, www.pbarolo. com.ar), and many others of faded grandeur. Avenida de Mayo crosses the **Avenida 9 de Julio**, one of the widest avenues in the world, which consists of three major carriageways with heavy traffic, separated in some parts by wide grass borders. Five blocks north of Avenida de Mayo the great **Plaza de la República**, with a 67-m obelisk commemorating the 400th anniversary of the city's founding, is at the junction of Avenida 9 de Julio with Avenidas Roque Sáenz Peña and Corrientes. **Teatro Colón** ① *Cerrito 628, entrance for guided visits Tucumán 1171, T4378 7127, www.teatrocolon.org.ar*, is one of the world's great opera houses. The interior is resplendent with red plush and gilt; the stage is huge, and salons, dressing rooms and banquet halls are equally sumptuous. A full building restoration was completed in 2010. Consult the website for details of performances, tickets and guided visits.

Close by is the **Museo Judío** ① *Libertad 769, T4123 0832, www.judaica.org.ar; for visits make an appointment with the rabbi (take identification)*, has religious objects relating to Jewish presence in Argentina in a 19th-century synagogue. Not far away is **Museo del Holocausto** (Shoah Museum) ① *Montevideo 919, T4811 3588, informaciones@fmh.org. ar, Mon-Thu 1100-1800, Fri 1100-1630, US$1.25 (ID required)*, a permanent exhibition of pictures, personal and religious items with texts in Spanish on the Holocaust, antisemitism in Argentina and the lives of many Argentine Jews in the pre- and post-war periods. There are also seminars, temporary art exhibitions and a library (open in the afternoon). **La Chacarita** ① *Guzmán 670, daily 0700-1800, take Subte Line B to the Federico Lacroze station*. This well known cemetery has the lovingly tended tomb of Carlos Gardel, the tango singer.

North of Plaza de Mayo

The city's traditional shopping centre, Calle Florida, is reserved for pedestrians, with clothes and souvenir shops, restaurants and the elegant Galerías Pacífico. More shops are to be found on Avenida Santa Fe, which crosses Florida at Plaza San Martín. Avenida Corrientes, a street of theatres, bookshops, restaurants and cafés, and nearby Calle Lavalle (partly reserved for pedestrians), used to be the entertainment centre, but both are now regarded as faded. Recoleta, Palermo and Puerto Madero have become much more fashionable (see below). The **Basílica Nuestra Señora de La Merced** *J D Perón y Reconquista 207, Mon-Fri 0800-1800*, founded 1604, rebuilt for the third time in the 18th century, has a beautiful interior with baroque and rococo features. In 1807 it was a command post against the invading British. Next door is the **Convento de San Ramón Nonato** (www.conventosanramon.org.ar). **Museo y Biblioteca Mitre** ① *San Martín 336, T4394 8240, www.museomitre.gov.ar, Mon-Fri 1300-1730, US$1.15*, preserves intact the household of President Bartolomé Mitre; has a coin and map collection and historical archives.

The **Plaza San Martín** has a monument to San Martín at the western corner of the main park and, at the north end, a memorial with an eternal flame to those who fell in the Falklands/ Malvinas War of 1982. On the plaza is **Palacio San Martín** ① *Arenales 761, T4819 8092, www.mrecic.gov.ar, free tours in Spanish and English (check times, in Feb 2012 Tue and Thu 1500)*. Built 1905-1909, it is three houses linked together, now the Foreign Ministry. It has collections of prehispanic and 20th-century art. On the opposite side of the plaza is the opulent **Palacio Paz** (Círculo Militar) ① *Av Santa Fe 750, T4311 1071, www.circulomilitar. org, guided tours Tue-Fri 1100, 1500; Wed, Sat 1100, US$9 (in English Wed and Thu 1530)*. The Círculo Militar includes **Museo de Armas** ① *Av Santa Fe 702, Mon-Fri 1300-1900*. It has all kinds of weaponry related to Argentine history, including the 1982 Falklands/ Malvinas War, plus Oriental weapons.

Plaza Fuerza Aérea Argentina (formerly Plaza Británica) has the clock tower presented by British and Anglo-Argentine residents, while in the **Plaza Canadá** (in front of the Retiro Station) there is a Pacific Northwest Indian totem pole, donated by the Canadian government. Behind Retiro station is **Museo Nacional Ferroviario** ① *ring the bell, free, Av del Libertador 405, T4318 3343, Mon-Fri 1030-1600, free*. For railway fans: locomotives, machinery, documents of the Argentine system's history, the building is in very poor condition. In a warehouse beside is the workshop of the sculptor Carlos Regazzoni who recycles refuse material from railways.

Museo de Arte Hispanoamericano Isaac Fernández Blanco ① *Suipacha 1422 (3 blocks west of Retiro), T4327 0228, www.museofernandezblanco.buenosaires.gob.ar Tue-Fri, 1400-1900, Sat, Sun and holidays 1100-1900, Thu free, US$0.25*, is one of the city's best museums. It contains a fascinating collection of colonial art, especially paintings and silver, also temporary exhibitions of Latin American art, in a beautiful neocolonial mansion (Palacio Noel, 1920s) with Spanish gardens; free concerts and tango lessons on Monday.

Recoleta and Palermo

Nuestra Señora del Pilar, Junín 1898, is a jewel of colonial architecture dating from 1732 (renovated in later centuries), facing onto the public gardens of Recoleta. A fine wooden image of San Pedro de Alcántara, attributed to the famous 17th-century Spanish sculptor Alonso Cano, is preserved in a side chapel on the left, and there are stunning gold altars. Upstairs is an interesting museum of religious art.

Next to it, the **Cemetery of the Recoleta** ① *entrance at Junín 1790, near Museo de Bellas Artes (see below), www.cementeriorecoleta.com.ar, 0700-1745, tours in Spanish and English*

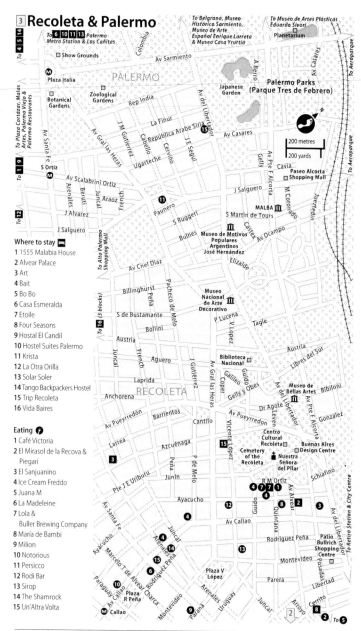

3 Recoleta & Palermo

To Belgrano, Museo Histórico Sarmiento, Museo de Arte Español Enrique Larreta & Museo Casa Yrurtia

To Museo de Artes Plásticas Eduardo Sívori

Planetarium

To 6 10 11 13 Palermo Metro Station & Las Cañitas

Colombia

Av Sarmiento

A Berro

Av Casares

To Aeroparque

Show Grounds

PALERMO

Plaza Italia

Palermo Parks (Parque Tres de Febrero)

Botanical Gardens

Zoological Gardens

Rep India

Japanese Garden

To Plaza Cortázar, Malas Artes, Palermo Viejo & Palermo Restaurants

J M Gutiérrez

La Finur

República Arabe Siria

Av Casares

J E Seguí

Av del Libertador

Cabello

Cerviño

200 metres

200 yards

Av Gral las Heras

Ugarteche

Av Santa Fe

To 1 9

S Ortiz

Gelly

Av Pte F Alcorta

M Coronado

Av Casares

Cavia

Paseo Alcorta Shopping Mall

Av Scalabrini Ortiz

Berutti

Arenales

Juncal

Araoz

French

Paunero

J Salguero

MALBA

S Martín de Tours

S Ruggeri

Museo de Motivos Populares Argentinos José Hernández

To 12

J Álvarez

Av Ocampo

J Salguero

Bulnes

Elizalde

To Alto Palermo Shopping Mall

Av Cnel Díaz

Pacheco de Melo

Billinghurst

Peña

Museo Nacional de Arte Decorativo

P Lucena

V López

Tagle

Where to stay

1 1555 Malabia House
2 Alvear Palace
3 Art
4 Bait
5 Bo Bo
6 Casa Esmeralda
7 Etoile
8 Four Seasons
9 Hostal El Candil
10 Hostel Suites Palermo
11 Krista
12 La Otra Orilla
13 Solar Soler
14 Tango Backpackers Hostel
15 Trip Recoleta
16 Vida Baires

S de Bustamante

Bollini

Austria

Biblioteca Nacional

Austria

To 16 (5 blocks)

Juncal

French

Aguero

J Gral las Heras

Galileo

Guido

Gelly y Obes

Libres del Sur

Museo de Bellas Artes

Bibiloni

Laprida

Anchorena

Coper

Dr Agote

González

RECOLETA

Av Pueyrredón

Barrientos

Larrea

Azcuénaga

Cantilo

Vicente López

Av Pueyrredón

Steven

Centro Cultural Recoleta

Buenos Aires Design Centre

Schiafino

Eating

1 Café Victoria
2 El Mirasol de la Recova & Piegari
3 El Sanjuanino
4 Ice Cream Freddo
5 Juana M
6 La Madeleine
7 Lola & Buller Brewing Company
8 María de Bambi
9 Milion
10 Notorious
11 Persicco
12 Rodi Bar
13 Sirop
14 The Shamrock
15 Un'Altra Volta

Pte J E Uriburu

Junín

Ayacucho

Av Santa Fe

Larrea

Ayacucho

Marcelo T de Alvear

Arenales

Av Callao

Cemetery of the Recoleta

Nuestra Señora del Pilar

R M Ortiz

Av Alvear

Av Libertador

To Retiro Station & City Centre

Quintana

Posadas

Paraguay

Callao

Plaza R Peña

Rodríguez Peña

Charca

Plaza V López

Parera

Montevideo

Patio Bullrich Shopping Centre

Arenales

Uruguay

Juncal

Parera

Libertad

Callao

Montevideo

Paraná

Arroyo

Cerrito

2

To 5

are available, T5614 8869), is one of the sights of Buenos Aires. With its streets and alleys separating family mausoleums built in every imaginable architectural style, La Recoleta is often compared to a miniature city. Among the famous names from Argentine history is Evita Perón who lies in the Duarte family mausoleum: to find it from the entrance go to the first tree-filled plaza; turn left and where this avenue meets a main avenue (go just beyond the Turriaca tomb), turn right; then take the third passage on the left. On Saturday and Sunday there is a good craft market in the park on Plaza Francia outside the cemetery (1000-1800), with street artists and performers. Next to the cemetery, the **Centro Cultural Recoleta** ① *T4803 1040, www.centroculturalrecoleta.org, Mon-Fri 1400-2100, Sat, Sun, holidays 1000-2100*, specializes in contemporary local art. Next door, the Buenos Aires Design Centre ① *www.designrecoleta.com.ar* has good design and handicraft shops.

Museo de Bellas Artes (National Gallery) ① *Av del Libertador 1473, T5288 9945, www. mnba.org.ar, Tue-Fri 1230-2030, Sat-Sun 0930-2030, free*. This excellent museum gives a taste of Argentine art, as well as a fine collection of European works, particularly post-Impressionist. Superb Argentine 19th and 20th-century paintings, sculpture and wooden carvings; also films, classical music concerts and art courses. **Biblioteca Nacional** (National Library) ① *Av del Libertador 1600 y Agüero 2502, T4808 6000, www.bn.gov.ar, Mon-Fri 0900-2100, Sat and Sun 1200-1900, closed Jan*. Housed in a modern building, only a fraction of the extensive stock can be seen. Art gallery, periodical archives; cultural events held. **Museo Nacional de Arte Decorativo** ① *Av del Libertador 1902, T4802 6606, www.mnad. org.ar, Tue-Sun 1400-1900 (closed Sun in Jan), US$1.15, students and seniors US$0.70, Tue free, guided visits US$3.50 in Spanish, Englsih and French, check times*. It contains collections of painting, furniture, porcelain, crystal, sculpture exhibited in sumptuous halls, once a family residence.

Palermo Chico is a delightful residential area with several houses of once wealthy families, dating from the early 20th-century. The predominant French style of the district was broken in 1929 by the rationalist lines of the **Casa de la Cultura** ① *Rufino de Elizalde 2831, T4808 0553, www.fnartes.gov.ar, Tue-Sun 1500-2000 (Jan closed)*. The original residence of the writer Victoria Ocampo was a gathering place for artists and intellectuals and is now an attractive cultural centre with art exhibitions and occasional concerts.

Museo de Arte Popular José Hernández ① *Av del Libertador 2373, T4803 2384, www. museohernandez.org.ar, Wed-Fri 1300-1900, Sat-Sun 1000-2000, US$0.25, free Sun; see website for exhibitions, events and workshops*. The widest collection of Argentine folkloric art, with rooms dedicated to indigenous, colonial and Gaucho artefacts; handicraft shop and library. **Museo de Arte Latinoamericano (MALBA)** ① *Av Figueroa Alcorta 3415, T4808 6500, www.malba.org.ar, Thu-Mon 1200-2000, US$5.75, students and seniors US$2.75 (Wed half price, students free, open till 2100); Tue closed*. One of the most important museums in the city houses renowned Latin American artists' works: powerful, moving and highly recommended. It's not a vast collection, but representative of the best from the continent. Good library, cinema (showing art house films as well as Argentine classics, US$4.60), seminars and shop, also has an elegant café, serving delicious food and cakes.

Of the fine **Palermo Parks**, the largest is Parque Tres de Febrero, famous for its extensive rose garden, Andalusian Patio, and delightful **Jardín Japonés** (with café) ① *T4804 4922, www.jardinjapones.org.ar, daily 1000-1800, US$3.70*. It is a charming place for a walk, delightful for children, and with a good café serving some Japanese dishes. Close by is the **Hipódromo Argentino** (Palermo racecourse) ① *T4778 2800, www.palermo.com.ar, races 10 days per month, free*. Opposite the parks are the Botanical and Zoological Gardens. At the entrance to the **Planetarium** ① *just off Belisario Roldán, in Palermo Park, T4771 9393,* *www.planetario.gov.ar, closed Jan 2012 for remodelling; small museum*, are several large meteorites from Campo del Cielo. **Museo de Artes Plásticas Eduardo Sívori** ① *Av Infanta Isabel 555 (Parque Tres de Febrero), T4774 9452, www.museosivori.org.ar, Tue-Fri 1200-2000, Sat and Sun 1000-2000 (1800 in winter), US$0.25, Wed and Sat free*. Emphasis on 19th and 20th-century Argentine art, sculpture and tapestry. The **Show Grounds** of the Argentine Rural Society, next to Palermo Park, entrance on Plaza Italia, stage the Annual Livestock Exhibition, known as Exposición Rural, in July. The **Botanical Gardens** ① *Santa Fe 3951, T4831 4527, entrance from Plaza Italia (take Subte, line D) or from C República Arabe Siria, daily 0800-1800, free guided visits Sat-Sun 1030; also nocturnal tours last Fri of each month at 2100 (booking required)*, contain characteristic specimens of the world's vegetation. The trees native to the different provinces of Argentina are brought together in one section. One block beyond is **Museo Evita** ① *Lafinur 2988, T4807 0306, www.museoevita.org, Tue-Sun 1100-1900, US$3.50 (US$8 with guided visit, only for groups of more than five people)*. In a former women's shelter run by Fundación Eva Perón, the exhibition of dresses, paintings and other items is quite interesting though lacks the expected passion; also a library and a café.

There are three important museums in Belgrano: **Museo Histórico Sarmiento** ① *Juramento 2180, T4782 2354, www.museosarmiento.gov.ar, Mon-Fri 1300-1800, Sat-Sun 1500-1900, US$1.15, guided visits Sun 1600*. The National Congress and presidential offices in 1880 now houses documents and personal effects of the former president, with a library of his work. **Museo de Arte Español Enrique Larreta** ① *Juramento 2291, T4784 4040, Mon-Fri, 1400-2000, Sat-Sun 1000-2000, guided visits Mon, Wed, Fri 1700, Sat-Sun 1600, 1800, US$0.75*. The home of the writer Larreta, with paintings and religious art from the 14th to the 20th century; also has a beautiful garden ① *open Mon-Fri 1200-1900, Sat, Sun 1000-2000 at Vuelta de Obligado 2155*. **Museo Casa Yrurtia** ① *O'Higgins 2390, esq Blanco Encalada, T4789 0094, Tue-Fri 1300-1900, Sun 1500-1900, US$0.50*. An old house crammed with sculpture, paintings, furniture and the collections of artist Rogelio Yrurtia and his wife; peaceful garden.

South of Plaza de Mayo

The church of **San Ignacio de Loyola**, begun 1664, is the oldest colonial building in Buenos Aires (renovated in 18th and 19th centuries). It stands in a block of Jesuit origin, called the **Manzana de las Luces** (Enlightenment Square – Moreno, Alsina, Perú and Bolívar). Also in this block are the **Colegio Nacional de Buenos Aires** ① *Bolívar 263, T4331 0734*, formerly the site of the Jesuits' Colegio Máximo, the Procuraduría de las Misiones (today the Mercado de las Luces, a crafts market) and 18th-century **tunnels**. For centuries the whole block was the centre of intellectual activity, though little remains today but a small **cultural centre with art courses, concerts, plays and film shows** ① *T4343 3620, www. manzanadelasluces.gov.ar, guided tours from Perú 272, Mon-Fri 1500, Sat and Sun 1500, 1630, 1800 in Spanish (in English by prior arrangement), arrive 15 mins before tour, US$2.75; the tours explore the tunnels and visit the buildings on C Perú, some include San Ignacio and its cloisters for US$0.35 extra*. The **Museo de la Ciudad** ① *Alsina 412, T4343 2123, Mon-Sun 1100-1900, US$1 for non-residents, free on Mon and Wed*. Permanent exhibition covering social history and popular culture, special exhibitions on daily life in Buenos Aires changed every two months, and a reference library open to the public. The church of **San Francisco** ① *Alsina y Defensa, T4331 0625, Wed-Sun 1100-1600, US$1.25*, run by the Franciscan Order, was built 1730-1754 and given a new façade in 1911.

Santo Domingo ① *Defensa y Belgrano, Mon-Fri 0900-1300, Sun 1000-1200*, was founded in 1751. During the British attack on Buenos Aires in 1806 some of Whitelocke's soldiers took refuge in the church. The local forces bombarded it, the British capitulated and their regimental colours were preserved in the church. General Belgrano is buried here.

Museo Etnográfico JB Ambrosetti ① *Moreno 350, T4345 8196, www.museoetnografico. filo.uba.ar, Tue-Fri 1300-1900, Sat-Sun 1500-1900 (closed Jan), US$0.75, guided visits Sat-Sun 1600.* Anthropological and ethnographic collections from the Mapuche and Argentina's northwest cultures (the latter a rich collection displayed on the first floor); also a small international room with a magnificent Japanese Buddhist altar.

San Telmo and La Boca
One of the few places which still has late colonial and Rosista buildings (mostly renovated in the 20th century) is the *barrio* of **San Telmo**, south of Plaza de Mayo. It's an atmospheric

④ **San Telmo**

200 metres
200 yards

Where to stay 🛏
1 Axel
2 Circus
3 El Hostal de Granados
4 Garden House
5 Garden House Art Factory
6 Hostel-Inn Buenos Aires
7 Kilca Hostel & Backpacker
8 La Casita de San Telmo
9 La Cayetana Historic House
10 Lola House
11 Lugar Gay
 de Buenos Aires
12 Mansión Dandi Royal
13 Ostinatto
14 Sabatico Travelers Hostel
15 Sandanzas
16 Telmho

Restaurants 🍴
1 Bar Británico
2 Brasserie Petanque
3 Dylan
4 El Desnivel &
 Bar La Resistencia
5 La Brigada
6 Nonna Bianca
7 Pride Café

Bars & clubs 🍸
8 Bar Dorrego
9 Bar Seddon
10 Plan B

place, with lots of cafés, antique shops and little art galleries. On Sundays, it has a great atmosphere, with an antiques market at the Plaza Dorrego (see page 41), free tango shows (1000-1800) and live music.

Parque Lezama, Defensa y Brasil, originally one of the most beautiful in the city, now rather run down and unsafe at night, has an imposing statue of Pedro de Mendoza, who (according to tradition) founded the original city in 1536 on this spot. In the park is the **Museo Histórico Nacional** ① *Defensa 1600, T4307 2301, Wed-Sun 1100-1800, US$0.50.* Argentine history, San Martín's uniforms and the original furniture and door of the house in which he died at Boulogne. In the park is the **Iglesia Ortodoxa Rusa** ① *Brasil 315; visits on Sat afternoon (women wearing trousers will be given skirts; men in shorts will be refused entry)*, with its five blue domes and a wonderful interior.

East of the Plaza de Mayo, behind the Casa Rosada, a broad avenue, Paseo Colón, runs south towards San Telmo and as Av Almirante Brown on to the old port district of **La Boca** ① *take a radio taxi from the centre or San Telmo and, to return, call for a taxi from the locutorio in the Centro Cultural de los Artistas, US$5 one way*, where the Riachuelo flows into the Plata. The much-photographed, brightly painted tin and wooden houses cover one block of the pedestrianized Caminito. As La Boca is the poorest and roughest area within central Buenos Aires, tourists are limited to this little street running from the Plaza La Vuelta de Rocha. You can also visit the **Museo de Bellas Artes Benito Quinquela Martín** ① *Pedro de Mendoza 1835, T4301 1080, Tue-Sun 1030-1730 (closed Jan), US$0.40*, with over 1000 works by Argentine artists, particularly Benito Quinquela Martín (1890-1977), who painted La Boca port life. Also sculptures and figureheads rescued from ships. Do not go anywhere else in La Boca and avoid it at night. The area is especially rowdy when the Boca Juniors football club is playing at home. At Boca Juniors stadium is **Museo de la Pasión Boquense** ① *Brandsen 805, T4362 1100, www.museoboquense.com, daily 1000-1800 (opening times may change during matches), US$8. Guided tour of the stadium in Spanish or English, 1100-1700, plus ticket to the museum, US$11.50.*

Docks and Costanera Sur
Fragata Presidente Sarmiento ① *dock 3, Juana Manuela Gorriti 600, Puerto Madero, T4334 9386, daily 1000-1900, US$1.* A naval training ship until 1961; now a museum. Nearby, in dock 4, is the **Corbeta Uruguay** ① *T4314 1090, daily 1000-1900, US$1, for both ships see www.ara. mil.ar*, the ship that rescued Otto Nordenskjold's Antarctic expedition in 1903. The **Puerto Madero** dock area has been renovated; the 19th-century warehouses are restaurants and bars, an attractive place for a stroll and popular nightspot. East of San Telmo on the far side of the docks, the Avenida Costanera runs as a long, spacious boulevard. A stretch of marshland reclaimed from the river forms the interesting **Costanera Sur Wildlife Reserve** ① *entrances at Av Tristán Achával Rodríguez 1550 (take Estados Unidos east from San Telmo) or next to the Buquebús ferry terminal (take Av Córdoba east), T4315 4129; for pedestrians and bikers only, Tue-Sun 0800-1800 (in summer, closes at 1900), free, take colectivos 4, 130 or 152*, where there are over 200 species of birds, including the curve-billed reed hunter. Free guided tours at weekends 1030, 1530, daily in summer, from the administration next to the southern entrance, but much can be seen from the road before then (binoculars useful). Also free nocturnal visits every month on the Friday closest to the full moon and the following Thursday (book Monday before, T4893 1588). It's half an hour walk from the entrance to the river shore and about three hours to walk the whole perimeter. In summer it's very hot with little shade. For details (particularly birdwatching) contact Aves Argentinas/AOP (see page 50).

Buenos Aires listings

For hotel and restaurant price codes and other relevant information, see pages 10-12.

● Where to stay

Shop around for hotels offering discounts on multi-night stays. If you pay in pesos in cash you may also get a reduction. The tourist offices at Ezeiza and Jorge Newbery airports book rooms. Room tax (VAT) is 21% and is not always included in the price. A/c is a must in high summer. Finding hotels for Fri, Sat, Sun nights can be difficult and hostels can get very busy, resulting in pressure on staff. A bed in a hostel dorm costs US$15-20. The range of `boutique' hotels and hostels is impressive, especially in Palermo and San Telmo. The same applies to restaurants, bars and clubs. There are fine examples of the **Four Seasons** (www.fourseasons.com/ buenosaires), **Hilton** (www.hilton.com), **Hyatt** (www. buenosaires.park.hyatt.com), **Marriott** (www.marriott.com), **NH** (www.nh- hoteles. com), **Pestana** (www.pestana.com), **Sofitel** (www.sofitel.com) and **Unique Hotels** (www.hotels-unique.com) chains. Hotels will store luggage, and most have English-speaking staff.

Note that prices listed for youth hostels are for dorms and prices for double rooms are given in the description.

Centre *p19, map p20*
$$$$ Alvear Palace, Av Alvear 1891, T4808 2100, www.alvearpalace.com. The height of elegance, an impeccably preserved 1920s Recoleta palace, sumptuous marble foyer, with Louis XV-style chairs, and a charming orangery where you can take tea with superb patisseries. Antique-filled bedrooms. Recommended.
$$$$ Aspen Towers, Paraguay 857, T5166 1900, www.aspentowers.com.ar. A modern hotel on 13 floors, with renovated bedrooms, all with hydromassage and Wi-Fi, and all facilities, including a good breakfast and a pool.
$$$$ Casa Calma, Suipacha 1015, T5199 2800, www.casacalma.com.ar. A relaxing haven in a downtown setting, homely yet luxurious, with a wellness centre and honesty bar.
$$$$ Faena Universe, Martha Salotti 445 (Puerto Madero), T4010 9000, www. faenahoteland universe.com. Set in a 100-year old silo, renovated by Philippe Starck, this is not for all budgets or tastes. Eclectic decoration, staff trained to be perfect, the whole place is unique.
$$$$ Panamericano, Carlos Pellegrini 551, T4348 5000, www.panamericano.us. Very smart and modern hotel, with luxurious and tasteful rooms, covered rooftop pool, and superb restaurant, **Tomo 1**. Excellent service too.
$$$$-$$$ Dolmen, Suipacha 1079, T4315 7117, www.hoteldolmen.com.ar. Good location, smart spacious entrance lobby, with a calm relaxing atmosphere, good professional service, modern, comfortable well-designed rooms, small pool.
$$$$-$$$ Etoile, R Ortiz 1835 in Recoleta, T4805 2626, www.etoile.com.ar. Outstanding location, rooftop pool, rooms with kitchenette.
$$$$-$$$ Moreno, Moreno 376, T6091 2000, www.morenobuenosaires.com. 150 m from the Plaza de Mayo, decorated in dark, rich tones, large rooms, good value, jacuzzi, gym and chic bar.
$$$ Art, Azcuénaga 1268, T4821 6248, www.art hotel.com.ar. Charming boutique hotel on a quiet residential street, only a few blocks from Recoleta or Av Santa Fe, simply but warmly decorated, good service, solarium, compact standard rooms.
$$$ Bisonte Palace, MT de Alvear 902, T4328 4751, www.hotelesbisonte.com. Charming, with calm entrance foyer, which

remains gracious thanks to courteous staff. Plain but spacious rooms, ample breakfast, good location. Very good value.

$$$ Colón, Carlos Pellegrini 507, T4320 3500, www.colon-hotel.com.ar. Splendid location overlooking Av 9 de Julio and Teatro Colón, extremely good value. Charming bedrooms, comfortable, pool, gym, great breakfasts, and perfect service. Highly recommended.

$$$ Castelar, Av de Mayo 1152, T4383 5000, www.castelarhotel.com.ar. A wonderfully elegant 1920s hotel which retains all the original features in the grand entrance and bar. Cosy bedrooms, charming staff, and excellent value. Also a spa with turkish baths and massage. Highly recommended.

$$$ Dorá, Maipú 963, T4312 7391, www.dora hotel.com.ar. Charming and old-fashioned with comfortable rooms, good service, attractive lounge with paintings. Warmly recommended.

$$$ El Conquistador, Suipacha 948, T4328 3012, www.elconquistador.com.ar. Stylish '70s hotel, which retains the wood and chrome foyer, but has bright modern rooms, and a lovely light restaurant on the 10th floor with great views. Well situated, good value.

$$$ Frossard, Tucumán 686, T4322 1811, www.hotelfrossard.com.ar. A lovely old 1940s building with high ceilings and the original doors, attractively modernized, and though the rooms are small (avoid No 11), the staff are welcoming, and this is good value, near C Florida.

$$$ Hispano, Av de Mayo 861, T4345 2020, www.hhispano.com.ar. Plain but comfortable rooms in this hotel which has been welcoming budget travellers since the 1950s, courtyard and small garden, central, Wi-Fi and other services.

$$$ Marbella, Av de Mayo 1261, T/F4383 3573, www.hotelmarbella.com.ar. Modernized, and central, though quiet, breakfast included, multi-lingual. Recommended.

$$$ Orly, Paraguay 474, T4312 5344, www.orly.com.ar. Good location, and comfortable plain rooms, with helpful service.

$$$ Plaza San Martín Suites, Suipacha 1092, T5093 7000, www.plazasanmartin.com.ar. Neat modern self-contained apartments right in the city centre, comfortable and attractively decorated, with lounge and little kitchen. Sauna, gym, room service. Good value.

$$$ Waldorf, Paraguay 450, T4312 2071, www.waldorf-hotel.com.ar. Welcoming staff and a comfortable mixture of traditional and modern in this centrally located hotel. Good value, with a buffet breakfast, English spoken. Recommended.

$$$-$$ Goya, Suipacha 748, T4322 9269, www.goya hotel.com.ar. Welcoming and central, worth paying more for superior rooms, though all are comfortable. Good breakfast, English spoken.

$$ O'Rei, Lavalle 733, T4393 7186, www.hotelorei.com.ar. **$** without bath, central, simple but comfortable, spotless, laundry facilities, helpful staff, no breakfast.

Youth hostels

$ pp 06 Central, Maipú 306, T5219 0052, www.06centralhostel.com. A few metres from the Obelisco and Av Corrientes, simple, spacious dorms (US$11-15), nicely decorated doubles (**$$**), use of kitchen, cosy communal area.

$ pp About Baires, Viamonte 982, T4328 4616, www.aboutbaireshostel.com. Conveniently located in a lovely building, mixed and same-sex dorms available (US$9-11), and doubles (**$$**), breakfast included.

$ pp BA Stop, Rivadavia 1194, T4382 7406, www.bastop.com. In a converted 1900s corner block, dorms, private rooms (**$$** double), breakfast included, large-screen TV, pool tables, bar, internet, English spoken, safe, very helpful staff. Repeatedly recommended.

$ pp Hostel Suites Obelisco, Av Corrientes 830, T4328 4040, www.hostelsuites.

com. Elegant hostel built in a completely restored old building in the heart of the city. Dorms, **$$** doubles and private apartments, breakfast included, DVD room, free internet and Wi-Fi, laundry service. HI discount.

$ pp Limehouse, Lima 11, T4383 4561, www.limehouse.com.ar. Dorms for up to 12 and doubles with and without bath (**$**, US$25), popular, typical city hostel with kitchen, internet, bar, roof terrace, "chilled", great if you like the party atmosphere, efficient staff. Recommended.

$ pp Milhouse Hostel, Hipólito Yrigoyen 959, T4383 9383, www.milhousehostel. com. In 1890 house, lovely rooms (**$$$** in double) and dorms, comfortable, free breakfast, cooking facilities, laundry, internet, tango lessons, HI discounts, very popular so reconfirm bookings at all times.

$ pp Portal del Sur, Hipólito Yrigoyen 855, T4342 8788, www.portaldelsurba. com.ar. Nice dorms and especially lovely doubles (**$$** pp) and singles in a converted 19th-century building. Recommended for single travellers.

$ pp Trip Recoleta, Vicente López 2180, T4807 8726, www.triprecoleta.com.ar. Spotless dorms and doubles (**$$**), chic, modern, next to many popular bars and cafés, Wi-Fi, nice terrace.

$ pp St Nicholas, B Mitre 1691, T4373 5920, www.snhostel.com. Beautifully converted old house, now a party hostel with spotless rooms, cooking facilities, large roof terrace and a pub with daily live shows, luggage store; also **$$** double rooms. Discounts for HI members.

$ pp V&S, Viamonte 887, T4322 0994, www.hostelclub.com. Central popular hostel (**$$$** in attractive double room, bath), breakfast, café, tiny kitchen, internet, lockers, tango classes, tours, warm atmosphere, welcoming. Recommended.

Palermo *p23, map p24*
$$$$ 1555 Malabia House, Malabia 1555, Palermo Viejo, T4833 2410, www. malabiahouse.com.ar. Elegant but

expensive B&B with individually designed bedrooms and calm sitting rooms, great breakfast, reliable and welcoming. Recommended.

$$$$ Bo Bo, Guatemala 4882, T4774 0505, www.bobo hotel.com. On a leafy street, 7 rooms decorated in contemporary style, some with private balconies, excellent restaurant.

$$$$ Legado Mítico, Gurruchaga 1848, T4833 1300, www.legadomitico.com. Stylish small hotel with 11 rooms named after Argentine cultural legends. They use local designs and products. Luxurious and recommended.

$$$$ Krista, Bonpland 1665, T4771 4697, www.kristahotel.com.ar. Intimate, hidden behind the plain façade of an elegant town-house, well-placed for restaurants. Good value, comfortable, individually-designed spacious rooms, Wi-Fi, wheelchair access.

$$$ Solar Soler, Soler 5676, T4776 3065, www.solarsoler.com.ar. Welcoming B&B in Palermo Hollywood, excellent service, free internet. Recommended.

$$$-$$ La Otra Orilla, Julián Alvarez 1779, Palermo Viejo, T4863 7426, www.otraorilla. com.ar. Quiet, French-style 1930s residence with 7 very different rooms, from a great suite to a cute single. Some have a balcony or street views, others are more secluded. The patio is delightful for having breakfast in summer. Very good value.

$$ Vida Baires, Gallo 1483, T4827 0750, www.vidabaires.com.ar. On a residential street, convenient for shops and transport, light, attractive rooms, welcoming, internet access, breakfast included.

Youth hostels
$ pp Bait, El Salvador 5115, T4774 2859, www.baitba.com. Small hostel 3 blocks from Plaza Serrano, simple rooms (**$$** doubles with and without bath), with breakfast, use of kitchen, internet, Wi-Fi, bar.

$ pp Casa Esmeralda, Honduras 5765, T4772 2446, www.casaesmeralda.com.ar.

Laid-back, dorms and **$$** doubles, neat garden with hammocks and pond. Offers basic comfort with great charm.

$ pp **Hostal El Candil**, Lerma 476, T4899 1547, www.hostalelcandil.com. Argentine-Italian owned hostel with shared rooms (US$11.50 pp) and doubles (**$$**), international atmosphere, quiet, comfortable, welcoming, with breakfast, rooftop terrace, Wi-Fi, tours arranged.

$ pp **Hostel Suites Palermo**, Charcas 4752, T4773 0806, www.suitespalermo.com. A beautiful century-old residence with the original grandeur partially preserved and a quiet atmosphere. Comfortable renovated dorms and private rooms with bath (**$$** doubles), good service, small travel agency, free internet, Wi-Fi, cooking and laundry facilities, DVD room and breakfast included.

$ pp **Tango Backpackers Hostel**, Paraguay 4601, T4776 6871, www.tangobp.com. Well situated for Palermo's nightlife, lots of activities, **$$** doubles, free internet access and Wi-Fi, open terrace with outdoor showers. HI discount.

San Telmo and around *p27, map p27*

$$$$ Axel Hotel, Venezuela 649, T4136 9393, www.axelhotels.com. Stunning gay hotel with 5 floors of stylishly designed rooms, each floor with a cosy living area, rooftop pool, gourmet restaurant. Recommended.

$$$$-$$$ La Cayetana Historic House, México 1330, T4383 2230, www.lacayetanahotel.com.ar. 11 suites in a beautifully restored 1820s house, each room individually designed, quiet, buffet breakfast, parking, Wi-Fi. Recommended.

$$$ La Casita de San Telmo, Cochabamba 286 T/F4307 5073, www.lacasitadesantelmo.com. 7 rooms in restored 1840's house, most open onto a garden with a beautiful fig tree, owners are tango fans; rooms rented by day, week or month.

$$$ Lola House, Castro Barros 1073, Boedo, T4932 2139, www.lolahouse.com.br.

Small boutique hotel in a nicely refurbished house, welcoming owners, comfortable, good breakfast, a/c, Wi-Fi, safe; 10 mins from centre on Subte E, also on bus routes.

$$$ Lugar Gay de Buenos Aires, Defensa 1120 (no sign), T4300 4747, www.lugargay.com.ar. A men-only gay B & B with 8 comfortable rooms, video room, jacuzzi, a stone's throw from Plaza Dorrego.

$$$ Mansión Dandi Royal, Piedras 922, T4307 7623, www.hotelmansiondandiroyal.com. A wonderfully restored 1903 residence, small upmarket hotel with an elegant tango atmosphere, small pool, good value. Daily tango lessons and *milonga* every Wed at 2140.

$$$ Telmho, Defensa 1086, T4116 5467, www.telmho-hotel.com.ar. Smart rooms overlooking Plaza Dorrego, huge beds, modern bathrooms, lovely roof garden, helpful staff.

$$ Garden House Art Factory, Piedras 545, T4343 1463, www.artfactoryba.com.ar. Large, early 1900s house converted into a hotel, charming owners (see **Garden House**, below), informal atmosphere with individually designed and brightly painted private rooms (some with bath), halfway between the centre and San Telmo. Wi-Fi, internet, breakfast included, no credit cards.

Youth hostels

$ pp **Circus**, Chacabuco 1020, T5430 0405, www.hostelcircus.com. Stylish rooms for 2 to 4 people, tastefully renovated building, small heated swimming pool.

$ pp **Garden House**, Av San Juan 1271, T4304 1824, www.gardenhouseba.com.ar. Small, welcoming independent hostel for those who don't want a party atmosphere; good barbecues on the terrace. Includes breakfast, free internet, dorms US$11-13, some **$$** doubles. Recommended.

$ pp **El Hostal de Granados**, Chile 374, T43625600, www.hostaldegranados.com.ar. Small, light, well-equipped rooms in an interesting building on a popular street, rooms for 2 (**$$**), dorms for 4 to 8 (US$11.50-19.50), with bath, breakfast included, kitchen, free internet and Wi-Fi, laundry.

$ pp Hostel-Inn Buenos Aires, Humberto Primo 820, T4300 7992, www.hibuenosaires.com. An old 2-storey mansion with an outdoor terrace, dorms for up to 8 people (US$10.50) and also private rooms (**$$**), activities, loud parties, free internet and Wi-Fi, breakfast included and individual lockers in every room. HI discount.

$ pp Kilca Hostel & Backpacker, Mexico 1545, between Saenz Peña and Virrey Cevallos, T4381 1966, www.kilcabackpacker.com. Lovingly restored 19th-century house with attractive landscaped patios. A variety of rooms from dorms (US$12) to doubles (**$$**); all bathrooms shared. Wi-Fi, breakfast included.

$ pp Ostinatto, Chile 680, T4362 9639, www.ostinatto.com. Shared rooms US$11.50-15, also has double rooms with and without bath (**$$**), also has apartments for rent. Minimalist contemporary design in a 1920s building, very nice, communal kitchen, free internet, Wi-Fi, promotes the arts, music, piano bar, movie room, tango lessons, arranges events, rooftop terrace.

$ pp Sabatico Travelers Hostel, México 1410, T4381 1138, www.sabaticohostel.com.ar. Also has double rooms with and without bath (**$$**), breakfast included.

$ pp Sandanzas, Balcarce 1351, T4300 7375, www.sandanzas.com.ar. Arty hostel run by a group of friends. Small but with a light airy feel, **$$** in double with bath, lounge and patio, free internet, Wi-Fi, breakfast and use of bikes, DVDs, kitchen.

Homestays and student residences
B&T Argentina, T4876 5000, www.bytargentina.com. Accommodation in student residences and host families; also furnished flats.

La Red Coret, www.angelfire.com/pq/coret. Run by Esther Corcias, a network of host families, with Spanish School and daytrips and meetings organized.

Apartments/self catering
Bahouse, T4815 7602, www.bahouse.com.ar. Very good flats, by the week or month, all furnished and well-located in San Telmo, Retiro, Recoleta, Belgrano, Palermo and the centre.

Casa 34, Juan Ramírez de Velasco 1054, T4854 0643, www.casa34.com. Helpful, with a big range.

Tu Casa Argentina, Fitzroy 2179, T4773 5544, www.tucasargentina.com. Furnished flats by the day, week, month (from US$50 per day). Credit cards not accepted, deposit and rent payable in dollars. Efficient and helpful.

❼ Restaurants

Eating out in Buenos Aires is one of the city's great pleasures, with a huge variety of restaurants from the chic to the cheap. To try some of Argentina's excellent steak, choose from one of the many *parrillas*, where your huge slab of lean meat will be expertly cooked over a wood fire. If in doubt about where to eat, head for Puerto Madero, where there are lots of good places serving international as well as local cuisine. Take a radio taxi to Palermo or Las Cañitas for a wide range of excellent restaurants all within strolling distance. For more information on the gastronomy of Buenos Aires see: www.guiaoleo.com.ar, restaurant guide in Spanish and English; www.vidalbuzzi.com.ar, in Spanish. 2 fantastic food-oriented blogs in English are: www.saltshaker.net, chef Dan Perlman who also runs a highly recommended private restaurant in his house, see website for details; and www.buenosairesfoodies.com.

Some restaurants are *tenedor libre*: eat as much as you like for a fixed price. Most cafés serve tea or coffee plus facturas, or pastries, for breakfast, US$2-3.50.

Retiro, and the area between Plaza de Mayo and Plaza San Martín *p19, map p20*

$$$ Dadá, San Martín 941. A restaurant and bar with eclectic decoration. Good for gourmet lunches.

$$$ La Chacra, Av Córdoba 941 (just off 9 de Julio). A superb traditional parrilla with excellent steaks, impeccable old-fashioned service, lively atmosphere.

$$$ La Estancia, Lavalle 941. A touristy but reliable *parrilla*, popular with business people at lunchtime, good grills.

$$$ Morizono, Reconquista 899. Japanese dishes. Recommended for their set lunch menus.

$$$ El Querandí, Perú 302 y Moreno. Good food in an intimate atmosphere in this place that was opened in the 1920s and is now also a tango venue in the evening. Next door is a wine bar serving lunch and dinner at **La Cava del Querandí**, Perú 322.

$$$ Sorrento Corrientes 668 (just off Florida). Intimate, elegant atmosphere, one of the most traditional places in the centre for very good pastas and seafood.

$$$ Tancat, Paraguay 645. Delicious Spanish food, very popular at lunchtime.

$$$ Tomo 1, Panamericano Hotel, Carlos Pellegrini 521, T4326 6695. Argentine regional dishes and international cuisine of a high standard in a sophisticated atmosphere. Very expensive.

$$$-$$ Abril, Suipacha y Arenales. A good small place serving a varied menu, mostly European dishes.

$$$-$$ La Casona del Nonno, Lavalle 827. Popular with tourists, for its central location and for its set price menu serving good food.

$$$-$$ El Palacio de la Papa Frita, Lavalle 735 and 954, Corrientes 1620. Great place for a filling feed, with a large menu, and quite atmospheric, despite bright lighting.

$$ Las Cuartetas, Av Corrientes 838. A local institution open early to very late for fantastic pizza, can be busy and noisy as it's so popular.

$$ Gianni´s, Viamonte 834 and Reconquista 1028. The set menu with the meal-of-the-day makes an ideal lunch. Good risottos and salads.

$$ Güerrín, Corrientes 1368. A Buenos Aires institution. Serves filling pizza and *faina* (chick pea polenta) which you eat standing up at a bar, or at tables, though you miss out on the colourful local life that way. Wonderful. For an extra service fee, upstairs room is less crowded or noisy.

$$-$ Pura Vida, Reconquista 516. Open Mon-Fri for salads, juices, sandwiches, wraps and soups, all natural ingredients.

Cafés

Aroma, Florida y M T de Alvear. A great place to relax, with a huge space upstairs, comfy chairs for watching the world go by.

Café Tortoni, Av de Mayo 825-9. This most famous Buenos Aires café has been the elegant haunt of artists and writers for over 100 years, with marble columns, stained glass ceilings, old leather chairs, and photographs of its famous clientele on the walls. Excellent coffee and cakes, good tea, excellent tango, live jazz in evenings, all rather pricey. Getting increasingly packed with tourists, but still worth a visit.

Clásica y Moderna, Callao 892, T4812 8707, www.clasicaymoderna.com. One of the city's most welcoming cafés, with a bookshop, great atmosphere, good breakfast through to drinks at night, daily live music and varied shows. Highly recommended.

Confitería Ideal, Suipacha 384. One of the most atmospheric cafés in the city. Wonderfully old-fashioned 1930s interior, serving good coffee and excellent cakes with good service. Upstairs, tango is taught and there's tango dancing at a *milonga* here. Highly recommended.

El Gato Negro, Av Corrientes 1669. A beautiful tearoom, serving a choice of coffees and teas, and good cakes. Delightfully scented from the wide range of spices on sale.

Florida Garden, Florida y Paraguay. Another well-known café, popular for lunch, and tea.

The Italian ice cream tradition has been marked for decades by 'heladerías' such as **Cadore**, Av Corrientes 1695 or **El Vesuvio**, Av Corrientes 1181, the oldest of all.

Puerto Madero *p28*

The revamped docks area is an attractive place to eat, and to stroll along the waterfront before dinner. There are good places here, generally in stylish interiors and with good service if a little overpriced.

$$$ El Clan, Olga Cossettini 1501, www.el-clan.com.ar. Home-made pastas, fish and meat dishes in a restaurant hung with long curtains and chandeliers.

$$$ La Parolaccia, Av Alicia Moreau de Justo 1052 and 1170. Excellent pasta and Italian-style dishes (seafood is the speciality at No 1170), executive lunch US$8 Mon-Fri, popular.

$$$-$$ Fresh Market, Azucena Villaflor y Olga Cossettini. Fresh fruits and vegetables served in the most varied ways in this small, trendy restaurant and deli, from breakfasts to dinners.

West of Plaza de Mayo *p22, map p24*

3 blocks west of Plaza San Martín, under the flyover at the northern end of Av 9 de Julio, between Arroyo and Av del Libertador in La Recova, are several good restaurants.

$$$ Juana M, Carlos Pellegrini 1535 (downstairs). Excellent choice, popular with locals for its good range of dishes, and its very good salad bar.

$$$ El Mirasol de la Recova, Posadas 1032. Serves top-quality parrilla in an elegant atmosphere.

$$$ Piegari, Posadas 1042. Great for Italian food served in generous portions; though a bit overpriced and a noisy place.

Recoleta *p23, map p24*

$$$ Lola, Roberto M Ortiz 1805. Well known for superb pasta dishes, lamb and fish.

$$$ Sirop, Pasaje del Correo, Vte Lopez 1661, T4813 5900. Delightful chic design, delicious French-inspired food, superb patisserie too. Highly recommended.

$$$-$$ El Sanjuanino, Posadas 1515. Atmospheric place offering typical dishes from the northwest: *humitas*, *tamales*, and *empanadas*, as well as unusual game dishes.

$$$-$$ Rodi Bar, Vicente López 1900. Excellent *bife* and other dishes in this typical *bodegón*, welcoming and unpretentious.

$$ La Madeleine, Av Santa Fe 1726. Bright and cheerful choice open 24 hrs; quite good pastas.

$$ María de Bambi, Ayacucho 1821. This small, quiet place is probably the best value in the area, serving very good and simple meals, also salon de té and patisserie. Open till 2130, closed on Sun.

Tea rooms, café-bars and ice cream

Café Victoria, Roberto M Ortiz 1865. Wonderful old-fashioned café, popular and refined, great cakes.

Ice Cream Freddo, in Recoleta at Roberto M Ortiz y Quintana, Arenales y Callao, Roberto M Ortiz y Guido, Santa Fe y Montevideo and at shopping malls. Known for the best ice cream.

Milion, Paraná 1048. Stylish bar and café in an elegant mansion with marble stairs and a garden, good drinks, mixed clientèle, recommended Fri after midnight.

Un'Altra Volta, in Recoleta at Av Santa Fe y Av Callao, Quintana y Ayacucho, Pacheco de Melo y Av Callao, also at Av Libertador 3060 in Palermo. Great ice creams, chocolates and pastries.

Palermo *p23, map p24*

This area of Buenos Aires is very popular, with many chic restaurants and bars in Palermo Viejo (referred to as 'Palermo Soho' for the area next to Plaza Cortázar and 'Palermo Hollywood' for the area beyond the railways and Av Juan B Justo) and the Las Cañitas district. It's a sprawling district, so you could take a taxi to one of these restaurants, and walk around before deciding where to eat. It's also a great place to stop for lunch, with cobbled streets, and 1900s buildings, now housing chic clothes shops.

The Las Cañitas area is fashionable, with a wide range of interesting restaurants mostly along CBaez, and most opening at around 2000, though only open for lunch at weekends:

$$$ Baez, Baez 240, Las Cañitas. Very trendy, with lots of orange neon, serving sophisticated Italian-style food and sushi.

$$$ Bio, Humboldt 2199, T4774 3880. Delicious gourmet organic food, on a sunny corner, open daily.

$$$ La Cabrera, Cabrera 5127 and 5099. Superb parrilla and pasta, huge portions, with 2 branches; very popular but reservations cannot be made. They offer a sparkling white wine while you wait.

$$$ Campo Bravo, Baez y Arevalo, Las Cañitas. Stylish, minimalist, superb steaks and vegetables on the *parrilla*. Popular and recommended, can be noisy.

$$$ Cluny, El Salvador 4618, T4831 7176. Very classy, a great place for lunch, fish and pasta with great sauces, mellow music.

$$$ Dominga, Honduras 5618, T4771 4443, www.domingarestaurant.com. Elegant, excellent food from a short but creative menu, professional service, good wine list, ideal for a romantic meal or treat, open evenings only.

$$$ Eh! Santino, Baez 194, Las Cañitas. Italian-style food in a trendy, small, if not cramped place, dark and cosy with lots of mirrors.

$$$ El Manto, Costa Rica 5801, T4774 2409. Genuine Armenian dishes, relaxed, good for a quiet evening.

$$$ Janio, Malabia 1805, T4833 6540. One of Palermo's first restaurants, open for breakfast through to the early hours, lunch US$6, sophisticated Argentine cuisine in the evening.

$$$ Novecento, Baez 199, Las Cañitas. A lively French-style bistro, stylish but unpretentious and cosy, good fish dishes among a broad menu.

$$$ El Preferido de Palermo, Borges y Guatemala, T4778 7101. Very popular bodegón serving both Argentine and Spanish-style dishes.

$$$ Social Paraíso, Honduras 5182. Simple delicious dishes in a relaxed chic atmosphere, with a lovely patio at the back. Good fish and tasty salads. Closed Sun evening and Mon.

$$$-$$ Morelia, Baez 260, Las Cañitas. Cooks superb pizzas on the *parrilla* or in wood ovens, and has a lovely roof terrace for summer. Also at Humboldt 2005.

$$$-$$ Omm, Honduras 5656, T4774 4224. Cosy wine and tapas bar with good food. Also Omm Carnes, Costa Rica 5198, T4773 0954, for meat dishes and steak, open from 1800, closed Sun.

$$ Krishna, Malabia 1833. A small, intimate place serving very good Indian-flavoured vegetarian dishes.

Tea rooms, café-bars and ice cream
Palermo has good cafés opposite the park on Av del Libertador, including the fabulous ice creams at **Un'Altra Volta**, Av del Libertador 3060 (another branch at Echeverría 2302, Belgrano).

Cusic, El Salvador 6016, T4139 9173, www.cusic.com.ar. For breakfast and lunches, breads, sandwiches, wraps, puddings, closed Tue.

Persicco, Salguero y Cabello, Maure y Migueletes and Av Rivadavia 4933 (Caballito). The grandsons of **Freddo's** founders also offer excellent ice cream.

San Telmo *p27, map p27*
$$$ Brasserie Petanque, Defensa y Mexico. Very attractive, informal French restaurant offering a varied menu with very good, creative dishes. Excellent value for their set lunch menus.

$$$ La Brigada, Estados Unidos 461, T4361 5557. Atmospheric parrilla, serving excellent Argentine cuisine and wines.

Very popular and compact, expensive, but recommended. Always reserve.

$$$ El Desnivel, Defensa 855. Popular parrilla, packed at weekends.

$$ Bar Británico, Brasil y Defensa 399. Open 24 hrs. A historic place with a good atmosphere at lunchtime.

$$ Pride Café, Balcarce y Giuffra. Wonderful sandwiches, juices, salads and brownies, with lots of magazines to read.

Ice creams

Dylan, Perú 1086. Very good. **Freddo**, a few blocks away, at Defensa y Estados Unidos. **Nonna Bianca**, Estados Unidos 425. For ice cream in an interent café.

Cheap eats

A few supermarkets have good, cheap restaurants: **Coto** supermarket, Viamonte y Paraná, upstairs. Many supermarkets have very good deli counters and other shops sell *fiambres* (smoked, cured meats) and cheeses for quick, cheap eating. The snack bars in underground stations are also cheap. **Delicity bakeries**, several branches, have very fresh *facturas* (pastries), cakes, breads, and American doughnuts. Another good bakery for breakfasts, sandwishes and salads is **Bonpler**, Florida 481, 0730-2300, with the daily papers, classical music. Other branches elsewhere.

🎧 Bars and clubs

Generally it is not worth going to clubs before 0230 at weekends. Dress is usually smart. A good way to visit some of the best bars is to join a pub crawl, eg **The Buenos Aires Pub Crawl**, www.pubcrawlBA.com, whose crawls several days a week are a safe night out. Entry can be from US$10-15, sometimes including a drink.

Centre, Retiro and Recoleta *p19, maps p20 and p24*
Buller Brewing Company, Roberto M Ortiz 1827, Recoleta. Brew pub.

Casa Bar, Rodríguez Peña 1150, Recoleta. Beers from around the world in a restored mansion, good place to watch international sports matches, also serves food.

La Cigale, 25 de Mayo 722, Centre, T4312 8275. Popular after office hours, good music, guest DJs on Tue.

The corner of Reconquista and Marcelo T de Alvear in Retiro is the centre of the small 'Irish' pub district, overcrowded on St Patrick's Day, 17 Mar. **Druid In**, Reconquista 1040, Centre, is by far the most attractive choice there, open for lunch and with live music weekly. **The Shamrock**, Rodríguez Peña 1220, in Recoleta, is another Irish-run, popular bar, happy hour for ISIC holders.

Palermo Viejo
Bangalore Bar, Humboldt 1416. English-style pub which serves wraps, curries and mojitos.

Mundo Bizarro, Serrano 1222. Famous for its weird films, cocktails, American-style food, electronic and pop music.

Sugar, Costa Rica 4619. Welcoming, cosy bar with cheap beer and drinks, happy hour nightly.

San Telmo *p27, map p27*
Bar Dorrego, Humberto Primo y Defensa. Bar/café with great atmosphere, seating on plaza outside, good for late-night coffee or drinks.

Bar Seddon, Defensa y Chile. Traditional bar open till late with live music on Fri.

La Resistencia, Defensa e Independencia. Local hangout with cheap drinks and rock music, lots of fun.

Plan B, Brasil 444. Alternative bar that doesn't look much from outside, but very friendly place where you can bring your own music, pool table.

La Trastienda, Balcarce 460, www. latrastienda.com. Theatre café with lots of live events, also serving meals and drinks from breakfast to dinner, great music, relaxed and cool, but busy lunchtime. Recommended.

Clubs

El Living, M T de Alvear 1540, Recoleta, T4811 4730. Relaxed bar, restaurant and small club, Thu-Sat.
Niceto Club (Club 69), Niceto Vega 5510, Palermo, T4779 9396, www.nicetoclub. com. Early live shows and funk or electronic music for dancing afterwards.

Gay clubs Most gay clubs charge from US$8 entry. **Amerika**, Gascón 1040, Almagro, www.ameri-k.com.ar. Thu-Sun, attracting over 2000 party-goers over 3 floors. **Bach Bar**, Cabrera 4390, www.bach-bar.com.ar. Friendly lesbian bar in Palermo Viejo, Wed-Sun. **Sitges**, Av Córdoba 4119, Palermo, T4861 3763, www.sitges online. com.ar. Gay and lesbian bar.

Jazz clubs **Notorious**, Av Callao 966, T4813 6888, www.notorious.com.ar. Live jazz at a music shop. **La Revuelta**, Alvarez Thomas 1368, T4553 5530. Live jazz, bossa nova and tango. **Thelonious**, Salguero 1884, T4829 1562. Live jazz and tango.

Salsa clubs La Salsera, Yatay 961, T4866 1829, www.lasalsera.com. Highly regarded.

⊙ Entertainment

Details of most events are given in Espectáculos/ Entretenimientos section of main newspapers, *Buenos Aires Herald* (English) on Fri and www. whatsupbuenosaires.com. At carnival time, look for the **Programa Carnaval Porteño**.

Cinemas

The selection of films is excellent, ranging from new Hollywood releases to Argentine and world cinema; details are listed daily in main newspapers. Films are shown uncensored and most foreign films are subtitled. Tickets best booked early afternoon to ensure good seats (average price US$5.50, more expensive at weekends, especially Sat night, discount on Wed and for 1st show daily).

Many cinemas in shopping malls, which tend to show more mainstream Hollywood films. Recent European and non-Hollywood films can be found elsewhere, mostly in the Atlas chain of cinemas: **Arteplex**, Av Cabildo 2829, Belgrano, T4781 6500; **Cineduplex**, Av Rivadavia 5050, T4902 5682; **Lorca**, Av Corrientes 1428. Most Argentine films are shown at **Complejo Tita Merello**, Suipacha 442, T4322 1195, and **Gaumont**, Av Rivadavia 1635, T4371 3050.

Independent foreign and national films are shown during the **Festival de Cine Independiente** (BAFICI), held every Apr, more information on the festival at www. bafici.gov.ar.

Cultural events

Centro Cultural Borges, Galerías Pacífico, Viamonte y San Martín, p 1, T5555 5359, www.ccborges.org.ar. Art exhibitions, concerts, film shows and ballet; some student discounts.
Centro Cultural Recoleta, Junín 1930, by Recoleta cemetery. Many free activities (see under Places in Buenos Aires).
Ciudad Cultural Konex, Sarmiento 3131 (Abasto), T4864 3200, www.ciudadcultural konex.org. A converted oil factory hosts this huge complex holding plays, live music shows, summer film projections under the stars, modern ballet, puppet theatre and, occasionally, massive parties.
Fundación Proa, Av Pedro de Mendoza 1929, T4104 1000, www.proa.org. Temporary exhibitions of contemporary art, photography and other cultural events in La Boca. Open Tue-Sun 1100-1900.
Luna Park stadium, Bouchard 465, near Correo Central, T5279 5279, www.lunapark. com.ar. Pop/jazz concerts, sports events, ballet and musicals.
Museo de Arte Latinoamericano, MALBA (address and website above), is a very active centre holding old or independent film exhibitions, seminars and conferences on arts.
Teatro Gral San Martín, Corrientes 1530, T4371 0111/8, www.teatrosan martin. ar. Cultural activities, many free, including

concerts, 50% ISIC discount for Thu, Fri and Sun (only in advance at 4th floor, Mon-Fri). The theatre's **Sala Leopoldo Lugones** shows international classic films, US$2.50.

Tango shows

There are two ways to enjoy tango: you can watch the dancing at a tango show. Most pride themselves on very high standards and although they are not cheap, this is tango at its best. Most prices include drinks and hotel transfers. Or you can learn to dance at a class and try your steps at a *milonga* (tango club). There is a tango information desk at **Centro Cultural San Martín**, Sarmiento 1551, T4373 2829, daily 1400-2100. The city tourist board's leaflet, *Passionate Buenos Aires*, lists classes and *milongas*. See also the websites **www. tangoguia.com**, **www.tangocity.com** and **www.todotango. com**. Every August there is a tango dancing competition, **Festival y Mundial de Baile**, open to both locals and foreigners, see **www.tangobuenosaires. gov.ar** for details.

Bar Sur, Estados Unidos 299, T4362 6086, www.bar-sur.com.ar. 2000-0300. Price including pizza, but drinks extra. Good fun, public sometimes join the professional dancers.

El Querandí, Perú 302, T5199 1770, www. querandi.com.ar. Tango show restaurant, daily show (2215) US$115 including dinner at 2030; show only costs US$75.

El Viejo Almacén, Independencia y Balcarce, T4307 7388, www.viejoalmacen. com. Daily, dinner from 2000, show 2200, US$115 with dinner and show; show only, US$74. Impressive dancing and singing, recommended.

Esquina Carlos Gardel, Carlos Gardel 3200 y Anchorena, T4867 6363, www. esquinacarlos gardel.com.ar. Opposite the former Mercado del Abasto, this is the most popular venue in Gardel's own neighbourhood; dinner at 2030 (dinner and show US$140), show at 2230 (US$96). Recommended.

Esquina Homero Manzi, Av San Juan 3601 (Subte Boedo), T4957 8488, www. esquinahomeromanzi.com.ar. Traditional show at 2200 with excellent musicians and dancers, dinner (2100) and show available, tango school. Recommended.

Evita Vive, Moreno 364, San Telmo, T4343 0463, www.evitavive.com. Tango show based around the life of Evita Perón, US$120 dinner and show, US$70 show only.

La Ventana, Balcarce 431, T4334 1314, www.la-ventana.com.ar. Daily dinner from 2000 (dinner and show US$120) or show with 2 drinks, 2200, US$70, very touristy but very good.

Piazzolla Tango, Florida 165 (basement), Galería Güemes, T4344 8201, www. piazzollatango.com. A beautifully restored belle époque hall hosts a smart tango show; dinner at 2045 (dinner and show US$110), show at 2215 (US$65).

Milongas are very popular with younger *porteños*. You can take a class and get a feel for the music before the dancing starts a couple of hours later. Both tango and *milonga* (the music that contributed to the origins of tango and is more cheerful) are played. Cost is from US$5; even beginners are welcome.

Centro Cultural Torquato Tasso, Defensa 1575, T4307 6506, www.torquatotasso. com.ar. See web for programme and prices (daily shows), English spoken.

Confitería Ideal, Suipacha 384, T4328 7750, www.confiteriaideal.com. Very atmospheric ballroom for daily milongas at this old central café. Most days dancing starts as early as 1500; lessons start 1200 on some days, 1500 on others and 1800 Sun. Also evening tango shows.

La Viruta (at Centro Armenio), Armenia 1366, Palermo Viejo, T4774 6357, www. lavirutatango. com. Very popular with a young and trendy crowd, classes every day except Mon, entry US$7 (check website for times), also salsa and rock dancing classes, with restaurant.

Tango Discovery, www.tangodiscovery. com. Offers unconventional method for tango lessons developed by dancer Mauricio Castro.

Theatre

About 20 commercial theatres play all year and there are many amateur theatres. The main theatre street is Av Corrientes. Book seats for theatre, ballet and opera as early as possible. Tickets for most popular shows (including rock and pop concerts) are sold also through **Ticketek**, T5237 7200, www.ticketek.com.ar. See also www.alternativateatral.com and www. mundoteatral.com.ar. For live Argentine and Latin American bands, best venues are: **La Trastienda**, www.latrastienda.com, or **ND Ateneo**, www.ndateneo.com.ar.

⊙ Shopping

The main, fashionable shopping streets are Florida and Santa Fe (from Av 9 de Julio to Av Pueyrredón). Palermo is the best area for chic boutiques and well-known international fashion labels; head for Calles Honduras and El Salvador, between Malabia and Serrano. C Defensa in San Telmo is known for its antique shops. It also has a few craft stalls around C Alsina, Fri 1200-1700. Pasaje de la Defensa, Defensa 1179, is a beautifully restored 1880s house containing small shops.

Bookshops

You'll find most bookshops along Florida, Av Corrientes (from Av 9 de Julio to Callao) or Av Santa Fe, and in shopping malls. Second- hand and discount bookshops are mostly along Av Corrientes and Av de Mayo. Rare books are sold in several specialized stores in the Microcentro (the area enclosed by Suipacha, Esmeralda, Tucumán and Paraguay). The main chains of bookshops, usually selling a small selection of foreign books, are: **Cúspide**, with several branches on Florida, Av Corrientes and some malls, and the biggest and most interesting store at Village Recoleta, Vicente López y Junín; **Distal**, Florida 738 and more branches on Florida and Av Corrientes; **Yenny-El Ateneo**, whose biggest store is on Av Santa Fe 1860, in an old theatre, there is café where the stage used to be; also in all shopping malls, they sell music too. For a larger selection of books in English: **Crack Up**, Costa Rica 4767, T4831 3502. Funky, open plan bookshop and café, open Mon-Wed till 2230, and till the early hrs the rest of the week. **Eterna Cadencia**, Honduras 5574, T4774 4100, www.eternacadencia.com. Excellent selection of novels, classics, contemporary fiction and translations of Spanish and Argentine authors. Highly recommended for its café too. **Walrus Books**, Estados Unidos 617, San Telmo, T4300 7135, www. walrus-books.com.ar. Second-hand books in English, including Latin American authors. Good children's section.

You can also try **ABC**, Maipú 866; **Joyce, Proust & Co**, Tucumán 1545 p 1 A, also sells books in other European languages; **Kel**, Marcelo T de Alvear 1369; **Librería Rodríguez**, Sarmiento 835; **LOLA**, Viamonte 976, Mon-Fri 1200-1830, small publishers specializing in Latin America natural history, also sell used and rare editions, most in English.

Foreign newspapers are available from news-stands on Florida, in Recoleta and the kiosk at Corrientes and Maipú.

Camping equipment

Good equipment from **Angel Baraldo**, Av Belgrano 270, T4342 4233, www.baraldo. com.ar. Argentine and imported stock. **Cacique Camping**, Esteban Echeverría 3360, Munro, T4762 1668, www.cacique.com. ar. Manufactured clothing and equipment. **Camping Center**, Esmeralda 945, www. camping-center.com.ar. Good selection of outdoor sports articles. **Costanera Uno**, at the southern end of Costanera Norte, T4312 4545, www.costanera uno.com. ar. For nautical sports, very good. **Ecrin**,

Av Santa Fe 2723 (Martínez), T4792 1935, www.ecrin.com.ar. Imported climbing equipment. **Fugate** (no sign), Gascón 238 (off Rivadavia 4000 block), T4982 0203, www.fugate.com.ar. Also repairs equipment. **Jorge Gallo**, Liniers 1522, Tigre, T4731 0323. GPS repair service. **Montagne**, Florida 719, Paraná 772, and several others, www.montagneoutdoors.com.ar. **Outside Mountain Equipment**, Otero 172 (Chacarita), T4856 6204, www.outside.com. ar. Camping gas available at **Britam**, B Mitre 1111, **El Pescador**, Paraguay y Libertad, and **Todo Gas**, Sarmiento 1540.

Handicrafts
Alhué, Juncal 1625. Very good indigenous-style crafts. **Arte y Esperanza**, Balcarce 234, www.arteyesperanza.com.ar. Crafts made by indigenous communities, sold by a Fair Trade organization. **Artesanías Argentinas**, Montevideo 1386, www. artesaniasargentinas. org. Aboriginal crafts and other traditional items sold by a Fair Trade organization. **Casa de San Antonio de los Cobres**, Pasaje de la Defensa, Defensa 1179, www.vivirenlos cobres.com. ar. Traditional Puna crafts in silver, llama or sheep wool. **El Boyero**, Florida 953, T4312 3564. High quality silver, leather, woodwork and other typical Argentine handicrafts. **Martín Fierro**, Santa Fe 992. Good handicrafts, stonework, etc. Recommended. **Plata Nativa**, Galería del Sol, Florida 860, local 41. For Latin American folk handicrafts and high quality jewellery.

Leather goods
Several shops are concentrated along Florida next to Plaza San Martín and also in Suipacha (900 block). **Aida**, Galería de la Flor, local 30, Florida 670. Quality, inexpensive leather products, can make a leather jacket to measure in the same day. **Dalla Fontana**, Reconquista 735. Leather factory, fast, efficient and reasonably priced for made-to-measure clothes. **Casa López**, MT de Alvear 640/658; also at

Patio Bullrich and Galerías Pacífico malls. The most traditional and finest leather shop, expensive but worth it. **Galería del Caminante**, Florida 844. Has a variety of good shops with leather goods, arts and crafts, souvenirs, etc. **La Curtiembre**, Juncal 1173, Paraguay 670. Affordable prices for good quality articles. **Prüne**, Florida 963 and in many shopping centres. Fashionable designs for women, many options in leather and not very expensive. **Uma**, in shopping malls and at Honduras 5225 (Palermo Viejo). For women, the trendiest of all.

Markets
Markets can be found in many of the city's parks and plazas, which hold weekend fairs. You wil find pretty much the same sort of handicrafts. The following offer something different. **Feria de Mataderos**, Lisandro de la Torre y Av de los Corrales 6436, T4342 9629, www.feriademataderos.com.ar, subte E to end of line then taxi (US$5), or buses 55, 63, 80, 92, 103, 117, 126, 141, 155, 180. Long way but few tourists, fair of Argentine handicrafts and traditions, music and dance festivals, gaucho horsemanship skills, every Sun 1100-2000 (Mar-Dec); nearby *Museo de los Corrales*, Av de los Corrales 6436, T4687 1949, Sun 1200-1830, US$0.35. **Mercado de las Luces**, Manzana de las Luces, Perú y Alsina, Mon-Fri 1100-1900, Sun 1400-1900. Handicrafts, second-hand books, plastic arts. **Parque Centenario**, Díaz Vélez y L Marechal. Sat 1100-2000, local crafts, cheap handmade clothes, used items of all sorts. **Parque Rivadavia**, Av Rivadavia 4900. Second-hand books, records, tapes, CDs and magazines, Sun 0900-1300. **Plaza Dorrego**, San Telmo. For souvenirs, antiques, etc, with free tango performances and live music, Sun 1000-1700, wonderfully atmospheric, and an array of 'antiques'. **Plaza Italia**, Santa Fe y Uriarte (Palermo). Second hand textbooks and magazines (daily), handicrafts market on Sat 1200-2000, Sun 1000-2000.

Shopping malls

Abasto de Buenos Aires, Av Corrientes 3247, T4959 3400, nearest Subte: Carlos Gardel, line B. In the city's impressive, Art Deco former fruit and vegetable market building: cheaper clothes, good choice, cinemas. **Alto Palermo**, Col Díaz y Santa Fe, T5777 8000, nearest Subte: opposite Bulnes, line D. Great for all the main clothes chain stores, and about 20 blocks' walk from Palermo's boutiques. **Galerías Pacífico**, on Florida, between Córdoba and Viamonte, T5555 5110, nearest Subte: Plaza San Martín, line C. A beautiful mall with fine murals and architecture, many exclusive shops and good food mall with wide choice and low prices in basement. Also good set-price restaurant on 2nd floor (lunches only). Free guided visits from the fountain on lower-ground floor (Mon-Fri 1130, 1630). **Paseo Alcorta**, Salguero y Figueroa Alcorta, T5777 6500. Huge mall, spanning four levels, with cinemas, supermarket, stores, many cheap restaurants (take colectivo 130 from Retiro or Correo Central, or 67 from Constitución or Recoleta). **Patio Bullrich**, Av Del Libertador 750 and Posadas 1245, T4814 7400, nearest Subte: 8 blocks from Plaza San Martín, line C. The most upmarket mall in the city, selling chic international and Argentine fashion designer clothes, boutiques selling high-quality leather goods, and small food court in elegant surroundings. **Unicenter**, Paraná 3745, Martínez, www.unicenter.com.ar. No Subte nearby, take bus No 60 from centre, 1 hr, or taxi US$9. The biggest of the lot, has everything you could possibly imagine.

⊙ What to do

Cricket

Asociación Argentina de Cricket, Paraguay 1270, T4816 4780, www.cricketargentina. com, for information. Cricket is played Nov-Mar.

Cycle hire and tours

La Bicicleta Naranja, Pasaje Giuffra 308, San Telmo and Nicaragua 4825, Palermo, T4362 1104, www.labicicletanaranja.com.ar. Bike hire and tours to all parts of the city, 4-5 hrs. **Lan&Kramer Bike Tours**, San Martín 910 p 6, and Chile 374 (San Telmo), T4311 5199, www.bike tours.com.ar. Daily at 0930 and 1400 next to the monument of San Martín (Plaza San Martín), 3½- 4-hr cycle tours to the south or the north of the city; also to San Isidro and Tigre, 4½-5 hrs; also, bike rental. **Urban biking**, Ramón Lista 5495, T4568 4321, www.urbanbiking.com. 4 ½-hr tours either to the south or to the north of the centre, starting daily 0900 and 1400 next to the English clock tower in Retiro. Night city tours, 3½ hrs, full day tours to San Isidro and Tigre (including kayak in the Delta), or occasionally, to the pampas. Also rents bikes.

Football and rugby

Football fans should see **Boca Juniors**, matches every other Sun 1500-1900 at their stadium (La Bombonera, Brandsen 805, La Boca, www.bocajuniors.com.ar, tickets for non-members only through tour operators, or the museum, T5777 1212 – see the murals; along Av Almirante Brown buses 29, 33, 53, 64, 86, 152, 168; along Av Patricios buses 10, 22, 39, 93), or their arch-rivals, **River Plate**, Av Figueroa Alcorta 7597, T4789 1200, www.cariver plate.com (to stadium take bus 29 from centre going north, or bus 15 from Palermo). Football season Mar to Jul, and Aug-Dec, most matches on Sun and sometimes Wed, Fri or Sat. Buy tickets (from US$8) from stadiums, sports stores near the grounds, ticket agencies or hostels and hotels, which may arrange guide/ transport (don't take a bus if traveling alone, phone a radio taxi; see also Tangol, below). Rugby season Apr-Oct/ Nov. For more information, **Unión Argentina de Rugby**, T4515 3500, www.uar.com.ar.

Horse racing

Hipódromo Argentino de Palermo, a large, modern racecourse, popular year round, and at **San Isidro**. Riding schools at both.

Polo

The high handicap season is Sep-Dec, but it is played all year round. Argentina has the top polo players in the world. A visit to the national finals at Palermo in Nov and Dec is recommended. For information, **Asociación Argentina de Polo**, T4777 8005, www. aapolo.com.

Swimming

Public baths near Aeroparque, **Punta Carrasco** (best, most expensive, also tennis courts) and **Parque Norte**, popular.
Club de Amigos, Av Figueroa Alcorta y Av Sarmiento, T4801 1213, www. clubdeamigos. org.ar. An indoor swimming pool is open all year round.

Tour operators and travel agents

An excellent way of seeing Buenos Aires and the surrounding area is by a 3-hr tour. Longer tours include dinner and a tango show, or a gaucho *fiesta* at a ranch (great food and dancing). Bookable through most travel agents. See also **BA Free Tour**, www. bafreetour.com, for a free walking tour of the city centre, 1000 Mon-Sat from Av Rivadavia y Rodríguez Peña.
Argentina Excepción, Juncal 4455, 5A, T4772 6620, www.argentina-excepcion. com. French/Argentine agency offering tailor-made, upper end tours, fly-drives, themed trips and other services. Also has a Santiago branch, www.chile-excepcion.com.
Argentina for Less, USA T1-877-661 6989 (Toll Free), UK 44-203-002-0571, World 1-512-535-0336, www.argentinaforless. com. Offers price guarantee on fully customised packages.
ATI, Esmeralda 567 (and other branches), T5297 9000, www.ati viajes.com. Mainly group travel, very efficient.

Barba Charters, T4824 3366. Boat trips and fishing in the Delta and Tigre areas.
BAT, Buenos Aires Tur, Lavalle 1444 of 10, T4371 2304, www.buenosairestur.com. City tours, twice daily; Tigre and Delta, daily, 5 hrs.
Buenos Aires Vision, Esmeralda 356, p 8, T4394 4682, www.buenosaires-vision. com.ar. City tours, Tigre and Delta, Tango (cheaper without dinner) and *Fiesta Gaucha*.
Cicerones de Buenos Aires, J J Biedma 883, T4331 9892, www.cicerones.org. ar. Non-profit organization offering volunteer "greeting"/ guiding service for visitors to the city; free, safe and a different experience.
Cultour, T156-365 6892 (mob), www. cultour. com.ar. A highly recommended walking tour of the city, 3-4 hrs led by a group of Argentine history/ tourism graduates. In English and Spanish.
Eternautas, Av Julio A Roca 584 p 7, T5031 9916, www.eternautas.com. Historical, cultural and artistic tours of the city and Pampas guided in English, French or Spanish by academics from the University of Buenos Aires, flexible.
Eves Turismo, Tucumán 702, T0800-345 3837, www.eves.com. Helpful and efficient, recommended for flights.
Flyer, Av Fondo De La Legua 425, San Isidro, T4512 8100, www.flyer.com.ar. English, Dutch, German spoken, repeatedly recommended, especially for estancias, fishing, polo, motorhome rental.
HI Travel Argentina, Florida 835 PB, T4511 8723, www.hitravel.com.ar. Hostel network office and advisors, specialised backpacker trips.
Kallpa, Tucumán 861, p 2, T5278 8010, www.kallpatour.com. Tailor-made tours to natural and cultural destinations throughout the country, with an emphasis on adventure, conservation and golf.
L'Open Tour, T5353 4443, www.lopentour. com.ar. Multilingual, 2-hr recorded tours

(headphones provided) on an open bus, to the south, the north or at night, from Plaza San Martín (opposite **Marriott Hotel**), from US$35. Book in advance.

Mai10, Av Córdoba 657, p 3, T4314 3390, www.mai10.com.ar. High-end, personalized tours for groups and individuals, covers the whole country, special interests include art, cuisine, estancias, photo safaris, fishing and many more.

Patagonia Chopper, www.patagonia chopper.com.ar. Helicopter tours of Buenos Aires and around, 15-45 mins (min 2 people; price includes transfer in/out to/from the city centre).

Say Hueque, Viamonte 749, p 6 of 1, and other branches in Palermo and San Telmo, T5199 2517/20, www.sayhueque.com. Recommended travel agency offering good-value tours aimed at independent travellers, friendly English-speaking staff. Specialize in tours to Patagonia, Iguazu and Mendoza.

Smile on Sea, T15-5018 8662, www.smileonsea.com. 2-hr private boat trips off Buenos Aires coast, leaving from Puerto Madero, on 32-ft sailing boats (up to 5 passengers). Also 8-hr trips to San Isidro and Delta.

South America.travel, Suipacha 530, p 2, T1-888-206 9253, T5984 3827, www.southamerica.travel. Custom and group tours through Argentina and throughout the region.

Tangol, Florida 971, ground floor, shop 31, T4363 6000, www.tangol.com. Friendly, independent agency specializing in football and tango, plus various sports, such as polo and paragliding. Can arrange tours, plane and bus tickets, accommodation. English spoken. Discounts for students. Overland tours in Patagonia Sep-Apr.

⊖ Transport

Air
Ezeiza (officially Ministro Pistarini, T5480 2500, www.aa2000.com.ar), the international airport, is 35 km southwest of the centre (also handles some domestic flights to El Calafate and Ushuaia in high season). The airport has 3 terminals: 'A' for all airlines except some **Aerolíneas Argentinas** international flights, **Air France**, Alitalia, KLM, which use 'B', and 'C' for **Aerolíneas Argentinas** international and national flights. There are duty free shops (expensive), exchange facilities (**Banco de la Nación**; Banco Piano; Global Exchange – rates of exchange in baggage reclaim are considerably poorer than elsewhere – only change the minimum to get you into the city) and ATMs (Visa and MasterCard), a Secretaría de Turismo desk, post office (open 0800-2000) and a left luggage office (US$3 per piece). No hotels nearby, but there is an attractive B&B 5 mins away with transfer included: **$$$ Bernie's**, Estrada 186, Barrio Uno, T4480 0420, www.posada bernies.com.ar, book in advance. There is a **Devolución IVA/Tax Free** desk (return of VAT) for purchases over the value of AR$70 (ask for a Global Refund check plus the invoice from the shop when you buy). Hotel booking service at Tourist Information desk – helpful, but prices are higher if booked in this way. A display in immigration shows choices and prices of transport into the city.

Airport buses Special buses to/from the centre are run by **Manuel Tienda León** (office in front of you as you arrive), company office and terminal at Av Madero 1299 y San Martín, behind Sheraton Hotel in Retiro, T4315 5115, www.tiendaleon.com.ar. To **Ezeiza**: 0400, 0500, then every 30 mins till 2315, 2400 (be 15 mins early); from Ezeiza: more-or-less hourly throughout the day and night, US$13.75 (US$26.50 return), 40-min journey, pay by pesos, dollars, euros or credit card. **Manuel Tienda León** will also collect passengers from addresses in centre for a small extra fee, book the previous day. Bus from Ezeiza to Aeroparque, 1 hr, US$16.

Fixed-price *remise taxis* for up to 4 passengers can be booked from the

Manuel Tienda León, Transfer Express, T0800-444 4872, reservas@transfer-express.com.ar, and other counters at Ezeiza. They charge US$42 to town or to Aeroparque. Radio taxis charge US$45, see Taxis below for more details on taxis. On no account take an unmarked car at Ezeiza, no matter how attractive the fare may sound. Drivers are adept at separating you from far more money than you can possibly owe them. Always ask to see the taxi driver's licence. If you take an ordinary taxi the Policía de Seguridad Aeroportuaria on duty notes down the car's licence and time of departure. There have been recent reports of taxi drivers taking Ezeiza airport-bound passengers to remote places, stealing all their luggage and leaving them there. Always take a *remise* or airport bus. A *remise* taxi from the centre to Ezeiza costs US$30-35.

Aeroparque (Jorge Newbery Airport), 4 km north of the centre, T5480 6111, www.aa2000.com.ar, handles all internal flights, and some flights to neighbouring countries. The terminal is divided into 3 sections. On the 1st floor there is a patio de comidas and many shops. At the airport also tourist information, car rental, bus companies, bank, ATMs, exchange facilities, post office, public phones and luggage deposit, US$4 per piece for 12 hrs. Manuel Tienda León buses to Aeroparque (see above for address), more-or-less hourly; from Aeroparque (departs from sector B, stops at AR), 0900-2350, 20-min journey, US$5.75. Local bus 45 run from outside the airport to the Retiro railway station. No 37 goes to Palermo and Recoleta and No 160 to Palermo and Almagro. If going to the airport, make sure it goes to Aeroparque by asking the driver, US$0.40. Remise taxis: are operated by Transfer Express and Manuel Tienda León, US$18 to centre, US$36 to Ezeiza. Taxi to centre US$6. Manuel Tienda León operates buses between Ezeiza and Aeroparque airports, US$16, stopping in city centre, US$5.75. AR/

Austral offer daily flights to the main cities; LAN has daily flights to some cities and tourist destinations; Andes flies to Salta and to Puerto Madryn, Sol flies to Rosario, Santa Fe and Córdoba (and in summer to Mar del Plata, Villa Gesell, Montevideo and Punta del Este), for details see text under intended destination. LADE offers weekly flights to **El Calafate**, **Ushuaia**, **Puerto Madryn** and **Bariloche** with several stops in Patagonia.

Bus

Local   City buses are called *colectivos* and cover a very wide radius. They are clean, frequent, efficient and very fast. The basic fare is about US$0.30, US$0.50 to the suburbs. Have coins ready for ticket machine as drivers do not sell tickets, but may give change. The bus number is not always sufficient indication of destination, as each number may have a variety of routes, but bus stops display routes of buses stopping there and little plaques are displayed in the driver's window. No 86 (white and blue) runs to the centre from outside the airport terminal to the left as you leave the building, 2 hrs, US$0.50, coins only, runs all day, every 20 mins during the day. To travel to Ezeiza, catch the bus at Av de Mayo y Perú, 1 block from Plaza de Mayo (many other stops, but this is central) – make sure it has 'Aeropuerto' red sign in the window as many 86s stop short of Ezeiza. See Information in Ins and outs, above, for city guides listing bus routes.

Long distance   Bus terminal at Ramos Mejía y Antártida Argentina (Subte Line C), behind Retiro station, T4310 0700, www.tebasa.com.ar. The terminal is on 3 floors. Bus information is at the Ramos Mejía entrance on the middle floor. Ticket offices are on the upper floor, but there are hundreds of them so you'll need to consult the list of companies and their office numbers at the top of the escalator. They are organized by region and are colour-coded. Buenos Aires city information desk is No 83 on the upper floor. It is advisable to go to the bus station the day before you travel to get to know where the platforms are so that when you are fully laden you know exactly where to go. At the basement and ground levels there are left-luggage lockers, US$2.50 for 1 day with tokens sold in kiosks; for large baggage, there's a *guarda equipaje* on the lower floor. For further details of bus services and fares, look under proposed destinations. There are no direct buses to either of the airports.

International buses International services are run by both local and foreign companies; heavily booked Dec-Mar (especially at weekends), when most fares usually rise sharply; fares shown here are for high season. Do not buy Uruguayan bus tickets in Buenos Aires; wait till you get to Colonia. To **Montevideo** Bus de la Carrera, **Belgrano** and **Cauvi**, US$45-50, 7½-9½ hrs; see Ferries, below.

Driving

Driving in Buenos Aires is no problem, provided you have eyes in the back of your head and good nerves. Traffic fines are high and police increasingly on the lookout for drivers without the correct papers. Car hire is cheaper if you arrange it when you arrive rather than from home. Also **Sixt**, Cerrito 1314, www.sixt.com.ar. There are several national rental agencies, eg **Dietrich**, Cerrito 1575, T0810-345 3438, www.onlinedietrich.com, or **Serra Lima**, Av Córdoba 3121, T4961 5276, serralima@ overnet.com.ar. **Ruta Sur**, San Martín 522, T5238 4071, www.rutasur.com. Rents 4WDs and motorhomes.

Ferry

To **Montevideo** and **Colonia** from Terminal Dársena Norte, Av Antártida Argentina 821 (2 blocks from Av Córdoba y Alem). **Buquebus**, T4316 6500, www.buquebus. com (tickets from Terminal, Retiro bus station, from offices at Av Córdoba 867 and Posadas 1452, by phone or online): 1) Direct to **Montevideo**, 1-4 a day, 3 hrs, US$185 tourist class, return, also carries vehicles and motorcycles. 2) To **Colonia**, services by 3 companies: **Buquebus**: minimum 5 crossings a day, from 1 to 3 hrs, US$78 tourist class return on slower vessel, US$108 tourist class return on faster vessel, with bus connection to **Montevideo**. (Buquebus now offers flights to Uruguay and Brazil with onward connections.) **Colonia Express**, www.coloniaexpress.com, makes 2-3 crossings a day between Buenos Aires and Colonia in a fast catamaran (no vehicles carried), 50 mins, prices range from US$43 to US$68 return, depending on type of service and where bought, or US$47-68 with bus connections to Montevideo. Office is at Av Córdoba 753, T4317 4100; Terminal Fluvial is at Av Pedro de Mendoza 330, T4317 4100. You must go there by taxi, US$5. **Seacat**, www.seacatcolonia.com, 2-3 fast ferries to Colonia, 1 hr, US$41-84, from the same terminal as Buquebus, with bus to Montevideo (US$46-114) and Punta del Este (US$82-126) on most crossings. Office: Av Córdoba 772, T4322 9555, phone sales: 4314 5100. See under Tigre, page 52, for services to Carmelo and Nueva Palmira.

Metro (Subte)

Six lines link the outer parts of the city to the centre. **Line 'A'** runs under Av Rivadavia, from Plaza de Mayo to Carabobo. **Line 'B'** from central Post Office, on Av L N Alem, under Av Corrientes to Federico Lacroze railway station at Chacarita, ending at Los Incas. **Line 'C'** links Plaza Constitución with the Retiro railway station, and provides connections with all the other lines but 'H'. **Line 'D'** runs from Plaza de Mayo (Catedral), under Av Roque Sáenz Peña (Diagonal Norte), Córdoba, Santa Fe and Palermo to Congreso de Tucumán (Belgrano). **Line 'E'** runs from Plaza de Mayo (Cabildo, on C Bolívar) through San Juan to Plaza de los Virreyes (connection to Premetro train service to the southwest end of the city).

Line 'H' runs from Corrientes, via Once to Parque Patricios, under Av Jujuy. Note that 3 stations, 9 de Julio (Line 'D'), Diagonal Norte (Line 'C') and Carlos Pellegrini (Line 'B') are linked by pedestrian tunnels. The fare is US$0.60, the same for any direct trip or combination between lines; magnetic cards (for 1, 2, 5, 10 or 30 journeys) must be bought at the station before boarding; only pesos accepted. Trains are operated by **Metrovías**, T4555 1616 or 0800-555 1616, and run Mon-Sat 0500-2250 (Sun 0800-2200). Line A, the oldest was built in 1913, the earliest in South America; it starts running Mon-Sat at 0600. Backpacks and luggage allowed. Free map (if available) from stations and tourist office. See www.subte.com.ar.

Taxi

Taxis are painted yellow and black, and carry Taxi flags. Fares are shown in pesos. The meter starts at US$1.70 when the flag goes down; make sure it isn't running when you get in. A fixed rate of US$0.17 for every 200 m or 1-min wait is charged thereafter. The fare from 2200 to 0600 starts at US$2. A charge is sometimes made for each piece of hand baggage (ask first). About 10% tip expected. It is not recommended to flag down a taxi on the street. For extra security, take a remise or radio taxi booked by phone or at the company's office. Some 'Radio Taxis' you see on the street are false. Check that the driver's licence is displayed. Lock doors on the inside. Worst places are the two airports and Retiro, but taxis from the official rank in the bus terminal are registered with police and safe.
Radio Taxis are managed by several different companies; basic fare US$2.55. Phone a radio taxi from your hotel (they can make recommendations), a phone box or locutorio, giving the address where you are, and you'll usually be collected within 5 mins. **Pídalo**, T4956 1200; **Sur**, T4638 2000; **5 Minutos**, T4523 1200; **Diez**, T4585 5007; **Premium**, T5238 000; **Tiempo**, T4854 3838.

Remise taxis operate all over the city, run from an office and have no meter. The companies are identified by signs on the pavement. Fares, which are fixed and can be cheaper than regular taxis, start at US$3.40 and can be verified by phoning the office, and items left in the car can easily be reclaimed. **La Terminal**, T4312 0711 is recommended, particularly from Retiro bus station.

Tram

Old-fashioned street cars operate Mar-Nov on Sat and holidays 1600-1930 and Sun 1000-1300, 1600-1930 and Dec-Feb on Sat and holidays 1700-2030, Sun 1000-1300, 1700-2030, free, on a circular route along the streets of Caballito district, from C Emilio Mitre 500, Subte Primera Junta (Line A) or Emilio Mitre (Line E), no stops en route. Operated by **Asociación Amigos del Tranvía**, T4431 1073, www.tranvia.org.ar. There is a new tram that runs along Av Alicia Moreau de Justo (Puerto Madero), with terminals at Av Córdoba and at Av Independencia, US$0.35.

Train

There are 4 main terminals: 1) **Retiro** (3 lines: **Mitre**, **Belgrano** and **San Martín** in separate buildings, for information T4311 8704). Mitre line (run by **TBA**, T0800-333 3822, www.tbanet.com.ar). Urban and suburban services include: **Belgrano**, **Mitre** (connection to Tren de la Costa, see below), **Olivos**, **San Isidro**, and **Tigre** (see below); long distance services to **Rosario Norte**, Mon-Thu 1400, Fri 1813, 6½ hrs, US$16.

2) **Constitución**, Roca line urban and suburban services to La Plata, Ezeiza, Ranelagh and Quilmes. Long distance services (run by **Ferrobaires**, T4304 0028, www.ferrobaires.gba.gov.ar): Bahía Blanca, 5 a week 1945, 12½ hrs, US$13.50-22; to Mar del Plata daily, 6-7 hrs, US$18-57.50; also to Bolívar and Daireaux.

3) **Federico Lacroze** Urquiza line and Metro headquarters (run by **Metrovías**,

T0800-555 1616, www.metrovias.com. ar). Suburban services: to General Lemos. **Trenes Especiales Argentinos**, T4554 8018, www.trenesdellitoral. com.ar, runs a train, *El Gran Capitán*, to **Posadas**, minimum 31 hrs, US$25-50 (sleeper US$75), from Lacroze via the towns along Río Uruguay, Tue 1050, Fri, 2205 (return Wed 2300, Sun 1500).

4) **Once**: Sarmiento line (run by *TBA*, see above). Urban and suburban services include **Luján** (connection at Moreno), **Mercedes** and **Lobos**. A fast service runs Mon-Fri between Puerto Madero (station at Av Alicia Moreau de Justo y Perón) and Castelar. Long distance services to Lincoln and Pehuajó (see www.ferrobaires.gba. gov.ar). Tickets checked before boarding and on train and collected at the end of the journey; urban and suburban fares are charged according different sections of each line; fares vary depending on the company.

⊙ Directory

Banks ATMs are widespread for MasterCard or Visa. The financial district lies within a small area north of Plaza de Mayo, between Rivadavia, 25 de Mayo, Av Corrientes and Florida. In non-central areas find banks/ATMs along the main avenues. Banks open Mon-Fri 1000-1500. General **MasterCard** office at Perú 151, T4348 7070, www.mastercard.com/ar, open 0930-1800. **Visa**, Corrientes 1437 p 2, T4379 3400, www.visa.com.ar. **American Express** offices are at Arenales 707 y Maipú, by Plaza San Martín, T0800-444 2450, www. american express.com.ar, where you can apply for a card, get financial services and change Amex TCs (1000-1500 only, no commission into US$ or pesos). *Casas de cambio* include **Banco Piano**, San Martín 345, T4325 6562 (has exchange facility at Ezeiza airport, 0600-2200), www.banco piano.com.ar, changes all TCs (commission 2%). **Eves**, Tucumán 702. **Forex**, MT de

Alvear 540, T4311 5543. **Banco Ciudad** at Av Córdoba 675 branch is open to tourists (with passport) for currency exchange and TCs, Mon, 1000-1800, Tue-Fri 1000-1700, Sat, Sun 1100-1800. Other South American currencies can only be exchanged in *casas de cambio*. **Cultural centres** British Council, M T de Alvear 590, p 4, T4114 8600, www.britishcouncil.org.ar (Mon-Fri 1000-1600). **British Arts Centre** (BAC), Suipacha 1333, T4393 6941, www.britisharts centre. org.ar. English plays and films, music concerts, photography exhibitions (closed Jan). **Goethe Institut**, Corrientes 319/43, T4318 5600, www.goethe.de/ins/ar/bue/ esindex.htm, open Mon-Fri 0900-1800. German library and newspapers (Mon, Tue, Thu 1230-1930, Fri 1230-1600, closed Jan), free German films shown, cultural programmes, German and Spanish language courses. Same building, upstairs, is the German Club, Corrientes 327. **Alliance Française**, Córdoba 946, T4322 0068, www. alianzafrancesa. org.ar. French library, film and art exhibitions. **Instituto Cultural Argentino Norteamericano** (ICANA), Maipú 672, T5382 1500, also at 3 de Febrero 821, T4576 5970, www.icana.org.ar. At the same addresses are branches of **Biblioteca Centro Lincoln**, T5382 1536, www.bcl.edu. ar, with library (including online, members' only borrowing), English/US newspapers. **Villa Ocampo**, Elortondo 1837, Beccar, Partido de San Isidro, T4732 4988, www. villaocampo.org. Former residence of writer and founder of Revista Sur Victoria Ocampo, now owned by UNESCO, in northern suburbs, Thu-Fri 1230-1800, Sat-Sun 1230-1900, US$2.75-4.15 entry, open for visits, courses, exhibitions, etc. **Embassies and consulates** For all foreign embassies and consulates in Buenos Aires, see http:// embassy.goabroad.com. **Internet and telephone** International and local calls, internet and fax from phone offices (*locutorios* or *telecentros*), many in the city centre. **Language schools** Academia

---

Buenos Aires, Hipólito Yrigoyen 571, p 4, T4345 5954, www.academiabuenosaires. com. **AISL**, (Argentina Improving Spanish Language), Rodríguez Peña 832, T5811 3940, www.argentin aisl.com. **All-Spanish**, Talcahuano 77 p 1, T4832 7794, www. all-spanish.com.ar. One to one classes. **Amauta Spanish School**, Federizo Lacroze 2129, T4777 2130, www.amautaspanish. com. Spanish classes, one-to-one or small groups, centres in Buenos Aires and Bariloche. **Argentina I.L.E.E**, T4782 7173, www.argentinailee.com. Recommended by individuals and organizations alike, with a school in Bariloche. **Cedic**, Reconquista 715, p 11 E, T4312 1016, www.cedic.com. ar. Recommended. **Elebaires**, Av de Mayo 1370, of 10, p 3, T4383 7706, www.elebaires. com.ar. Small school with focused classes, also offers 1-to-1 lessons and excursions. Recommended. **Español Andando**, T5278 9886, www.espanol-andando.com. Offers a different approach to classes, courses run for a week and each day you will meet your fellow students and your teacher in a different part of the city. Recommended. **Expanish**, Perón 698, T5252 3040, www.expanish.com. Well-organized courses which can involve excursions, accommodation and Spanish lessons in sister schools in Peru and Chile. Highly recommended. **IBL (Argentina Spanish School)**, Florida 165, p 3, of 328, T4331 4250, www.ibl.com.ar. Group and one-to-one lessons, all levels, recommended. **Bue Spanish School**, Av Belgrano 1431, p 2, apt18, T4381 6347, www.buespanish. com.ar. Intensive and regular Spanish courses, culture programme, free materials. **Lenguas Vivas**, Carlos Pellegrini 1515, T4322 3992, http://ieslvf.caba.infd.edu. ar. Very good cheap courses. **Universidad de Buenos Aires**, 25 de Mayo 221, T4334 7512 or T4343 1196, www.idiomas. filo. uba.ar. Offers cheap, coherent courses, including summer intensive courses. For other schools teaching Spanish, and for

private tutors look in *Buenos Aires Herald* in the classified advertisements. Enquire also at *Asatej* (see Useful addresses) and at **South American Explorers**. For claims or suggestions on Spanish courses, contact the student ombudsman at **Defensoría del Estudiante**, defensoria@spanishinargentina. org.ar. **Medical services** Urgent medical service: for free municipal ambulance service to an emergency hospital department (day and night) **Casualty ward, Sala de guardia**, T107 or T4923 1051/58 (SAME). Inoculations: **Hospital Rivadavia**, Av Las Heras 2670, T4809 2000, Mon-Fri, 0700-1200 (bus 10, 37, 59, 60, 62, 92, 93 or 102 from Plaza Constitución), or **Dirección de Sanidad de Fronteras y Terminales de Transporte**, Ing Huergo 690, T4343 1190, Mon 1400-1500, Tue-Wed 1100-1200, Thu and Fri 1500-1600, bus 20 from Retiro, no appointment required (yellow fever only; take passport). If not provided, buy the vaccines in **Laboratorio Biol**, Uriburu 153, T4953 7215, or in larger chemists. Many chemists have signs indicating that they give injections. Any hospital with an infectology department will give hepatitis A. **Centros Médicos Stamboulian**, 25 de Mayo 464, T4515 3000, French 3085, T5236 7772, also in Belgrano and Flores, www.stamboulian.com.ar. Private health advice for travellers and inoculations centre. Public Hospitals: **Hospital Argerich**, Almte Brown esq Pi y Margall 750, T4121 0700. **Hospital Juan A Fernández**, Cerviño y Bulnes, T4808 2600/2650, probably the best free medical attention in the city. **British Hospital**, Perdriel 74, T4309 6400, www. hospital britanico.org.ar. US$42 a visit. **German Hospital**, Av Pueyrredón 1640, between Beruti and Juncal, T4827 7000, www.hospitalale man.com.ar. Both have first-aid centres (*centros asistenciales*) as do other main hospitals. Dental treatment: excellent dental treatment centre at **Carroll Forest**, Vuelta de Obligado 1551 (Belgrano), T4781 9037, info@carroll-forest.

com.ar. **Dental Argentina**, T4828 0821, www.dental-argentina.com.ar. **Useful addresses Migraciones**: (Immigration), Antártida Argentina 1355, edif 4 (visas extended mornings only), T4317 0234, www.migraciones.gov.ar, 0730-1400 (see Visas and immigration, page 15). **Central Police Station**: Moreno 1550, Virrey Cevallos 362, T4370 5911/5800 (emergency, T101 from any phone, free). See page 13 for **Comisaría del Turista** (tourist police). **Aves Argentinas/AOP** (a BirdLife International partner), Matheu 1246, T4943 7216, www.aves argentinas.org.ar. For information on birdwatching and specialist tours, good library, open Mon-Fri 1030-1330, 1430-2030 (closed Jan). Student organizations: **Asatej**: Helpful Argentine Youth and Student Travel Organization, runs a Student Flight Centre, Florida 835, p 2, oficina 205, T4114 7528, www.asatej.com, Mon-Fri 0900-1900 (with many branches in BA and around the country). Booking for flights (student discounts) including cheap 1-way flights (long waiting lists), hotels and travel; information for all South America, notice board for travellers, ISIC cards sold (giving extensive discounts; Argentine ISIC guide available here), English and French spoken. Cheap fares also at **TIJE**, San Martín 601, T5272 8400 or branches at Av Santa Fe 898, T5272 8450, and elsewhere in the city, Argentina and Chile, www.tije.com. **YMCA**: (Central), Reconquista 439, T4311 4785, www.ymca.org.ar. **YWCA**: Humberto 1º 2360, T4941 3776, www.ywca.org.ar.

Around Buenos Aires

Tigre → *Population: 31,000 (Partido de Tigre – Tigre county – 301,000).*

This touristy little town, 32 km northwest of Buenos Aires, is a popular weekend destination lying on the lush jungly banks of the Río Luján, with a fun fair and an excellent fruit and handicrafts market (Puerto de Frutos) daily 1100-2000 with access from Calles Sarmiento or Perú. There are restaurants on the waterfront in Tigre across the Río Tigre from the railway line, along Lavalle and Paseo Victorica; cheaper places can be found on Italia and Cazón on the near side, or at the Puerto de Frutos. North of the town is the delta of the Río Paraná: innumerable canals and rivulets, with holiday homes and restaurants on the banks and a fruit- growing centre. The fishing is excellent and the peace is only disturbed by motor-boats at weekends. Regattas are held in November. Take a trip on one of the regular launch services (*lanchas colectivas*) which run to all parts of the delta, including taxi launches – watch prices for these – from the wharf (*Estación Fluvial*). Tourist catamarans, many companies with daily services, 1-2 hour trips, eg US$11.50-17.25, from Lavalle 499 on Río Tigre, T4731 0261/63, www.tigreencatamaran.com.ar, and three to eight services daily, 1½-hour trips, US$17.25, from Puerto de Frutos, *Río Tur* (T4731 0280, www.rioturcatamaranes.com.ar). *Sturla* (Estación Fluvial, oficina 10, T4731 1300, www. sturla viajes.com.ar) runs three 1-hour trips a day, US$14.50 (including bus tour); they also have trips with lunch, night-time boat trips, full-day excursions from the centre of Buenos Aires, and more. You can also hire kayaks, canoes or rowing boats, rent houses, or visit *recreos*, little resorts with swimming pools, tennis courts, bar and restaurant. **Tigre tourist office** ⓘ *by the Estación Fluvial, Mitre 305, T0800-888 84473, www.tigre.gov.ar, also at Juncal 1600 and the Puerto de Frutos*, with a full list of houses to rent, activities, etc. **Centro de Guías de Tigre y Delta** ⓘ *Estación Fluvial oficina 2, T4731 3555, www.tododelta.com.ar.* For guided walks and launch trips.

Museo Naval ⓘ *Paseo Victorica 602, T4749 0608, Mon-Fri 0830-1730, Sat-Sun 1030-1830, US$0.80.* Worth a visit to see the displays on the Argentine navy. There are also relics of the 1982 Falklands/ Malvinas War. **Museo de Arte** ⓘ *Paseo Victorica 972, T4512 4528, www. mat.gov.ar, Wed-Fri 0900-1900, Sat-Sun 1200-1900, US$2.75,* hosts a collection of Argentine figurative art in the former Tigre Club Casino, a beautiful belle époque building. **Museo del Mate** ⓘ *Lavalle 289, T4506 9594, www.elmuseodelmate.com, Tue-Sun 1100-1800 (1100-1900 in summer), US$2.60,* tells the history of mate and has an interesting collection of the associated paraphernalia.

Isla Martín García

This island in the Río de la Plata (Juan Díaz de Solís' landfall in 1516) used to be a military base. Now it is an ecological/historical centre and an ideal excursion from the capital, with many trails through the cane brakes, trees and rocky outcrops – interesting birds and flowers. Boat trips: four weekly from Tigre at 0900, returning 2000, three-hour journey, US$57 return including lunch, *asado* and guide; US$98 pp including weekend overnight at inn, full board. Reservations only through *Cacciola* (address under Tigre, Transport, below), who also handle bookings for the inn and restaurant on the island. There is also a campsite.

For hotel and restaurant price codes and other relevant information, see pages 10-12.

🛏 Where to stay

Tigre *p51*

$$$$ La Becasina, Arroyo Las Cañas (Delta islands second section), T4328 2687, www.labecasina.com . One of Argentina's most delightful places to stay, an hour by launch from Tigre, buried deep from the outside world, with 15 individual lodges on stilts in the water, connected by wooden walkways, all comforts and luxuries provided and tasteful décor, with intimate dining room, jacuzzi and pool amidst the trees. Full board, excellent food and service. Recommended.

$$$$ Villa Julia, Paseo Victorica 800, in Tigre itself, T4749 0642, www.villajulia.com. ar. A 1906 villa converted into a chic hotel, beautifully restored fittings, comfortable, good restaurant open to non-residents.

$$$ Los Pecanes, on Arroyo Felicaria, T4728 1932, www.hosterialospecanes.com. On a secluded island visited regularly by hummingbirds. Ana and Richard offer a few comfortable rooms and delicious food. Ideal base for boat excursions and birdwatching. Cheaper Mon-Fri.

$$$ Posada de 1860, Av Libertador 190, T4749 4034, www.tigrehostel.com.ar. A beautiful stylish villa with suites and an associated **Hostel Tigre** at No 137 (same phone and website) with dorms for up to 6 at **$** pp, and private rooms (**$$$** double); breakfast, cooking facilities and Wi-Fi. Discounts on rooms Mon-Thu, HI affiliated.

$$ Casona La Ruchi, Lavalle 557, T4749 2499, www.casonalaruchi.com.ar. The Escauriza family are the hosts of this lovely 1892 villa, central, homely, cosy rooms, a garden with a pool.

$$ TAMET, Río Carapachay Km 24, T4728 0055, www.tamet.com.ar. For a relaxing stay on an island with sandy beaches and quite comfortable premises, with breakfast, games and canoes. Also has camping.

🚌 Transport

Tigre *p51*
Bus
From central **Buenos Aires**: take No 60 from Constitución: the 60 'bajo' is a little longer than the 60 'alto' but is better for sightseeing.

Ferry
To **Carmelo** (Uruguay) from Terminal Internacional, Lavalle 520, Tigre. **Cacciola**, T4749 0931, www.cacciolaviajes.com (in Buenos Aires at Florida 520, p 1, of 113, T4393 6100), 0830, 1630, and 2355 Dec-Feb, 4 hrs, US$31.50 (US$56.25 return). To Montevideo, US$42.50, US$77 return. Also offers bus connections from central Buenos Aires and to various Uruguayan cities and overnight packages to Carmelo, Colonia and Montevideo.

To **Nueva Palmira** (Uruguay) from Terminal Internacional. **Líneas Delta Argentino**, oficina 6 at Estación Fluvial, T4731 1236, www.lineas delta.com.ar. Daily at 0730, 3 hrs, US$25, US$40 return. To **Carmelo** US$30, US$46 return, and **Colonia**, 4½ hrs from Tigre, US$38, US$55 return, both daily 0730.

Note Argentine port taxes are generally included in the fares for Argentine departures.

Train
From **Buenos Aires**: take train from Retiro (FC Mitre section) to Tigre, or to Bartolomé Mitre and change to the Maipú station (the stations are linked) for the **Tren de la Costa**, T4002 6000, US$3.65 one way, every 20 mins from Maipú Mon-Thu 0710- 2300, Fri 0710-2400, Sat-Sun 0830-0010, 25 mins.

From Palermo or Recoleta, take Subte line D to Carranza, which connects with the Mitre line. (Buses to Tren de la Costa are 60 from Constitución, 19 or 71 from Once, 152 from centre.) Several stations have shopping centres (eg San Isidro), and terminus, Estación Delta, has the huge fun fair, El Parque de la Costa, and a casino. You can get off the train as many times as you want on the same ticket. Cheaper but slower, 50 mins, is the **TBA** train from Retiro direct to Tigre, every 7 mins Mon-Fri, every 15 mins Sat-Sun, US$0.35.

The Pampas

South and west of Buenos Aires the flat, fertile lands of the pampa húmeda stretch seemingly without end, the horizon broken only by a lonely windpump or a line of poplar trees. This is home to the gaucho, whose traditions of music and fine craftsmanship remain alive. Argentina's agricultural heartland is punctuated by quiet pioneer towns, like Chascomús, and the houses of grand estancias. Argentina's former wealth lay in these splendid places, where you can stay as a guest, go horse riding, and get a great insight into the country's history and gaucho culture. The mountain range at Tandil offers great walking and marvellous views.

San Antonio de Areco → *Phone code: 02326. Population: 18,000.*

San Antonio de Areco, 113 km northwest of Buenos Aires, is a completely authentic, late 19th-century town, with single-storey buildings around a plaza filled with palms and plane trees, streets lined with orange trees, and an attractive *costanera* along the river bank. There are several estancias and a couple of villages with accommodation nearby and the town itself has historical *boliches* (combined bar and provisions store, eg *Los Principios, Moreno y Mitre*). The gaucho traditions are maintained in silver, textiles and leather handicrafts of the highest quality, as well as frequent gaucho activities, the most important of which is the **Day of Tradition** in the second week of November (book accommodation ahead), with traditional parades, gaucho games, events on horseback, music and dance. **Museo Gauchesco Ricardo Güiraldes** ⓘ *on Camino Güiraldes, T455839, www.museoguiraldes. com.ar, closed for restoration*, is a replica of a typical estancia of the late 18th century, surrounded by a neat park, with impressive *gaucho* artefacts, paintings by Pedro Figari and displays on the life of Güiraldes, the writer whose best-known book, *Don Segundo Sombra*, celebrates the gaucho. He lived in the **Estancia La Porteña** ⓘ *8 km from town, T011-15-5626 7347, www.laporteniadeareco.com*, which dates from 1823. It is a national historic monument and offers day visits and accommodation in three different houses (**$$$$**, huge banquets with lots of meat). Superb gaucho **silverwork** for sale at the workshop and museum of **Juan José Draghi** ⓘ *Lavalle 387, T454219, www.draghiplaterosorfebres.com, 0900-1300, 1530-2000 (Sun 1000-1300 only), US$1.70 for a guided visit*. Excellent **chocolates** at **La Olla de Cobre** ⓘ *Matheu 433, T453105, www.laolladecobre.com.ar*, with a charming little café for drinking chocolate and the most amazing home-made *alfajores*. There is a large park spanning the river near the **tourist information centre**. The **Centro Cultural y Museo Usina Vieja**, ⓘ *Alsina 66, Tue-Sun 1100-1700, US$0.50*, is the city museum. There are ATMs on the plaza, but nowhere to change TCs. The **tourist office** ⓘ *Zerboni y Arellano, T453165, www.san antoniodeareco.com*, is by the river. Also see www.visiteareco.com.

La Plata → *Phone code: 0221. Population: 642,000.*

La Plata, near the shores of the Río de la Plata, was founded in 1882 as capital of Buenos Aires province and is now an important administrative centre, with an excellent university.

It's a well-planned city, reminiscent of Paris in places, with the French-style **legislature** and the elegant **Casa de Gobierno** on Plaza San Martín, central in a series of plazas along the spine of the city. On **Plaza Moreno** to the south there's an impressive Italianate palace housing the **Municipalidad**, and the **Cathedral**, a striking neo-Gothic brick construction. North of Plaza San Martín is La Plata's splendid park, the **Paseo del Bosque**, with mature trees, a zoo and a botanical garden, a boating lake and the **Museo de La Plata** ① *T425 7744, www.fcnym. unlp.edu.ar, Tue-Sun 1000-1800 and holiday Mondays, closed 1 Jan, 1 May, 24, 25, 31 Dec, US$1*, which is highly recommended. This museum houses an outstanding collection of stuffed animals, wonderful dinosaur skeletons and artefacts from pre-Columbian peoples throughout the Americas. 8 km northwest of the city is the **República de los Niños** ① *Camino Gral Belgrano y Calle 501, www.republica.laplata.gov.ar, daily 1000-2200, US$1.30, getting there: take a train from La Plata or Buenos Aires to Gonnet station, US$0.50, or bus 338 from La Plata, car park US$1.30*. This is Eva Peron's legacy, a delightful children's village with scaled-down castles, oriental palaces, a train, boat lake, restaurant and workshops. Fun for a picnic. The **Parque Ecológico** ① *Camino Centenario y San Luis, Villa Elisa, T473 2449, www.parquecologico. laplata.gov.ar, 0900-1930, free, getting there: take bus 273 D or E*, is another good place for families, with native *tala* forest and plenty of birds.

The municipal **tourist offices** are ① *Diagonal 79 entre 5 y 56, Palacio Campodónico, T4229764, Mon-Fri 0900-1700*, and *Pasaje Dardo Rocha, T427 1535, daily 1000-2000, www. laplata.gov.ar*. The latter, in an Italianate palace, also houses a gallery of contemporary **Latin American art** ① *C 50 entre 6 y 7, T427 1843, www.macla.laplata.gov.ar, Tue-Fri 1000-2000, Sat-Sun 1400- 2100 (1600-2200 in summer), free*.

Chascomús, Dolores and Tandil

To get to the heart of the pampas, stay in one of many estancias scattered over the plains. There are several accessible from the main roads to the coast, fast Ruta 2 (be prepared for tolls) and Ruta 11, near two well-preserved historic towns, Chascomús and Dolores. At Punta Indio, 165 km from Buenos Aires, is 1920s Tudor style **Estancia Juan Gerónimo** ① *T02221-481414, 011-154 937 4326, www.juangeronimo.com.ar, ($$$$) full board, activities included, English and French spoken*. Set on the coast in a beautiful nature reserve which protects a huge variety of fauna, the estancia offers walks and horse rides in 4000 ha. Accommodation is simple and elegant, and the food exquisite.

Chascomús is a beautifully preserved town from the 1900s, with a rather Wild West feel to it, Chascomús is a lively place built on a huge lake, perfect for fishing and water sports. There's a great little museum **Museo Pampeano** ① *Av Lastra y Muñiz, T425110, Tue-Fri 0800-1400, Sat-Sun 1000-1400, 1700-1900 (Tue Fri 0900-1500, Sat-Sun 1030-1630 in winter), US$0.50*, with gaucho artefacts, old maps and fabulous antique furniture. **Tourist office** ① *Av Costanera by the pier, T02241-430405, 0900-1900 daily, www.chascomus. gov.ar*. Dolores is a delightful small town, like stepping back in time to the 1900s, very tranquil. **Museo Libres del Sur** ① *daily 1000-1700*, is an old house in Parque Libres del Sur, full of gaucho silver, plaited leather *talero*, branding irons, and a huge cart from 1868. The **Sierras de Tandil** are 2000 million years old, among the world's oldest mountains, beautiful curved hills of granite and basalt, offering wonderful walking and riding. Tandil itself is an attractive, breezy town, a good base for exploring the sierras, with a couple of marvellous estancias close by. There's a park, **Parque Independencia**, with great views from the hill with its Moorish-style castle, and an amphitheatre, where there's a famous community theatre event throughout Easter week (book hotels ahead). The peaks nearby offer wild countryside for riding, climbing, walking, or ascent by 1.2-km cable car ride (at

Cerro El Centinela, 5 km away). Very helpful **tourist information** at ① *Av Espora 1120, on the way into town, T02293-432073, also at Plaza Independencia and at the bus terminal, www.turismo.tandil.gov.ar.* Look up estancias and gaucho-related activities in the region at www.caminodelgaucho.com.ar.

The Pampas listings

For hotel and restaurant price codes and other relevant information, see pages 10-12.

● Where to stay

San Antonio de Areco *p53*
Most hotels offer discounts Mon-Thu or Fri.
$$$ Antigua Casona, Segundo Sombra 495, T456600, www.antiguacasona.com. Charmingly restored 1897 house with five rooms opening onto a delightful patio and exuberant garden, most relaxing and romantic. Bikes to borrow.
$$$ Paradores Draghi, Lavalle 387, T455583, www.paradoresdraghi.com.ar. Traditional-style, comfortable rooms face a manicured lawn with a pool. Just metres away Draghi family has its silversmith workshop. Recommended.
$$$ Patio de Moreno, Moreno 251, T455197, www.patiodemoreno.com. The top hotel in town is a stylish place with spacious, minimalist rooms, a large patio with a pool and great service.
$$$-$$ San Carlos, Zerboni y Zapiola, T453106, www.hotel-sancarlos.com.ar. On the riverside park, convenient for young families, has pool for kids, bikes to borrow (1st hr free), restaurant.
$$ Hostal de Areco, Zapiola 25, T456118, www.hostaldeareco.com.ar. Popular, with a warm welcome, good value.
$$ Los Abuelos, Zerboni y Zapiola T456390. Very good, welcoming, small pool, plain but comfortable rooms with TV, facing riverside park.

Camping
2 sites in the park by the river: best is **Club River Plate**, on Costanera, T454998, sports club, shady sites with all facilities, pool.

Estancias
Some of the province's finest estancias are within easy reach for day visits, offering horse riding, an *asado* lunch, and other activities. Stay overnight to really appreciate the peace and beauty of these historical places. See **Estancia La Porteña**, above. Look online at: www.sanantoniodeareco.com/turismo/estancias/index.htm, or www.turismo.gov.ar/eng/menu.htm (go to Active Tourism, Rural Tourism).
$$$$ El Ombú, T492080, T011-4737 0436 (BsAs office), www.estanciaelombu.com. Fine house with magnificent terrace dating from 1890, comfortable rooms, horse riding, English- speaking owners; price includes full board and activities but not transfer. Recommended.
$$$$ La Bamba, T454895, www.la-bamba.com.ar. Dating from 1830, in grand parkland, charming rooms, English-speaking owners who have lived here for generations, superb meals, price is for full board. Recommended.

La Plata *p53*
$$$ Argentino, C 46 No 536, ebtre 5 y 6, T423 4111, www.hotelargentino.com. Central, comfortable, bright rooms. Also has apartments for rent.
$$$ La Plata Hotel, Av 51 No 783, T422 9090, www.weblaplatahotel.com.ar. Modern, well furnished, comfortable, spacious rooms and nice bathrooms. Price includes a dinner (drinks extra).
$ pp **La Plata Hostel**, C 50 No 1066, T457 1424, www.laplata-hostel.com.ar. Well-organized, convenient hostel in a historic house, high ceilings, small garden, simple but comfortable dorms for 4 or 8.

Estancias

$$$$ Casa de Campo La China, 60 km from La Plata on Ruta 11, T0221-421 2931, www.casadecamp olachina.com. ar. A charming 1930s adobe house set in eucalyptus woods, with beautifully decorated spacious rooms off an open gallery, day visits (US$45) to ride horses, or in carriages, eat *asado*, or stay the night, guests of Cecilia and Marcelo, who speak perfect English. Delicious food, meals included in price. Highly recommended.

Chascomús *p54*

For a full list see www.chascomus.com.ar.
$$$ Chascomús, Av Lastra 367, T422968, www.chascomus.com.ar (under 'hoteles'). The town's most comfortable hotel, atmospheric, welcoming, with stylish turn-of-the-century public rooms and lovely terrace.
$$$ La Posada, Costanera España 18, T423503, www.chascomus.com.ar (under 'cabañas'). On the laguna, delightful, very comfortable cabañas with cooking facilities.
$$$ Roble Blanco, Mazzini 130, T436235, www.robleblanco.com.ar. A very good choice, in a refurbished 100-year-old house, modern comfortable rooms, a large heated pool with attractive deck and welcoming common areas. Also has a spa. Recommended.
$$ Laguna, Libres del Sur y Maipú, T426113, www.lgnhotel.com.ar. Traditional, old fashioned, sleepy hotel by the station. Pleasant, quiet rooms.

Estancias

Both estancias will collect you from Chascomús.
$$$$ Haras La Viviana, in Castelli, 65 km from Chascomús, T011-4702 9633, http://harasla viviana.com.ar. Perfect for horse riding, since fine polo ponies are bred here. Tiny cabins in gardens by a huge laguna where you can kayak or fish, very peaceful, good service, wonderful welcome from lady novelist owner, fluent English spoken.

$$$ La Horqueta, 3 km from Chascomús on Ruta 20, T011-4777 0150, www.la horqueta.com. Full board, mansion in lovely grounds with laguna for fishing, horse riding, bikes to borrow, English-speaking hosts, safe gardens especially good for children, plain food.

Dolores *p54*

$$$$ Dos Talas, 10 km from town, T02245-443020, www.dostalas.com.ar. The most beautiful estancia in the pampas, and one of the oldest. An elegant house in grand parkland designed by Charles Thays, with fascinating history. The owners are descendents of the original owner, Pedro Luro. The rooms and the service are impeccable, regional food with traditional, family recipes. Pool, gaucho-style riding, English spoken.

Tandil *p54*

Many to choose from, see www.tandil.com or www.cybertandil.com.ar.
$$$ Las Acacias, Av Brasil 642, T02293-423373, www.posadalasacacias.com. ar. Attractive hostería in restored 1890s dairy farm near golf club, excellent service with good food and lovely park with pool, Italian and English spoken.
$$ Plaza de las Carretas, Av Santamarina 728, T447850, www.plazadelascarretas. com.ar. An early 20th-century family house, good rooms, quiet, comfy, nice garden.

Estancias

$$$$ Ave María, 16 km from Tandil, past Cerro El Centinela, T02293-422843, www. avemaria tandil.com.ar. In beautiful gardens overlooking the rocky summits of the sierras. You're encouraged to feel at home and relax, swim in the pool or walk in the grounds, hills and woodland. Impeccable rooms, superb food and discreet staff who speak English. Highly recommended.
$$$$ Siempre Verde, T02292-498555, www.estanciasiempreverde.com. A 1900's house, 45 km south-west of Tandil (next to

Barker) with traditional-style rooms, good views. The owners, descendants of one of Argentina's most important families, are very hospitable and helpful. Wonderful horse riding and walking among the sierras, fishing, *asados* on the hillside, camping. Highly recommended.

🍴 Restaurants

San Antonio de Areco *p53*
Many *parrillas* on the bank of the Río Areco.
$$ Almacén de Ramos Generales, Zapiola 143, T456376 (best to book ahead). Perfect place, popular with locals, very atmospheric, superb meat, very good pastas and a long wine list.
$$ Café de las Artes, Bolívar 70, T456398 (better book ahead). In a hidden spot, this cosy place serves delicious pastas with a large wine selection.
$$ La Costa, Zerboni y Belgrano (on the riverside park). A very good traditional *parrilla* with an attractive terrace.
$$ La Ochava de Cocota, Alsina y Alem. Relaxing, attractive, excellent service, superb *empanadas* and vegetable pies. It is also a café.
$ La Esquina de Merti, Arellano y Segundo Sombra. The ideal place for a beer on the main plaza. Go early to get a table outside.
$ La Vieja Sodería, Bolívar y General Paz. An atmospheric and agreeable corner for varied picadas and sandwiches. It's also a bar and a café serving great cakes.

La Plata *p53*
$$ Cervecería Modelo, C 54 y C5. Traditional German-style *cervecería*, with good menu and beer.
$$ Don Quijote, Plaza Paso. Delicious food in lovely surroundings, well known.
$$ El Chaparral Platense, C 60 y C 116 (Paseo del Bosque). Good *parrilla* in the park, great steaks.
$$ La Aguada, C 50 entre 7 y 8. The oldest restaurant in town, good for *minutas* (light meals), famous for its *papas fritas*.

Confitería París, C 7 y 48. The best croissants, and a lovely place for coffee.

Chascomús *p54*
$$ Colonial, Estados Unidos y Artigas. Great food, pastas and cakes are recommended.
$$ El Viejo Lobo, Mitre y Dolores. Very good fish.

Tandil *p54*
Plenty of *pizzerías*, and good local sausages and cheeses served in *picadas* (nibbles) with drinks.
$$ 1905, Santamarina 609, T448725. In a charming old house, minimalist style, fine, elaborate meals.
$$ Carajo, Saavedra Lamas s/n (at Club Náutico). *Parrilla* in a great location by the lake. Also tea house serving cakes in the afternoons.
$$ El Manco Paz, Paz 1145. Very good and elegant parrilla.
$$ El Molino, Juncal 936. Broad menu, meat cooked *al disco*, on an open fire, delicious.
$$ Epoca de Quesos, San Martín y 14 de Julio, T448750. Atmospheric, delicious local produce, wines and *picadas*.
$$ Taberna Pizzuela, Paz y Pinto. Attractive old place serving good simple dishes, including pizza, their speciality.
$$ Vieja Cantera, Monseñor de Andrea 315 *Picadas*, simple meals and a tea room in a beautiful spote at the foot of Monte Calvario.

🎯 What to do

The Pampas *p53*
Horse riding
All estancias offer horse riding. Other operators can be contacted from the hotels in the Pampas towns.

Trekking and mountain biking
Contact an approved guide who will take you to otherwise inaccessible privately

owned land for trekking. **Horizonte Vertical**, Tandil, T432762, www.horizonte- vertical. com.ar. For climbing, mountain biking, canoeing and walking.

⊖ Transport

San Antonio de Areco p53
Bus

From **Buenos Aires** (Retiro bus terminal), 1½-2 hrs, US$8, every hour with Chevallier or Pullman General Belgrano.

Remise taxis
Sol, San Martín y Alsina, T455444.

La Plata p53
Bus

Terminal at Calle 4 and Diagonal 74, T427 3186/427 3198. To **Buenos Aires**, very frequent during the day, hourly at night, Costera Metropolitana and Plaza, 1½ hrs either to Retiro terminal or to Centro (stops along Av 9 de Julio), via Autopista (a little shorter), US$3.50, or via Centenario.

Train

To/from **Buenos Aires** (Constitución), frequent, US$1.50, 1 hr 10 mins (ticket office hidden behind shops opposite platform 6).

Chascomús p54
Bus

Frequent service, several per day to **Buenos Aires**, 2 hrs, US$9, **La Plata**, **Mar del Plata**, and daily to **Bahía Blanca** and **Villa Gesell**; terminal T422595.

Train

Station T422220. Daily with Ferrobaires, www.ferrobaires.gba.gov.ar, to **Buenos Aires** (Constitución), US$6, and to **Mar del Plata**, passing Dolores en route.

Tandil p54
Bus

Frequent to **Buenos Aires** (6 hrs, US$24-27), **Bahía Blanca** (6 hrs, US$19), **Mar del Plata** (4 hrs, US$9), **Necochea**. Bus terminal Av Buzón 650, T432092.

Train

Once a week from **Buenos Aires** on Fri, return Mon, US$12.

Northeast Argentina

The river systems of the Paraná, Paraguay and Uruguay, with hundreds of minor tributaries, small lakes and marshlands, dominate the Northeast. Between the Paraná and Uruguay rivers is Argentine Mesopotamia containing the provinces of Entre Ríos, Corrientes and Misiones, this last named after Jesuit foundations, whose red stone ruins have been rescued from the jungle. The great attraction of this region is undoubtedly the Iguazú Falls, which tumble into a gorge on a tributary of the Alto Paraná on the border with Brazil. But the region offers other opportunities for wildlife watching, such as the national parks of the Wet Chaco and the amazing flooded plains of the Esteros del Iberá. This is also the region of mate tea, sentimental chamamé music and tiny chipá bread.

Up the Río Uruguay

This river forms the frontier with Uruguay and there are many crossings as you head upstream to the point where Argentina, Uruguay and Brazil meet. On the way, you'll find riverside promenades, sandy beaches, hot springs and palm forests.

Gualeguaychú → *Phone code: 03446. Population: 109,461 (department).*
On the Río Gualeguaychú, 19 km above its confluence with the Río Uruguay and 236 km north of Buenos Aires, this is a pleasant town with a massive pre-Lenten carnival. Parades are held in the Corsódromo (see www.carnavaldelpais.com.ar or www.grancarnaval. com.ar for details of participating groups, prices of tickets, etc). Some 33 km southeast the Libertador Gral San Martín Bridge (5.4 km long) provides the most southerly route across the Río Uruguay, to Fray Bentos (vehicles US$6; pedestrians and cyclists may cross only on vehicles, officials may arrange lifts). **Tourist office** ① *Paseo del Puerto, T422900, www.gualeguaychuturismo.com, 0800-2000 (2200 in summer, 2400 Fri-Sat).* The **Uruguayan consulate** is at Luis N Palma 500, T426168, conuruguale@entrerios.net.
Nice walks can be taken along the *costanera* between the bridge and the small port, from where short boat excursions and city tours leave (some also from the *balneario norte*), **Gualeguaychú Aventura**, T429886, www.gchuaventura.com.ar, or **Lancha C de Gualeguaychú**, T423248, high season only. **El Patio del Mate** ① *G Méndez y Costanera, T424371, www.elpatiodel mate.com.ar, daily 0800-2000 (2200 in summer)*, is a workshop dedicated to the *mate* gourd. On the outskirts are thermal pools at **Termas del Guaychú** ① *Ruta 14 Km 63.5, www.termasdelguaychu.com.ar*, and **Termas del Gualeguaychú** ① *Ruta 42 Km 2.5, T499167.*

Concepción del Uruguay → *Phone code: 03442. Population: 100,728 (department).*
The first Argentine port of any size on the Río Uruguay was founded in 1783. Overlooking Plaza Ramírez is the church of the Immaculate Conception which contains the remains of Gen Urquiza. **Palacio San José** ① *32 km west of town, T432620, www.palacios anjose.com. ar, Mon-Fri 0800-1900, Sat-Sun 0900-1800, US$1, free guided visits 1000, 1100, 1500, 1600, plus 1200, 1400 at weekends, and night visits at Easter, Jan-Feb (on Fri) and Oct-Dec (one Sat a month).* Urquiza's former mansion, set in beautiful grounds with a lake, is now a museum, with artefacts from Urquiza's life and a collection of period furniture, recommended. Take Ruta 39 west and turn right after Caseros train station. Buses to Paraná or Rosario del Tala stop at El Cruce or Caseros, 4 or 8 km away respectively (no shade for a comfortable

summer walk), US$2 (**Turismo Pioneros**, Mitre 908, T433914, www.turismopioneros.com.ar, runs combis from Concepción del Uruguay, US$13 plus entry fee). **Tourist office** ① *9 de Julio 844, T425820, and Galarza y Daniel Elías, T440812, www.concepcionturismo.gov.ar, 0800-2000 (0700-2200 in high season).*

Colón → *Phone code: 03447. Population: 62,160 (department).*

Founded in 1863, Colón is 45 km north of Concepción del Uruguay. It has shady streets, an attractive *costanera* and long sandy beaches. At Avenida 12 de Abril y Paso is **La Casona** (1868), with a handicraft exhibition and shop. Next to the port, Calle Belgrano leads to the **Complejo Termal** ① *closed for refurbishment 2011-2012; check reopening at termascolon@gmail.com.* **Tourist office** ① *Av Costanera Quirós y Gouchón, T421233, www.colon.gov.ar, 0600-2000 (2200 in high season).* The **Uruguayan consulate** is at San Martín 417, T421999, crou@ciudad.com.ar.

Parque Nacional El Palmar

① *58 km north of Colón, T493049, www.elpalmarapn.com.ar. US$10. Buses from Colón, 1 hr, US$2, will drop you at the entrance and is easy to hitch the last 12 km to the park administration. LHL tour agency (T422222) charges US$40 pp for a half day excursion; entry extra. Remise taxis from Colón offer tours, 4-hr return trip, including tour or waiting time for US$60 for up to 4 people (entry extra), eg Remises Colón, T422221 or Palmares, T424808. There are camping facilities (electricity, hot water), with restaurant opposite, and a small shop.*

This park of 8500 ha is on the Río Uruguay, entrance gates off Ruta 14, where you'll be given a map and information on walks. The park contains varied scenery with a mature palm forest, sandy beaches on the Uruguay river, indigenous tombs and the remains of an 18th-century quarry and port, a good museum and many rheas and other birds. The Yatay palms grow up to 12 m and some are hundreds of years old. It became a Ramsar site in 2011. It is best to stay overnight as wildlife is more easily seen in the early morning or at sunset. Very popular at weekends in summer.

Refugio de Vida Silvestre La Aurora del Palmar ① *T03447-154 31689, www.auroradelpalmar. com.ar, free,* is opposite the Parque Nacional El Palmar, 3 km south of Ubajay at Km 202 Ruta 14. A private reserve protecting a similar environment to that of its neighbour, La Aurora covers 1300 ha, of which 200 are covered with a mature palm forest. There are also gallery forests along the streams and patches of *espinal* or scrub. Birds are easily seen, as are capybaras along the streams. The administration centre is only 500 m from Ruta 14 and services are well organized. There are guided excursions on horseback, by 4WD and on foot combined, or canoe, two hours, US$13 per person, minimum four people. Camping US$9 is per person per day plus US$9 per tent, also private rooms at **$$$ Casona La Estación** (rate for 4 people) or **$$$-$$** in doubles or dorms in old railway carriages. Buses from Colón or those coming from the north will drop you at the entrance. Tell the driver you are going to La Aurora del Palmar (ask for Ruta 14 Kilómetro 202), to avoid confusion with the national park. *Remise* taxi from Ubajay costs US$7. Book in advance.

Concordia → *Phone code: 0345. Population: 170,033 (Department).*

Just downriver from Salto, Uruguay, Concordia, 120 km north of Colón, is a large city with few fine turn-of-the-20th century buildings and a beautiful 70-ha riverside park, northeast of town, where ruins of Mansión San Carlos can be seen. About 20 km upriver Salto Grande international hydroelectric dam provides road and railway crossings to Uruguay. Fishing and nautical sports on the river and from villages on the large lake, including a popular thermal resort at Federación, 64 km north of Concordia. **Tourist office** ① *Pellegrini y Bartolomé Mitre, T4213905, www.concordia.gov.ar/turismo, daily 0800-2100*. The Uruguayan consulate is at Asunción 131, T422 1426, conurucon@arnet.com.ar.

Upstream from Concordia in the province of Corrientes is the port of **Monte Caseros**, with the Uruguayan town of Bella Unión, Brazilian border, almost opposite. An international bridge is planned; in the meanwhile, small launches provide the border crossing (four a day, not on Sunday) and at Alvear (Monday-Friday) further upstream. Less adventurous, there are two international bridges at Paso de los Libres and Santo Tomé, the former being very busy and used by most bus companies crossing to Uruguaiana and Brazilian tourist destinations.

Up the Río Uruguay listings

For hotel and restaurant price codes and other relevant information, see pages 10-12.

● Where to stay

Gualeguaychú *p59*
Accommodation is scarce during carnival. Prices 25% higher Dec-Mar, Easter and long weekends. The tourist office can contact estate agents for short stays in private flats.
$$$ Puerto Sol, San Lorenzo 477, T434017, www.hotelpuertosol.com.ar. Good rooms, a/c, Wi-Fi, next to the port, has a small resort on a nearby island (transfer included) for relaxing drink.
$$$ Tykuá, Luis N Palma 150, T422625, www.tykuahotel.com.ar. Breakfast included, 3 blocks from the bridge, a/c, Wi-Fi, laundry.

Camping
Several sites on riverside, others next to the bridge and north of it. El Ñandubaysal, T423298, www.nandu baysal.com.ar. The smartest, on the Río Uruguay, 15 km southeast (US$17-25 per tent).

Concepción del Uruguay *p59*
$$$$-$$ Grand Hotel Casino, Eva Perón 114, T425586, www.grandhotelcasino.com. ar. Originally a French-style mansion with adjacent theatre, superior rooms have a/c and TV, VIP rooms have new bathrooms, includes breakfast, Wi-Fi.

$$$ Antigua Posta del Torreón, España y Almafuerte, T432618, www. postadeltorreon.com.ar. Nine confortable rooms (a/c, TV, Wi-Fi) in a stylish boutique hotel with a pool.
$$ Nuevo Residencial Centro, Moreno 130, T427429, www.nuevorescentro.com.ar. One of the cheapest options in town. Basic rooms, some with a/c, in a traditional 19th-century building with a lovely patio, 1½ blocks from the plaza. No breakfast.

Colón *p60*
$$$ Holimasú, Belgrano 28, T421305, www.hotel holimasu.com.ar. Nice patio, breakfast included, Wi-Fi, a/c extra, **$$** in low season.
$$$ Hostería Restaurant del Puerto, Alejo Peyret 158, T422698, www. hosteriadecolon.com.ar. Great value, lovely atmosphere in old house, breakfast included, Wi-Fi, pool, no credit cards.
$$ La Posada de David, Alejo Peyret 97, T423930, www.colonentrerios.com.ar/ posadadedavid. Nice family house, garden, welcoming, good double rooms with breakfast, great value.

Camping
Several sites, some with cabins, on river bank, from US$7 daily.

🍽 Restaurants

Concepción del Uruguay *p59*
$$$ El Conventillo de Baco, España 193, T433809. A refined choice with some outside tables and a chance to try fish from the river.

Colón *p60*
$$$ Chiva Chiva, Gral Urquiza y Brown. An artist's refuge; her inspiration is in the meals and drinks and in the pottery on display.
$$$ La Cosquilla del Angel, Alejo Peyret 180. The smartest place in town, meals include fish, set menu, live piano music.
$$$ Viejo Almacén, Gral Urquiza y Paso. Cosy, good cooking and excellent service.

🚌 Transport

Gualeguaychú *p59*
Bus
Bus terminal at Bv Artigas y Bv Jurado, T440688 (30-min walk to centre, *remise* taxi US$3). To **Concepción del Uruguay**, 1 hr, US$3. To **Buenos Aires**, US$20-22, 3½ hrs, several daily. To **Fray Bentos**, US$7, 1½ hrs, and **Mercedes**, US$9, 2 hrs, Ciudad de Gualeguay and ETA CUT (not Sun). To **Montevideo**, US$46-55, 6 ½ hrs, **Plus Ultra**.

Concepción del Uruguay *p59*
Bus
Terminal at Rocamora y Los Constituyentes (remise, US$2). To **Buenos Aires**, frequent, 4-4½ hrs, US$25-28. To **Colón**, 1 hr, US$2.

Colón *p60*
Bus
Terminal at Paysandú y Sourigues (10 blocks north of main plaza), T421716, left luggage at **Remises Base** (opposite Terminal) on 9 de Julio. Not all long distance buses enter Colón. **Buenos Aires**, US$28-32, 5-6 hrs. **Mercedes** (for Iberá), several companies, 7-8 hrs, US$21. **Paraná**, 4-6 hrs, US$10. **Uruguay**: via the Artigas Bridge (US$6 toll, open 24 hrs) all formalities dealt with on Uruguayan side. *Migraciones* officials board the bus, but non-Argentines/Uruguayans should get off bus for stamp. Bus to **Paysandú**, Copay and Río Uruguay, US$4, 1 hr.

Concordia *p60*
Bus
Terminal at Justo y Yrigoyen, T4217235, 15 blocks north- west of Plaza 25 de Mayo (reached by No 2 bus). **Buenos Aires**, US$34-41, 5-7½ hrs. **Paraná** US$11-18, 4½ hrs.

Train
Station about 10 blocks southeast of centre, tickets at Bus Terminal, T4220317, www.trenbinacional.com. 1 service on Mon to **Pilar** with a bus connection to **Buenos Aires** downtown, US$27, 11 hrs. On Thu 1 service to **Salto**, US$4, 1½ hrs.

To Uruguay
By **ferry** to Salto, US$4, 15 mins, 4 a day, not Sun. Port is 15 blocks southeast of centre. The **bus** service via the Salto Grande dam, US$4, 1½ hrs, is run by **Flecha Bus** and **Chadre**, 2 day each, not Sun; all formalities on the Argentine side, open 24 hrs. Passengers have to get off the bus to go through immigration. **Bikes** are not allowed to cross the international bridge but officials will help cyclists find a lift.

Up the Río Paraná

Several historic cities stand on the banks of the Paraná, which flows south from its confluence with the Río Paraguay. National parks protecting endangered marshes, especially at Iberá, are the highlight of the zone.

Rosario → *Phone code: 0341. Population: 1.2 million.*

The largest city in the province of Santa Fe and the third largest city in Argentina, Rosario, 295 km northwest of Buenos Aires, is a great industrial and export centre. It has a lively cultural scene with several theatres and bars where there are daily shows. The **tourist office** ① *Av Belgrano y Buenos Aires, T480 2230, www.rosarioturismo.com,* is on the riverside park next to the Monumento a la Bandera. See www.viarosario.com for the latest events information.

The old city centre is Plaza 25 de Mayo. Around it are the **cathedral** and the **Palacio Municipal**. On the north side is the **Museo de Arte Decorativo** ① *Santa Fe 748, T480 2547, www.museoestevez.gov.ar, Wed-Fri 1500-2000, Sat-Sun 1000-2000, free.* This sumptuous former residence houses a valuable private collection of paintings, furniture, tapestries sculptures and silverwork, brought mainly from Europe. Left of the cathedral, the **Pasaje Juramento** opens the pedestrian way to the imposing **Monumento a la Bandera** ① *T480 2238, www.monumentoalabandera.gov.ar, Mon 1400-1800, Tue-Sun 0900-1800 (in summer till 1900), US$1 (tower), free (Salón de las Banderas).* This commemorates the site on which, in 1812, General Belgrano, on his way to fight the Spaniards in Jujuy, raised the Argentine flag for the first time. A 70 m-tower has excellent panoramic views. In the first half of November in the Parque a la Bandera (opposite the monument) *Fiesta de las Colectividades* lasts 10 nights, with stalls offering food and a stage for folk music and dances. From Plaza 25 de Mayo, Córdoba leads west towards Plaza San Martín and beyond, the Boulevard Oroño. These 14 blocks are known as the **Paseo del Siglo** and have the largest concentration of late 19th- and early 20th-century buildings in the city. **Museo de Bellas Artes J B Castagnino** ① *Av Pellegrini 2202, T480 2542, www.museocastagnino.org. ar, closed Tue, open 1400-2000, Sat-Sun 1300-1900, US$1.15.* Just outside the 126-ha Parque Independencia, it has an impressive collection of French impressionist, Italian baroque and Flemish works, and one of best collections of Argentine paintings and sculpture. Upriver is the **Museo de Arte Contemporáneo** (MACRO) ① *Blvd Oroño on the river shore, T480 4981, www.macromuseo.org.ar, Thu-Tue 1500-2100 (1400-2000 in winter), US$1.* Inside a massive old silo, this remarkable museum is 10 levels high with a small gallery on each level, and at the top is a viewing deck.

Che Guevara was born here in 1928. The large white house at Entre Ríos y Urquiza where he lived for the first two years of his life before his family moved to Alta Gracia, near Córdoba, is now an insurance company office. There are dozens of riverside resorts on the islands and sandbars opposite Rosario. Boats to the resorts depart daily in summer (otherwise just at weekends) from *La Fluvial,* Av de los Inmigrantes 410, opposite Monumento a la Bandera, T447 3838, or from *Costa Alta,* between La Florida and the suspension bridge.

Parque Nacional Islas de Santa Fe, 60 km north of Rosario, is Argentina's newest national park, opened in October 2010. Its 2900 ha protect the wildlife of the islands formed by the meandering branches of the Río Paraná and its access point is Puerto Gaboto.

Paraná → *Phone code: 0343. Population: 339,930 (department).*

About 30 km southeast of Santa Fe, the capital of Entre Ríos was, from 1854-1861, capital of the Republic. The centre is on a hill offering views over the Río Paraná and beyond to Santa Fe. In the centre is the **Plaza Primero de Mayo**, around which are the **Municipalidad**, the large **Cathedral** and the Colegio del Huerto, seat of the Senate of the Argentine Confederation between 1854 and 1861. The **Casa de Gobierno** at Santa Fe y Laprida has a grand façade. Take pedestrianized San Martín and half block west of the corner with 25 de Junio is the fine **Teatro 3 de Febrero** (1908). Two blocks north is the **Plaza Alvear**; on the west side of which is the **Museo de Bellas Artes** ① *Buenos Aires 355, T420 7868, Tue-Fri*

0700-1300, 1500-1900, Sat 1000-1400, 1700-2000, Sun 1000-1300, US$0.75. It houses a vast collection of Argentine artists' work, with many by painter Cesario Bernaldo de Quirós. The city's glory is **Parque Urquiza**, along the cliffs above the Río Paraná. It has a statue to Gen Urquiza, and a bas-relief showing the battle of Caseros, at which he finally defeated Rosas. **Tourist offices**, in the centre at ① *Buenos Aires 132, T423 0183*; at Parque Urquiza ① *Av Laurencena y Juan de San Martín, T420 1837; at the bus terminal, T420 1862; and at the Hernandarias tunnel, www.turismoenparana.com.* Provincial office ① *Laprida 5, T420 7989, www.unatierradiferente.com.*

Santa Fe → *Phone code: 0342. Population: 525,093.*

From Paraná to Santa Fe, the road goes under the Río Paraná by the Herandarias tunnel (toll) and then crosses a number of bridges (bus service by Etacer and Fluviales, US$3.50, 50 minutes). Santa Fe, capital of its province, was founded by settlers from Asunción in 1573, though its present site was not occupied until 1653. The south part of the city, around the **Plaza 25 de Mayo** is the historic centre. On the Plaza itself is the majestic **Casa de Gobierno**, built in 1911-1917 in French style on the site of the historic Cabildo, in which the 1853 constitution was drafted. Opposite is the **Cathedral**. **Museo Histórico Provincial** ① *3 de Febrero 2553, T457 3529, all year 0830-1200, afternoon hours change frequently, closed Mon, free.* The building, dating from 1690, is one of the oldest surviving civil buildings in the country. About 100 m south is the **Iglesia y Convento de San Francisco** (1673 to 1695), with fine wooden ceilings, built from timber floated down the river from Paraguay, carved by indigenous craftsmen and fitted without the use of nails. On the opposite side of the park is the superb **Museo Etnográfico y Colonial** ① *Tue-Fri 0830-1200, 1530-1900, Sat-Sun 1530-1830, US$0.50*, with an exhibition of artefacts from 2000 BC to the first Spanish settlers of Santa Fe la Vieja. **Tourist offices**, at the bus terminal ① *T457 4124, 0800-2000* and at Boca del Tigre ① *Av JJ Paso 3500, T457 1862, www.santafeturismo.gov.ar, 0800-2000,* all good. **Provincial office** ① *San Martín 1399, T458 9475, turismo@santafe.gov.ar.*

Esteros del Iberá

The **Reserva Natural del Iberá** protects nearly 13,000 sq km of wetlands known as the **Esteros del Iberá**, similar to the Pantanal in Brazil. Over sixty small lakes, no more than a few metres deep, cover 20-30% of the protected area, which is rich in aquatic plants. Like islands in the *lagunas, embalsados* are floating vegetation, thick enough to support large animals and trees. Wildlife includes black caiman, marsh deer, capybara and about 370 species of bird, among them the *yabirú* or *Juan Grande*, the largest stork in the western hemisphere. More difficult to see are the endangered maned wolf, the 3-m long yellow anaconda, the *yacaré* ñato and the river otter. There is a visitors' centre by the bridge at the access to Carlos Pellegrini (see below), open 0730-1200, 1400-1800, helpful and informative park rangers. **Mercedes** *(Phone code: 03773, Population: 47,425),* 250 km southeast of Corrientes, gives the best access and is the only point for getting regular transport to Carlos Pellegrini. There are a couple of decent places to stay, a few restaurants, ATMs and internet facilities; also a small tourist office at Sarmiento 650, T420100. The surrounding countryside is mostly grassy *pampas*, where rheas can be seen, with rocks emerging from the plains from time to time. **Carlos Pellegrini**, 120 km northeast of Mercedes (rough road), stands on beautiful *Laguna Iberá*. A one-day visit allows for a three-hour boat excursion (US$22.50 pp if not included in hotel rates), but some hotels offer more activities for longer stays, eg horse rides or guided walks. Iberá Expediciones, Yaguarete y Pindó, T154 01405, www.ibera expediciones.com, offers guided treks, horse riding, night-time 4WD trips and information.

Parque Nacional Mburucuyá

ⓘ *12 km east of the town of Mburucuyá, T03782-498907, mburucuya@apn.gov.ar, free, 2 hotels. Buses San Antonio from Corrientes go daily to Mburucuyá, 2½ hrs, US$4; remises to the park, US$12.*

West of the Esteros del Iberá and 180 km southeast of Corrientes, this park covers 17,660 ha, stretching north from the marshes of the Río Santa Lucía. It includes savanna with *yatay* palms, 'islands' of wet Chaco forest, and *esteros*. The mburucuyá or passionflower gives the name to the park. Wildlife is easy to see. Formerly two estancias, Santa María and Santa Teresa, the land was donated by their owner, the Danish botanist Troels Pedersen, who identified 1300 different plants here. Provincial route 86 (unpaved) crosses the park for 18 km leading to the information centre and free campsite (hot water and electricity).

Corrientes → *Phone code: 0379. Population: 356,310.*

Corrientes, founded in 1588 is some 30 km below the confluence of the Ríos Paraguay and Alto Paraná. The 2.75-km General Belgrano bridge across the Río Paraná (toll) links the city with Resistencia (25 km), from where Ruta 11 goes north to Formosa and Asunción. East of Corrientes, Ruta 12 follows the Alto Paraná to Posadas and Iguazú. The river can make the air heavy, moist and oppressive, but in winter the climate is pleasant. The city, known as the capital of Carnaval in Argentina, is also capital of Corrientes province and the setting for Graham Greene's novel, *The Honorary Consul*. **Tourist offices**, city tourist office at ⓘ *Carlos Pellegrini 542, T442 3779, daily 0700-2100*, good map. **Provincial office** ⓘ *25 de Mayo 1330, T442 7200, province and city information, Mon-Fri 0700-1300, and in the bus station, T441 4839, open 0700-2200, www.corrientes.gov.ar.*

On the **Plaza 25 de Mayo**, one of the best preserved in Argentina, the **Jefatura de Policía**, built in 19th-century French style, the Italianate **Casa de Gobierno** and the church of **La Merced**. The **Museo de Artesanías** ⓘ *Quintana 905, Mon-Fri 0800-1200, 1600-2000, free*, is a large old house with an exhibition of handicrafts made from the most diverse materials imaginable, by indigenous groups and contemporary urban and rural artisans. Six blocks south is the leafy Plaza de la Cruz, on which the church of **La Cruz de los Milagros** (1897) houses a cross, the Santo Madero, placed there by the founder of the city, Juan Torres de Vera – *indígenas* who tried to burn it were killed by lightning from a cloudless sky. The **Museo de Ciencias Naturales 'Amadeo Bonpland'** ⓘ *San Martín 850, Mon-Sat 0900-1200, 1600-2000*, contains botanical, zoological, archaeological and mineralogical collections including 5800 insects and huge wasp nest. A beautiful walk eastwards, along the Avenida Costanera, beside the Paraná river leads to **Parque Mitre**, from where there are views of sunset.

Up the Río Paraná listings

For hotel and restaurant price codes and other relevant information, see pages 10-12.

😊 Where to stay

Rosario *p63*
Rosario has a good range of business hotels (eg 4 in the Solans group, www.solans.com) and a number of hostels at the budget end.

$$$$-$$$ Ros Tower, Mitre 299, T529 9000, http://rostower.com.ar. Central 5-star hotel with pool and bar on the roof, good services, spa and restaurant.
$$$ Esplendor Savoy Rosario, San Lorenzo 1022, T448 0071, www.esplendor savoy rosario.com. Early 20th-century mansion, once Rosario's best, now completely remodelled as a luxury hotel with all modern services: gym, Wi-Fi, etc.

$$$ Garden, Callao 45, T437 0025, www.
hotel gardensa.com. Good option a little
way from the centre, in the Pichincha
district (next to Blv Oroño) with superior
rooms and comfortable standard rooms.
Also restaurant and children's play area.
$$$-$$ Merit Majestic, San Lorenzo 980,
T440 5872, www.amerian.com. Modern,
inviting 3-star, newly refurbished, well
designed rooms in an ornate turn-of-the-
century building, stylish.
$$ Boulevard, San Lorenzo 2194, T447
5795, www.hotelboulevard. com.ar. Small
1920s house, tastefully renovated as a
charming B&B with doubles and triples,
Wi-Fi. Recommended.
$ pp Hostel Point, Catamarca 1837, T440
9337, www.hostelpoint.com.ar. Central,
nicely designed, brightly coloured dorms
(US$11.50-13.75) and a lovely double (**$$**).
Recommended.
$ pp Anamundana Guest House,
Montevideo 1248, T424 3077, www.
anamundanahostel.com. In an old terraced
house, sparsely but stylishly decorated,
dorms (US$11.50) and doubles (**$$**) with
high ceilings and original windows and
doors. It can be noisy at times.
$ pp La Lechuza, Corrientes 561, T448
4714, www.lalechuzahostel.com.ar.
Welcoming, sociable hostel with helpful
owner, dorms only, from US$10.50, Wi-Fi,
bar and kitchen.
$ pp Passers Hostel, 1 Mayo 1117, T440
4590, www.passershostel.com.ar. Funky
wallpaper and furniture, spacious dorms,
with breakfast, Wi-Fi, kitcjen. Only a few
metres from the Monumento a la Bandera.
$ pp Punto Clave, Ituzaingó 246, T481
9569, www.puntoclavehostel. com.ar. A
fun, cheerful hostel with large dorms, a
comfortable common area with big bean
bags and helpful owners. Recommended.

Paraná *p63*
$$$ Gran Hotel Paraná, Urquiza 976,
T422 3900, www.hotelesparana.com.

ar. Overlooking Plaza Primero de Mayo, 3
room categories (breakfast included), smart
restaurant *La Fourchette*, gym.
$$ San Jorge, Belgrano 368, T422 1685,
www.sanjorgehotel.com.ar. Renovated
house, helpful staff, older rooms are
cheaper than the modern ones at the back
with TV, breakfast, Wi-Fi, kitchen.
$ Paraná Hostel, Andrés Pazos 159, T455
0847, www.paranahostel.com.ar. Small,
central, nice living room with cable TV
and comfy sofas. Smart dorms and private
rooms (**$$**) available. Best budget option
in the area.

Santa Fe *p64*
$$$ Castelar, 25 de Mayo 2349, T456 0999,
www.castelarsantafe.com.ar. On a small
plaza, 1930's hotel, good value, comfortable,
breakfast included, restaurant.
$$$ Riogrande, San Gerónimo 2580, T450
0700, www.hotel-riogrande.com.ar. Santa
Fe's best hotel has very good rooms, with
slightly smaller standard ones. A large
breakfast is included.
$$$-$$ Hostal Santa Fe de la Veracruz,
San Martín 2954, T455 1740, www.hostalsf.
com. Traditional favourite, 2 types of room,
both good value, large breakfast, restaurant,
sauna (extra).

Esteros del Iberá *p64*
Mercedes
$$ Sol, San Martín 519 (entre Batalla
de Salta y B Mitre), T420283, www.
mimercedes.com.ar/hotelsol. Comfortable
rooms around a wonderful patio with
black and white tiles, and lots of plants,
Wi-Fi. Lovely.
$$ La Casa de China, Mitre y Fray L
Beltrán, call for directions, T156 27269,
lacasadechina@hotmail.com. A delightful
historical old house with clean rooms and
a lovely patio, breakfast included, Wi-Fi.
Recommended.

Carlos Pellegrini

$$$$ pp **Posada Aguapé**, T03773-499412, www.iberaesteros.com.ar. On a lagoon with a garden and pool, comfortable rooms, attractive dining room, rates are for full board and include 2 excursions. Recommended.

$$$$ pp **Posada de la Laguna**, T03773-499413, www.posadadelalaguna.com. A beautiful place run by Elsa Güiraldes (grand-daughter of famous Argentine novelist, Ricardo Güiraldes) and set on the lake, very comfortable, large neat garden and a swimming pool, full board and all excursions included, English and some French spoken, excellent country cooking. Highly recommended.

$$$$ pp **Rincón del Socorro**, T03782-497161, www.rincondel socorro.com. Incredibly luxurious, beautifully set in its own 12,000 ha 35 km south of Carlos Pellegrini, with 6 spacious bedrooms, each with a little sitting room, 3 cabañas, and elegant sitting rooms and dining rooms. Delicious home-produced organic food, excellent trips on the lagunas with bilingual guides, *asados* at lunchtime, night safaris and horse riding. Gorgeous gardens, pool with superb views all around. Highly recommended.

$$$$-$$$ **Irupé Lodge**, T03752-438312 or 93773-402193, www.ibera-argentina. com. Rustic, simple rooms, great views of the laguna from dining room, offers conventional and alternative trips, camping on islands, diving, fishing, several languages spoken. Offers all-inclusives and combined Iberá and Iguazú tours.

$$$ pp **Hostería Ñandé Retá**, T03773-499411, www.nandereta.com. Large old wooden house in a shady grove, play room, full board, home cooking, excursions.

$$$ pp **Posada Ypá Sapukai**, Sarmiento 212, T03773-1551 4212, www.ypasapukai. com.ar. Private rooms and shared. Good value, nice atmosphere, excellent staff. Rates are for full board and include 2 3-hr boat trips, or a walk or horse riding.

$$$ **Rancho Iberá**, Caraguatá y Aguará, T03783-1531 8594, www.posadarancho ibera.com.ar. Designed like an old Argentine country house, *posada* with double and triple bedrooms and a well-maintained garden. Also has a cottage for 5.

$$$ **Rancho Inambú**, T03773-1543 6159, Yeruti, entre Aguapé y Pehuajó, www. ranchoinambu.com.ar. Services include tours, 24-hr water, a lovely common area and a great bar (open to non-guests). Nice rustic rooms set in lush gardens.

$$$ pp **San Lorenzo**, at Galarza, T03756-481292, www.estanciasanlorenzo.com. Next to 2 lakes on the northeast edge of the region, splendid for wildlife watching, full board, only 3 rooms, horse rides, walks, boat trips all included. Boat excursions by night are charged separately. Access from Gobernador Virasoro (90 km), via Rutas 37 and 41. Transfer can be arranged to/from Gobernador Virasoro or Posadas for an extra charge. Closed Jan-Feb.

$ pp **Don Justino Hostel**, Curupi y Yaguareté, T03773-1562 8823. Small hostel 3 blocks from the lake, 2 from the plaza. Organizes tours and boat trips.

Corrientes *p65*

$$$$ **La Alondra**, 2 de abril 827, T443 0555, www.laalondra.com.ar. The best place to stay in town. 7 beautiful rooms and a wonderful communal area. Antique furniture throughout, exquisite styling and a homely feel. Lovely patio and 12-m pool.

$$$ **Gran Hotel Guaraní**, Mendoza 970, T443 3800, www.hguarani.com.ar. 4-star, business-oriented with restaurant, pool and gym, parking, breakfast.

$ pp **Bienvenida Golondrina**, La Rioja 455, T443 5316, http://bvngolondrina. blogspot.com/. The only hostel in the city. Half a block from the port, in a carefully remodelled old building. Bright dorms, cheaper with fan, private rooms (**$$**), ultra-modern kitchen, Wi-Fi, a roof-top terrace and lots of internal patios to relax in.

⊘ Restaurants

Rosario *p63*

$$$ Escauriza, Bajada Escauriza y Paseo Ribereño, La Florida, 30 mins' drive from centre, near bridge over the Paraná, T454 1777. Said to be the 'oldest and best' fish restaurant, with terrace overlooking the river.

$$ Amarra, Av Belgrano y Buenos Aires, T447 7550. Good food, including fish and seafood, quite formal, cheap set menus Mon-Fri noon.

$$ La Estancia, Av Pellegrini 1510 y Paraguay. Typical good *parrilla* popular with locals a few blocks east of Parque Independencia.

$$ Rich, San Juan 1031, T411 5151. A classic, widely varied menu, superb food, reputed to be one of the best restaurants in the whole country. Set meals including pastas, meats and salads, closed Mon. Recommended.

$ New Taipei, Laprida 1121. Decent Chinese food for a change from the usual Argentine fare, lunch menú US$4.50.

$ Patio, at Gallega supermarkets, Pellegrini y Mitre and Pellegrini y Moreno. Cheap self-service restaurants with good range of salads.

Cafés and bars

Antares, Callao y Catamarca, T437 0945. A good choice of their own label beers, happy hour, friendly, also serves food, live music on Sun evening.

El Born, Pellegrini 1574. Tapas bar, open daily 0800-0300, from 1800 Sat-Sun, also has a clothes shop.

Kaffa, Córdoba 1473. Good coffee served inside the large bookshop **El Ateneo Yenny**.

La Maltería del Siglo, Roca 1601 y Santa Fé. Open every day for food, drinks and background music, livens up when major football matches are on.

Rock'n'Feller's, Oroño y Jujuy. Flash new location for this popular restobar, upmarket, international fare including Tex-Mex

options. Popular at night too.

Verde que te quiero Verde, Córdoba 1358. Great vegetarian café open 0800-2100, closed Sun, serving a fantastic brunch and lots of good veggie options. Recommended.

Santa Fe *p64*

Many good eating places, with excellent meals with wine. Many places in the centre close on Sun.

$$ El Quincho de Chiquito, Av Almirante Brown y Obispo Príncipe (Costanera Oeste). Classic fish restaurant, excellent food, generous helpings and good value.

$$ España, San Martín 2644. An elegant place, serving good food.

$ El Brigadier, San Martín 1670. This colonial- style place next to the Plaza 25 de Mayo serves superb *surubí al paquete* (stuffed fish) and many *parrilla* dishes.

$ Club Sirio Libanés, 25 de Mayo 2740. Very good Middle Eastern food, popular Sun lunch for families.

Corrientes *p65*

$ El Solar, San Lorenzo 830. Informal, busy at lunchtime, meals by weight.

$ Martha de Bianchetti, 9 de Julio y Mendoza. Smart café and bakery.

Panambí, Junín near Córdoba. A traditional, central *confitería*, serving good pastries and regional breads.

⊖ Transport

Rosario *p63*

Air

Airport at Fisherton, 15 km west of centre, T451 3220. *Remises* charge US$16. Daily flights to Buenos Aires with **AR** and **Sol**, 45 mins. Also **Gol** to Porto Alegre.

Bus

Terminal at Santa Fe y Cafferata, about 30 blocks west of the *Monumento de la Bandera*, T437 3030, www.terminalrosario. gov.ar. For local buses you must buy magnetic card sold at kiosks in the centre or near bus stops (US$0.50 per journey), several bus lines to centre with stops on Córdoba (eg 101, 103, 115); from centre, take buses on Plaza 25 de Mayo, via C Santa Fe. *Remise* US$5. **Buenos Aires**, 4 hrs, US$25-33. **Córdoba**, 6 hrs, US$32-39. **Santa Fe**, 2½ hrs, US$13.

Train
Rosario Norte station, Av del Valle 2750. To/from Buenos Aires, operated by **Ferrocentral**, T436 1661, www. ferrocentralsa.com.ar, ticket office at the station open daily except Wed (different times each day). To **Buenos Aires** Wed 1134 and Sat 1418, US$16; to Tucumán Mon and Fri 1626. Taxis charge US$2.

Paraná *p63*
Bus
Terminal at Av Ramírez 2598 (10 blocks southeast of Plaza Primero de Mayo), T422 1282. Buses 1, 6 to/from centre, US$1. *Remise* US$5. To **Colón** on Río Uruguay, 4-5 hrs, US$10. To **Buenos Aires**, 6-7 hrs, US$38-49.

Santa Fe *p64*
Air
Airport at Sauce Viejo, 17 km south. T499 5064. Taxi US$5 from bus terminal. Daily **AR** (25 de Mayo 2287, T0810-222 86527) and **Sol** (Suipacha 2993, T0810-444 4765) to and from **Buenos Aires**.

Bus
Terminal near the centre, Gen M Belgrano 2910, T457 4124. To **Córdoba**, US$22-36, 5 hrs. Many buses to **Buenos Aires** US$35-46, 6 hrs; to **Paraná** frequent service US$3, 50 mins; to **Rosario**, 2½ hrs, US$13.

Esteros del Iberá *p64*
Bus
Mercedes to **Carlos Pellegrini**: Itatí II combis Mon-Sat 1230 (schedules change frequently) from Pujol 1166, T420184, T156

29598, 4-5 hrs, US$10. Combi spends an hour picking up passengers all around Mercedes after leaving the office. Returns from Pellegrini at 0430, book by 2200 the night before at the local grocery (ask for directions). Mercedes to **Buenos Aires**, 9-10 hrs, US$52-66. Mercedes to **Corrientes**, 3 hrs, US$12. To **Puerto Iguazú**, best to go via Corrientes, otherwise via any important town along Ruta 14, eg Paso de los Libres, 130 km southeast. There is a direct bus from Carlos Pellegrini to **Posadas**.

Corrientes *p65*
Air
Camba Punta Airport, 10 km east of city, T445 8684. (Remise US$5.) **AR** (T442 4647) to/from Buenos Aires.

Bus
Terminal: Av Maipú 2400. To **Resistencia**, Chaco–Corrientes, every 15 mins from Av Costanera y La Rioja at the port, 40 mins, US$3. Main terminal on Av Maipú, 5 km southeast of centre, bus No 103 (be sure to ask the driver if goes to terminal as same line has many different routes), 20 mins, US$0.50. To **Posadas** US$23-32, 3½-4 hrs, several companies. To **Buenos Aires**, several companies, 11-12 hrs, US$78-103. **Crucero del Norte** (www.crucerodelnorte. com.ar) and **El Pulqui** (www.elpulquisrl. com.ar) run Corrientes-Resistencia-**Asunción** (Paraguay) daily, US$18.

⊙ Directory

Airline offices Aerolíneas Argentinas, Córdoba 852, T420 8135. **Gol**, Santa Fe 1515, T530 1150. **Sol**, Entre Ríos 986, T0810-444 4765. **Banks** Many banks along C Córdoba, east of plaza San Martín. Exchange at **Transatlántica**, Mitre y Rioja. TCs exchanged at **Banex**, Mitre y Santa Fe. **Bike hire and repair** Bike House, San Juan 973, T424 5280, info@bikehouse.com.ar. Bike Rosario, Zeballos 327, T155 713812,

www.bikerosario.com.ar, Sebastián Clérico.
Bike rental (US$14 per day), bike tours, also
kayak trips. **Speedway Bike Center**, Roca
1269, T426 8415, info@speedwaybikecenter.
com.ar.

Santa Fe *p64*
Banks Banking district around San Martín
y Tucumán. Exchange money and TCs at
Tourfé, San Martín 2500, or at **Columbia**,
San Martín 2275.

The Chaco

Much of the Chaco is inaccessible because of poor roads (many of them impassable during
summer rains) and lack of public transport, but it has two attractive national parks which
are reachable all year round. Resistencia and Formosa are the main cities at the eastern rim,
from where Rutas 16 and 81 respectively go west almost straight across the plains to the
hills in Salta province. Buses to Salta take Ruta 16, while Ruta 81 has long unpaved sections
west of Las Lomitas, which make for a very hard journey after heavy rains. Presidencia
Roque Sáenz Peña, 170 km northwest of Resistencia, is a reasonable place to stop over.
The Chaco has two distinct natural zones. The Wet Chaco spreads along the Ríos Paraná
and Paraguay covered mainly by marsh-lands with savanna and groves of caranday
palms, where birdwatching is excellent. Further west, as rainfall diminishes, scrubland of
algarrobo, white quebracho, palo borracho and various types of cacti characterise the Dry
Chaco, where South America's highest temperatures, exceeding 45°C, have been recorded.
Winters are mild, with only an occasional touch of frost in the south. The Chaco is one of
the main centres of indigenous population in Argentina: the Toba are settled in towns by
the Río Paraná and the semi-nomadic Wichí live in the western region. Less numerous are
the Mocoví in Chaco and the Pilagá in central Formosa. For introductory articles see www.
chaco.gov.ar/MinisterioDeGobierno/PueblosOriginarios/, www.saludindigena.org.ar and
www.chacolinks.org.uk.

Resistencia → *Phone code: 0362. Population: 386,390.*
The hot and energetic capital of the Province of Chaco, Resistencia is 6.5 km up the
Barranqueras stream on the west bank of the Paraná and 544 km north of Santa Fe. On
the Paraná itself is the little port of Barranqueras. Resistencia is known as the 'city of the
statues', there being over 200 of these in the streets. Four blocks from the central Plaza 25
de Mayo is the **Fogón de los Arrieros** ① *Brown 350 (between López y Planes and French),
T442 6418, open to non-members Mon-Sat 0900-1200, Mon-Fri 2100-2300, US$2.* This
famous club and informal cultural centre deserves a visit, for its occasional exhibitions
and meetings. The **Museo Del Hombre Chaqueño** ① *Juan B Justo 280, Mon-Fri 0800-1200,
1600-2000, free,* is a small anthropological museum with an exhibition of handicrafts by
native Wichí, Toba and Mocoví people. It has a fascinating mythology section in which
small statues represent Guaraní beliefs (still found in rural areas). There are banks and
cambios in the centre for exchange. **Tourist office** ① *Plaza 25 de Mayo, T445 8289, Mon-Fri
0800-2000.* **Provincial tourist office** ① *Av Sarmiento 1675, T443 8880, www.chaco.travel,
Mon-Fri 0800-1300, 1400-2000, Sat 0800-1200.*

Parque Nacional Chaco
① *T03725-499161, chaco@apn.gov.ar, 24 hrs, free, 115 km northwest of Resistencia, best
visited between Apr-Oct to avoid intense summer heat and voracious mosquitoes.*
The park extends over 15,000 ha and protects one of the last remaining untouched areas

of the Wet Chaco with exceptional *quebracho colorado* trees, *caranday* palms and dense riverine forests with orchids along the banks of the Río Negro. Some 340 species of bird have been sighted in the park. Mammals include *carayá* monkeys and, much harder to see, collared peccary, puma and jaguarundi. 300 m from the entrance is the visitors' centre and a free campsite with hot showers and electricity. There you can hire bicycles or horses for US$5 per hour. The paved Ruta 16 goes northwest from Resistencia and after about 60 km Ruta 9 branches off, leading north to Colonia Elisa and Capitán Solari, 5 km east of the park entrance, via a dirt road. If in a group, call the park in advance to be picked up at Capitán Solari. *La Estrella* run daily buses Resistencia-Capitán Solari, where *remise* taxis should not charge more than US$3 to the park, a short journey that can also be done on foot. Tour operators run day-long excursions to the park from Resistencia.

Formosa → *Phone code: 0370. Population: 233,028.*
The capital of Formosa Province, 186 km above Corrientes, is the only Argentine port of any note on the Río Paraguay. It is oppressively hot from November to March. **Tourist offices** ① *José M Uriburu 820 (Plaza San Martín), 1600-2000, T442 5192, www.formosa. gob.ar/turismo, Mon-Fri 0730-1300.* Ask about guided excursions and accommodation at estancias.

Border with Paraguay
The easiest crossing is by road via the Puente Loyola, 4 km north of **Clorinda** (phone code: 03718). From Puerto Falcón, at the Paraguayan end of the bridge, the road runs 40 km northeast, crossing the Río Paraguay, before reaching Asunción. **Immigration** formalities for entering Argentina are dealt with at the Argentine end, those for leaving Argentina at the Paraguayan end. Crossing, open 24 hours. **Buses** from Clorinda to Puerto Falcón cost US$0.75 and from Falcón to Asunción, *Empresa Falcón* run every hour, US$1.50, last bus to the centre of Asunción 1830.

Parque Nacional Río Pilcomayo
① *Access to the park is free, 24 hrs, administration centre in Laguna Blanca, Av Pueyrredón y Ruta 86, T03718-470045, riopilcomayo@apn.gov.ar, Mon-Fri 0700-1430.*
Some 48,000 ha, 65 km northwest of Clorinda is this national park is recognised as a natural wetland, with lakes, marshes and low-lying parts which flood during the rainy season. The remainder is grassland with caranday palm forests and Chaco woodland. Among the protected species are aguará-guazú, giant anteaters and coatis. Caimans, black howler monkeys, rheas and a variety of birds can also be seen. The park has two entrances leading to different areas. Easiest to reach on foot is Laguna Blanca, where there is an information point and a free campsite with electricity and cold water. From there, a footpath goes to the Laguna Blanca, the biggest lake in the park. A bit further is the second entrance, leading to the area of Estero Poí, with another information point and a campsite without facilities. **Godoy** buses run from Formosa or Resistencia to the small towns of Laguna Naick-Neck, 5 km from the park (for going to Laguna Blanca) and Laguna Blanca, 8 km from the park (for going to Estero Poí). **Remise** taxis from both towns should charge no more than US$4 for these short journeys. There are police controls on the way to the park because of the proximity to the Paraguay border.

The Chaco listings

For hotel and restaurant price codes and other relevant information, see pages 10-12.

🛏 Where to stay

Resistencia *p70*
$$$ Covadonga, Güemes 200, T444 4444, www.hotelcovadonga.com.ar. Comfortable, a/c, breakfast, swimming pool, sauna, gym.
$$$-$$ Niyat Urban Hotel, Hipólito Yrigoyen 83, T444 8451, www.niyaturban.com.ar. The newest and best hotel in town. Modern, spacious and stylish rooms overlooking the park. Buffet breakfast, cable TV and efficient staff.
$$-$ Bariloche, Obligado 239, T442 1412, jag@cpsarg.com. Good budget choice, welcoming owner, decent rooms with a/c. No breakfast, but there's a nearby café at Gran Hotel Royal.

Formosa *p71*
$$$ Turismo, San Martín 759, T443 1122, hotelturismo@elpajaritosa.com.ar. Large building by the river, good views, a/c and breakfast.
$$ Plaza, José M Uriburu 920, T442 6767, plaza_formosa@hotmail.com. On Plaza, good, pool, with breakfast, very helpful, some English spoken, secure parking.
$$ Colón, Belgrano 1068, T442 6547, www.hotelcolonformosa.com. Comfortable rooms, a/c, breakfast included, Wi-Fi.
$ El Extranjero, Av Gutnisky 2660, T452276. Opposite bus terminal, OK, with a/c.

🍴 Restaurants

Resistencia *p70*
$$ Kebon, Don Bosco and Güemes, T442 2385. One of the better restaurants in the city, wide choice, popular for lunch and with families.
$$-$ Charly, Güemes 213, T443 4019. Parrilla and international food, excellent, a/c.

$ San José, Roca y Av Alberdi. A popular café and confitería on Plaza 25 de Mayo with excellent pastries and ice creams.

Formosa *p71*
$ El Tano Marino, Av 25 de Mayo 63. Italian, pastas are the speciality.

🎉 Festivals

Resistencia *p70*
Fiesta Nacional de Pescado de los Grandes is celebrated **10-12 Oct**, Río Antequeros, 14 km away.

Formosa *p71*
The world's longest **Via Crucis** pilgrimage with 14 stops along Ruta 81 (registered in the Guinness Book of Records) takes place every Easter week, starting in Formosa and ending at the border with the province of Salta, 501 km northwest. **Festival de la caña con ruda** is held on the last night of **Jul**, when Paraguayan *caña* flavoured by the *ruda* plant is drunk as a protection against the mid-winter blues. A good chance to try regional dishes. **Nov Festival Provincial de Folclore**. Held at Pirané (115 km northwest), the major music festival in the northeast, attracting national stars.

🚌 Transport

Resistencia *p70*
Air
Airport 8 km west of town (taxi US$3), T444 6 009. **AR**, T444 5551, to/from **Buenos Aires**, 1¼ hrs.

Bus
To **Corrientes**, Chaco-Corrientes buses stop opposite *Norte* supermarket on Av Alberdi e Illia, 40 mins, US$3. Modern terminal on Av Malvinas Argentinas y Av Maclean in western outskirts (bus 3

or 10 from Oro y Perón, 1 block west of plaza, 20 mins, US$0.75; *remise* US$3). To **Buenos Aires** 12-13 hrs, US$78-93 several companies. To **Formosa** 2-2½ hrs, US$11.50-17.25. To **Iguazú**, 8-10½ hrs, US$40-66, several companies, some require change of bus in **Posadas**, 5½ hrs, US$21-32. To **Salta**, FlechaBus and La Veloz del Norte, 12½ hrs, US$73-85. To **Asunción** 3 companies, 5-5½ hrs, US$16-18.

Formosa *p71*
Air
El Pucu airport, 5 km southwest, T445 2490; *remise*, US$3. **AR** (T742 9314) to **Buenos Aires** 1½ hrs.

Bus
Terminal at Av Gutnisky 2615, 15 blocks west of Plaza San Martín, T445 1766, www.terminalformosa.com.ar (*remise* US$2). **Asunción**, 3 hrs, US$13. **Buenos Aires** 15-17 hrs, US$92-121.

Misiones

While Posadas is one of the main crossing points to Paraguay, most people will head northeast, through the province of the Jesuit Missions, towards Iguazú. This is a land of ruined religious establishments, gemstones and waterfalls.

Posadas → *Phone code: 0376. Population: 324,756 (department).*
This is the main Argentine port on the south bank of the Alto Paraná, 377 km above Corrientes, and the capital of the province of Misiones. On the opposite bank of the river lies the Paraguayan town of Encarnación, reached by the San Roque bridge. The city's centre is **Plaza 9 de Julio**, on which stand the Cathedral and the **Gobernación**, in imitation French style. The riverside and adjacent districts are good for a stroll. Follow Rivadavia or Buenos Aires north to Avenida Andrés Guaçurarí (referred also to as Roque Pérez), a pleasant boulevard, lively at night with several bars. Immediately north of it is the small and hilly **Bajada Vieja** or old port district. There is a good **Museo Regional Aníbal Cambas** ⓘ *Alberdi 600 in the Parque República del Paraguay, 11 blocks north of Plaza 9 de Julio, T444 7539, Mon-Fri 0700-1900*, its permanent exhibition of Guaraní artefacts and pieces collected from the nearby Jesuit missions is worth seeing. **Tourist office** ⓘ *Colón 1985, T444 7540, www.turismo. misiones.gov.ar, daily 0800-2000.*

Border with Paraguay
Argentine immigration and customs are on the Argentine side of the bridge to Encarnación. Buses across the bridge (see Transport page 77) do not stop for formalities; you must get exit stamps. Get off the bus, keep your ticket and luggage, and catch a later bus. Pedestrians and cyclists are not allowed to cross; cyclists must ask officials for assistance. Boats cross to Encarnación, 6-8 minutes, hourly Monday-Friday 0800-1800, US$1. Formalities and ticket office at main building. Port access from Avenida Costanera y Avenida Andrés Guaçurarí, T442 5044 (*Prefectura*).

San Ignacio Miní → *Phone code: 0376.*
ⓘ *0700-1900, US$11.50 with tour (ask for English version), leaves from entrance every 20 mins. Allow 1½ hrs. Go early to avoid crowds and the best light for pictures (also late afternoon); good birdwatching. Son et lumière show at the ruins, daily 1900 autumn and winter, 2000 spring and summer, in 5 languages, cancelled if raining US$11.50, T447 0186.*
The little town of San Ignacio is the site of the most impressive Jesuit ruins in the region,

63 km northeast of Posadas. It is a good base for visiting the other Jesuit ruins and for walking. San Ignacio, together with the missions of Santa Ana and Loreto, is a UNESCO World Heritage Site. There are heavy rains in February. Mosquitoes can be a problem. The local festival is 30-31 July. Tourist office at Independencia 605, T447 0130.

San Ignacio Miní was founded on its present site in 1696. The 100 sq-m, grass-covered plaza is flanked north, east and west by 30 parallel blocks of stone buildings with four to 10 small, one-room dwellings in each block. The roofs have gone, but the massive metre-thick walls are still standing except where they have been torn down by the *ibapoi* trees. The public buildings, some of them 10 m high, are on the south side of the plaza. In the centre are the ruins of a large church finished about 1724. The masonry, sandstone from the Río Paraná, was held together by mud. Inside the entrance, 200 m from the ruins, is the **Centro de Interpretación Jesuítico-Guaraní**, with displays on the lives of the Guaraníes before the arrival of the Spanish, the work of the Jesuits and the consequences of their expulsion, as well as a fine model of the mission. **Museo Provincial** contains a small collection of artefacts from Jesuit reducciones.

The ruins of two other Jesuit missions are worth visiting. **Loreto** ① *US$6, or with ticket to San Ignacio within 15 days, 0700-1830*, can be reached by a 3-km dirt road (signposted) which turns off Ruta 12, 10 km south of San Ignacio. Little remains other than a few walls; excavations are in progress. There are no buses to Loreto; the bus drops you off on Ruta 12, or take a tour from Posadas or a *remise*. **Santa Ana** ① *US$5, or with San Ignacio ticket, 16 km south of San Ignacio, 0730-1930 (1830 in winter), buses stop on Ruta 12*, was the site of the Jesuit iron foundry. Impressive high walls still stand and beautiful steps lead from the church to the wide open plaza The ruins are 700 m along a path from Ruta 12 (signposted).

Near San Ignacio, is the **Casa de Horacio Quiroga** ① *T470124, 0800-1900, US$1 (includes 40-min guided tour; ask in advance for English). Take Calle San Martín (opposite direction to the ruins) to the Gendarmería HQ. Turn right and on your right are 2 attractive wood and stone houses. After 200 m the road turns left and 300 m later, a signposted narrow road branches off.* The house of this Uruguayan writer, who lived part of his tragic life here as a farmer and carpenter between 1910 and 1916 and in the 1930s, is worth a visit. Many of his short stories were inspired by the subtropical environment and its inhabitants.

San Ignacio to Puerto Iguazú

Ruta 12 continues northeast, running parallel to Río Alto Paraná, towards Puerto Iguazú. With its bright red soil and lush vegetation, this attractive route is known as the Región de las Flores. You get a good view of the local economy: plantations of *yerba mate*, manioc and citrus fruits, timber yards, manioc mills and *yerba mate* factories. The road passes through several small modern towns including Jardín America, Puerto Rico, Montecarlo and Eldorado, with accommodation, campsites, places to eat and regular bus services. Just outside Eldorado, **Estancia Las Mercedes** ① *T03751-1541 8224, www.estancialasmercedes. com*, is an old *yerba mate* farm with period furnishings, open for day visits with activities like riding, boating, and for overnight stays with full board (**$$$**). **Wanda**, 50 km north of Eldorado, was named after a Polish princess and is famous as the site of open-cast amethyst and quartz mines which sell gems. There are guided tours to two of them, **Tierra Colorada** and **Compañía Minera Wanda** ① *daily 0700-1900*.

Gran Salto del Moconá

For 3 km the waters of the Río Uruguay in a remote part of Misiones create magnificent falls (known in Brazil as Yucumã) up to 20 m high. They are surrounded by dense woodland protected by the Parque Estadual do Turvo (Brazil) and the Parque Provincial Mocaná, the Reserva Provincial Esmeralda and the Reserva de la Biósfera Yabotí (Argentina). Mocaná has roads and footpaths, accommodation where outdoor activities can be arranged, such as excursions to the falls, trekking in the forests, kayaking, birdwatching and 4WD trips. Alternative bases are El Soberbio (70 km southwest) or San Pedro (92 km northwest). Roads from both towns to Mocaná are impassable after heavy rain and if the river is high (May-October) the falls may be under water. Regular bus service from Posadas to El Soberbio or San Pedro, and from Puerto Iguazú to San Pedro, but no bus all the way to the falls.

Misiones listings

For hotel and restaurant price codes and other relevant information, see pages 10-12.

🛏 Where to stay

Posadas *p73*
$$$ Continental, Bolívar 1879 (on Plaza 9 de Julio), T444 0990, www.hoteleramisiones.com.ar. Standard rooms and more spacious VIP rooms, some have river views, restaurant on 1st floor.
$$$ Julio César, Entre Ríos 1951, T442 7930, www.juliocesarhotel.com.ar. 4-star hotel, pool and gym, spacious reasonably priced rooms, some with river views, breakfast included. Recommended.
$$ City, Colón 1754, T433901, citysa@arnet.com.ar. Gloomy reception, but good rooms, some overlooking plaza, with breakfast and a/c, restaurant on 1st floor, parking.
$$ Le Petit, Santiago del Estero 1630, T436031, lepetithotel@ciudad.com.ar. Good value, small, a short walk from centre on a quiet street, a/c, with breakfast.
$$ Residencial Colón, Colón 2169, T442 5085, www.residencialcolon.blogspot.com. Small but affordable rooms with a/c and TV, Wi-Fi, parking. Apartments for up to 6.
$ pp **Hostel Vuelo el Pez**, 25 de Mayo 1216, T443 8706, www.vuelaelpez.com.ar. Small hostel with basic but comfortable facilities, brightly coloured walls and lots of advice. Doubles (**$$**) also available.
$ pp **Residencial Misiones**, Félix de Azara 1960, T430133. Dark rooms, fan, central, old house with a patio, no breakfast, poorly equipped kitchen.

San Ignacio Miní *p73*
$$ La Toscana, H Irigoyen y Uruguay, T447 0777, www.hotellatoscana.com.ar. Family-run, 12-bedroom hotel with rustic, inviting rooms and a wonderful pool with a terrace. It's an easy 10-min walk from the tourist office and main plaza. Highly recommended.
$$ San Ignacio, San Martín 823, T447 0422, hotelsanignacio@arnet.com.ar. Good if not dated rooms with a/c and self-catering apartments for 4-5 people. Breakfast extra. Phone booths and an interesting view of town from the reception.
$ pp **Adventure Hostel**, Independencia 469, T447 0955, www.sihostel.com.ar. Large hostel with a fantastic pool and a games area. Spacious communal areas, comfy double rooms (**$$**). Camping available (US$5). Short walk to centre of town.
$ pp **Hostel El Jesuita**, San Martín 1291, T1542 24571. Welcoming owners, Darío and Graciela, run this small hostel. Fully equipped kitchen, spacious double rooms (**$$**) with their own exit to the garden, small comfy dorm, 1½ blocks from the ruins. Call when you arrive to be picked up. Travel advice. 3 camping spots. Recommended.

Camping
Complejo Los Jesuitas, C Emilia Mayer, T446 0847, www.complejolosjesuitas.com.ar. Campsite and cabins for 4 people.

Gran Salto del Mocaná *p74*
$$$ pp **El Refugio Mocaná**, 3 km from access to the reserve, 8 km from the falls (or

contact at Bolívar 1495, in Posadas), T0376-442 1829, www.refugiomocona.com.ar. Price for 3-day package. Rustic rooms for 4-5 with shared bath, campsite, tents for rent, meals available. Many activities, such as 30-min boat trips to the falls, 1-hr walk to the falls, and several other excursions on foot and by 4WD. There is also a kayak journey down the river Yabotí. Transfer with sightseeing to and from San Pedro, 2 hrs.

$$ Hostería Puesta del Sol, C Suipacha s/n, El Soberbio, T03755-495161 (T011-4300 1377 in Buenos Aires). A splendid vantage point overlooking town, with a swimming pool and restaurant. Comfortable rooms, with breakfast and a/c. Full board available. They also run boat excursions arranged to the falls, 7-8 hrs, landing and meal included (minimum 4 people). The journey to the falls is by a boat crossing to Brazil, then by vehicle to Parque do Turvo, 7 hrs, meal included. Otherwise, a 4WD journey on the Argentine side with more chances for trekking takes 7 hrs, with a meal included. There are other lodges in the vicinity, for example: www.donenriquelodge.com. ar, www.lodgelamision.com.ar, www. posadalabonita.net

Restaurants

Posadas *p73*
Most places offer *espeto corrido*, eat as much as you can *parrilla* with meat brought to the table.

$$, De La Costa, Av Costanera. Hugely popular with locals, this place on the riverbank has 2 floors, with great views from the upper floor and a cheerful buzz on Sat.

$$ El Mensú, Fleming y Cnel Reguera (in the Bajada Vieja district). Attractive house with a varied menu of fish and pasta, large selection of wines. Closed Mon.

$$, La Querencia, Bolívar 1849 (on Plaza 9 de Julio). A large traditional restaurant offering *parrilla*, *surubí* and pastas.

$$, Plaza Café, Bolívar 1979 just outside the shopping centre. Great salads and large mains. Busy during the day and busier at night. Highly recommended.

$, Bar Español, Bolívar 2085. Open since 1958, this restaurant has tasty Spanish-influenced food. Have an ice cream for dessert next door at **Duomo**.

$, La Nouvelle Vitrage, Colón y Bolívar. Good pizzas, sandwiches and coffee. Friendly staff, good view of the plaza, free Wi-Fi.

San Ignacio Miní *p73*
There are several restaurants catering for tourists on the streets by the Jesuit ruins, eg **La Carpa Azul**, Rivadavia 1295, and **La Misionera**, Rivadavia 1105, both good.

$, La Aldea, Rivadavia y Alberdi, opposite ruins. An attractive house serving good and cheap pizzas, *empanadas* or other simple meals.

What to do

Posadas *p73*
Abra, Colón 1975, T442 2221, www. abratours.com.ar. Tours to San Ignacio, including Santa Ana Jesuit ruins, also those in Paraguay and in Brazil, plus tours to waterfalls.

Guayrá, San Lorenzo 2208, T443 3415, www.guayra.com.ar. Tours to Iberá, to Saltos del Moconá, to both sites in a 5-day excursion, and to other sites in Misiones, also car rental and transfer to Carlos Pellegrini (for Iberá).

San Ignacio Miní *p73*
Misiones Excursions, Ruta 12 esq Santa María de Mayer, T1543 73448, www. misionesexcursions.com.ar. Excellent, small company, personalized tours to the missions, including to Trinidad in Paraguay. Also visits to Guaraní villages, a *yerba* estancia, kayaking, cycling and 2-night excursions to the Esteros de Iberá (book in advance). Recommended.

Posadas *p73*

Air

Gen San Martín Airport, 12 km west, T445 7413, reached by *remise* US$10. To **Buenos Aires**, AR (Ayacucho 1724, T442 2036), direct or via Corrientes or Formosa, 1 hr 50 mins.

Bus

Terminal about 5 km out of the city at Av Santa Catalina y Av Quaranta (T445 6106, municipal tourist office), on the road to Corrientes. *Remise* US$5. For bus into town, cross the street from the terminal and look for Nos 15, 21 or 8 to the centre, US$1.50. Travel agencies in the centre can book bus tickets. To **Buenos Aires**, 12-13 hrs, US$87-114. Services to **San Ignacio Miní**, 1 hr, US$5, and **Puerto Iguazú**, US$16.75-18, 5-6 hrs.

San Ignacio Miní *p73*

Bus Stop in front of the church, leaving almost hourly to **Posadas** (US$5) or to **Puerto Iguazú** (US$15). Do not rely on bus terminal at the end of Av Sarmiento, only a few stop there. More buses stop on Ruta 12 at the access road (Av Sarmiento).

To **Paraguay**, a ferry crosses the Río Paraná at **Corpus** to **Bella Vista**, foot passengers US$2 (for cars weekdays only), which is a good route to the Paraguayan Jesuit missions. There are immigration and customs facilities.

Posadas *p73*

Banks Casa de cambio Mazza, Bolívar 1932. For money exchange, TCs accepted. **Consulates** Paraguay, San Lorenzo 1561, T442 3858. Mon-Fri 0700-1400. Same-day visas. **Immigration** Dirección Nacional de Migraciones, Buenos Aires 1633, T442 7414, 0630-1330. **Medical services** Hospital Dr Ramón Madariaga, Av L Torres 1177, T444 7000.

Iguazú Falls

The mighty Iguazú Falls are the most overwhelmingly magnificent in all of South America. So impressive are they that Eleanor Roosevelt remarked "poor Niagara" on witnessing them (they are four times wider). In 2012 they were confirmed as one of the New7Wonders of Nature. Viewed from below, the tumbling water is majestically beautiful in its setting of begonias, orchids, ferns and palms. Toucans, flocks of parrots and cacique birds and great dusky swifts dodge in and out along with myriad butterflies (there are at least 500 different species). Above the impact of the water, upon basalt rock, hovers a perpetual 30-m high cloud of mist in which the sun creates blazing rainbows.

Arriving at Iguazú Falls

Information Entry is US$23, payable in pesos only. Argentines, Mercosur and Misiones inhabitants pay less. Entry next day is half price with same ticket, which you must get stamped at the end of the first day. Open daily 0800-1800. Visitor Centre includes information and photographs of the flora and fauna, as well as books for sale. There are places to eat, toilets, shops and a locutorio in the park. In the rainy season, when water levels are high, waterproof coats or swimming costumes are advisable for some of the lower catwalks and for boat trips. Cameras should be carried in a plastic bag. **Tourist offices** ⓘ *Aguirre 311, Puerto Iguazú, T420800*, and **Municipal office** ⓘ *Av Victoria Aguirre y Balbino Brañas, T422938, 0900-2200, www.iguazuturismo. gov.ar; at the Falls, T0800-266 4482, www.iguazuargentina.com.* National park office: ⓘ *Victoria Aguirre 66, T420722, iguazu@apn.gov.ar.*

The falls, on the Argentina-Brazil border, are 19 km upstream from the confluence of the Río Iguazú with the Río Alto Paraná. The Río Iguazú (*I* is Guaraní for water and *guazú* is Guaraní for big), which rises in the Brazilian hills near Curitiba, receives the waters of some 30 rivers as it crosses the plateau. Above the main falls, the river, sown with wooded islets, opens out to a width of 4 km. There are rapids for 3.5 km above the 74 m precipice over which the water plunges in 275 falls over a frontage of 2470 m, at a rate of 1750 cu m a second (rising to 12,750 cu m in the rainy season).

Around the falls → *In Oct-Mar (daylight saving dates change each year) Brazil is 1 hr ahead.*
On both sides of the falls there are national parks. Transport between the two is via the Ponte Tancredo Neves as there is no crossing at the falls themselves. The Brazilian park offers a superb panoramic view of the whole falls and is best visited in the morning when the light is better for photography. The Argentine park (which requires at least a day to explore properly) offers closer views of the individual falls in their forest setting with its wildlife and butterflies, though to appreciate these properly you need to go early and get well away from the visitor areas. Busiest times are holidays and Sundays. Both parks have visitors' centres and tourist facilities are constantly being improved, including for the disabled.

1 **Around the Iguazú Falls**

Where to stay
1 Camping e Pousada Internacional
2 Complejo Americano & Hostel Inn Iguazú
3 Del Parque Ibirá Retá
4 Hostel Natura & Paudimar Campestre
5 Hotel Das Cataratas
6 Posada 21 Oranges
7 Pousada Evelina
8 Sheraton Internacional Iguazú Resort

Parque Nacional Iguazú covers an area of 67,620 ha. The fauna includes jaguars, tapirs, brown capuchin monkeys, collared anteaters and coatimundis, but these are rarely seen around the falls. There is a huge variety of birds; among the butterflies are shiny blue morphos and red/black heliconius. From the Visitor Centre a small gas-run train (free), the **Tren de la Selva**, whisks visitors on a 25-minute trip through the jungle to the Estación del Diablo, where it's a 1-km walk along catwalks across the Río Iguazú to the park's centrepiece, the **Garanta del Diablo**. A visit here is particularly recommended in the evening when the light is best and the swifts are returning to roost on the cliffs, some behind the water. Trains leave on the hour and 30 minutes past the hour. However, it's best to see the falls from a distance first, with excellent views from the two well-organized trails along the **Circuito Superior** and **Circuito Inferior**, each taking around an hour and a half. To reach these, get off the train at the **Estación Cataratas** (after 10 minutes' journey) and walk down the **Sendero Verde**. The Circuito Superior is a level path which takes you along the easternmost line of falls, Bossetti, Bernabé Mandez, Mbiguá (Guaraní for cormorant) and San Martín, allowing you to see these falls from above. This path is safe for those with walking difficulties, wheelchairs and pushchairs, though you should wear supportive non-slippery shoes. The Circuito Inferior takes you down to the water's edge via a series of steep stairs and walkways with superb views of both San Martín falls and the Gaganta del Diablo from a distance. Wheelchair users, pram pushers, and those who aren't good with steps should go down by the exit route for a smooth and easy descent. You could then return to the Estación Cataratas to take the train to Estación Garganta, 10 and 40 minutes past the hour, and see the falls close up. Every month on the five nights of full moon, there are 1½-hour guided walks (bilingual) that may include or not a dinner afterwards or before the walk, at the Restaurant La Selva, depending on the time of departure. See www.iguazuargentina.com for dates, times and email booking form; reservations also in person at the park, T03757-491469, or through agencies: US$62 with dinner; US$46 without.

At the very bottom of the Circuito Inferior, a free ferry crosses 0930-1530 on demand to the small, hilly **Isla San Martín** where trails lead to miradores with good close views of the San Martín falls (boats go 0930-1530). The park has two further trails: **Sendero Macuco**, 7 km return (the park says 2-3 hours, allow much more), starting from near the Visitor Centre and leading to the river via a natural pool (El Pozón) fed

by a slender waterfall, **Salto Arrechea** (a good place for bathing and the only permitted place in the park). **Sendero Yacaratiá** starts from the same place, but reaches the river by a different route, and ends at Puerto Macuco, where you could take the *Jungle Explorer* boat to the see the Falls themselves (see below). This trail is really for vehicles (30 km in total) and is best visited on an organized safari.

Puerto Iguazú → *Phone code: 03757. Population: 82,227.*

This modern town is 18 km northwest of the falls high above the river on the Argentine side near the confluence of the Ríos Iguazú and Alto Paraná. It serves mainly as a centre for visitors to the falls. The port lies to the north of the town centre at the foot of a hill: from the port you can follow the Río Iguazú downstream towards Hito-Tres Fronteras, a *mirador* with views over the point where the Ríos Iguazú and Alto Paraná meet and over neighbouring Brazil and Paraguay. There are souvenir shops, toilets and pubs are here; bus US$0.50. **La Aripuca** ① *T423488, www.aripuca.com.ar, US$3, turn off Ruta 12 just after Hotel Cataratas, entrance after 250 m, 0900-1800, English and German spoken*, is a large

2 **Puerto Iguazú**

Where to stay
1 Garden Stone
2 Hostería Casa Blanca
3 Iguazú Jungle Lodge
4 Marco Polo Inn
5 Panoramic
6 Peter Pan
7 Pirayú Resort
8 Res Familiar Noelia
9 Saint George
10 Secret Garden
11 Stop Hostel
12 Timbó Posada

Restaurants
1 Aqva
2 El Quincho del Tío Querido
3 Fatto in Casa
4 La Esquina
5 La Rueda
6 Pizza Color
7 Pizzería La Costa
8 Tango Bar Iguazú

wooden structure housing a centre for the appreciation of the native tree species and their environment. **Güirá Oga** (Casa de los Pájaros) ① *US$2, daily 0830-1700, turn off Ruta 12 at Hotel Orquídeas Palace, entrance is 800 m further along the road from Aripuca; T423980, www. guiraoga.fundacionazara.org.ar*, is a sanctuary for birds that have been injured, where they are treated and reintroduced to the wild; exquisite parrots and magnificent birds of prey. There is also a trail in the forest and a breeding centre for endangered species.

Iguazú Falls listings

For hotel and restaurant price codes and other relevant information, see pages 10-12.

🛏 Where to stay

Puerto Iguazú *p80, maps p78 and p80*
$$$$ Panoramic, Paraguay 372, T498050, www.panoramic-hoteliguazu.com. On a hill overlooking the river, this hotel is stunning. Serene outdoor pool with great views, large well-designed rooms and 5-star inclusions.
$$$$ Posada Puerto Bemberg, Fundadores Bemberg s/n, Puerto Libertad (some 35 km south of Iguazú), T03757-496500, www.puertobemberg.com. Wonderful luxury accommodation and gourmet cuisine in a 1940s bungalow surrounded by lush gardens. Huge living areas, beautifully decorated rooms and helpful staff. Also offers 3-night stays in **Casa Bemberg**, the original house. Good birdwatching. Highly recommended.
$$$$ Sheraton Internacional Iguazú Resort, T491800, www.sheraton.com/ iguazu. Fine position overlooking the falls, excellent, good restaurant and breakfast, sports facilities and spa. Taxi to airport available. Recommended.
$$$$ Yacutinga Lodge, 30 km from town, pick up by jeep, www.yacutinga. com. A beautiful lodge in the middle of the rainforest, with activities, learning about the bird and plant life and Guaraní culture. Accommodation is in rustic adobe houses in tropical gardens, superb food and drinks included, as well as boat trips and walks. Recommended.
$$$$-$$$ Saint George, Córdoba 148, T420633, www.hotelsaintgeorge.com.

Comfortable modern-ish rooms around a leafy pool area, with attentive service and a pleasant atmosphere. Half-board available. By the bus station. Tours arranged.
$$$ Iguazú Jungle Lodge, Hipólito lyrigoyen y San Lorenzo, T420600, www. iguazujungle lodge.com. A well-designed complex of *cabañas* and loft apartments, 7 blocks from the centre, by a river, with lovely pool. Comfortable and stylish, a/c, Wi-Fi, DVDs, great service, restaurant, breakfast included. Houses sleep 7, good value if full. Warmly recommended.
$$$ Pirayú Resort, Av Tres Fronteras 550, on the way to the Hito, T420393, www. pirayu.com.ar. Well-equipped, comfortable *cabañas*, lovely river views, sports and games, pool, entertainment.
$$$ Posada 21 Oranges, C Montecarlo y Av los Inmigrantes, T155 71403, www. riotropic.com.ar. 10 simple but comfortable rooms set around a pool, lovely garden, Wi-Fi, welcoming. US$5 taxi ride or 20-min walk to town.
$$$ Secret Garden, Los Lapachos 623, T423099, www.secretgardeniguazu.com. Small B&B with attentive owners, fern garden surrounding the house. Spacious rooms, good breakfast and cocktails, relaxing atmosphere.
$$ Del Parque Ibirá Retá, R12, Km 4.5, T420872, www.ibirareta.com.ar. Intimate lodge snuggled in the middle of Parque Botánico Ibirá Retá, decorated in simple modern colours, with TV, a/c, breakfast included and there is the option of including dinners as well.
$$ Hostería Casa Blanca, Guaraní 121, near bus station, T421320, www.

casablancaiguazu.com.ar. With breakfast, family run, spotless, large rooms, good showers, beautifully maintained.

$$ Timbó Posada, Misiones 147, T422698, www.timboiguazu.com.ar. 100 m from the bus station. Doubles have a/c and Wi-Fi, dorms are US$12 pp. Kitchen, good breakfasts.

$ pp Hostel Inn Iguazú, R 12, Km 5, T421823, http://hiiguazu.com. 20% discount to HI members and 10% discount on long-distance buses, a/c doubles **$$$**. Large, well-organized hostel which used to be a casino. Huge pool and free internet, pool tables, ping-pong and a range of free DVDs to watch. They also organize package tours to the falls, which include accommodation. Recommended.

$ pp Marco Polo Inn, Av Córdoba 158, T425559, www.hostel-inn.com. The biggest and most central hostel in town, right in front of the bus station, a/c doubles **$$$**. Wi-Fi throughout, nice pool, fun bar at night (open to non-residents). It gets busy so reserve in advance. Recommended.

$ pp Garden Stone, Av Córdoba 441, T420425, www.gardenstonehostel.com. Lovely hostel with a homely feel set in nice gardens, with a large outdoor eating area. They have plans for a pool but in the meantime the garden is the perfect place to relax in. Recommended for a tranquil stay.

$ pp Peter Pan, Av Córdoba 267, T423 616, www.peterpanhostel.com. Just down the hill from the bus station, spotless, central pool and large open kitchen. The doubles (**$$**) are lovely. Helpful staff.

$ pp Residencial Familiar Noelia, Fray Luis Beltrán 119, T420729, residencialfamiliarnoelia@yahoo.com. Cheap, well-kept and helpful, good breakfast, family-run, good value.

$ pp Stop Hostel, Av Victoria Aguirre 304, T424616, www.stophostel.com. Single and mixed dorms at US$8 per bed, private rooms US$18 pp, with breakfast, bar, Wi-Fi, iPod docks, luggage lockers, English spoken, tourist information, good.

Camping

Complejo Americano, Ruta 12, Km 5, T420190, www.complejoamericano.com. ar. 3 pools, wooded gardens, *cabañas* (**$$$**), camping US$9 pp, food shop, electricity, barbecue.

🍽 Restaurants

Puerto Iguazú *p80, maps p78 and p80*

$$ Aqva, Av Córdoba y Carlos Thays, T422064. Just down from the bus station, this lovely restaurant serves dishes made with ingredients from the area.

$$ El Quincho del Tío Querido, Bompland 110, T420151. Recommended for *parrilla* and local fish, very popular, great value.

$$ La Esquina, Córdoba 148, next to *Hotel St George*, T425778. Extensive buffet, beef, fish, salads, friendly service.

$$ La Rueda, Córdoba 28, T422531. Good food and prices, fish, steaks and pastas, often with mellow live music. Highly recommended.

$$ Tango Bar Iguazú, Av Brasil 1, T422008. New bar which serves pizzas and pastas. It turns into a milonga with tango classes and dancing at night.

$$-$ Fatto in Casa, Av Brasil 126. Italian food in a lively part of town. Often recommended by locals.

$ Pizza Color, Córdoba y Amarante. Popular for pizza and *parrilla*.

$ Pizzería La Costa, Av Río Iguazú, on costanera. Popular, informal, high above the river on the coast road, looks basic, but the pizzas are superb.

⚙ What to do

Iguazú Falls *p77, map p78*
Explorador Expediciones, Perito Moreno 217, T421632, www.rainforestevt.com. ar. Offers 2 small-group tours: *Safari a la Cascada* which takes you by jeep to the Arrechea waterfall, stopping along the way to look at wildlife, with a short walk to the falls, 2 hrs. And *Safari en la Selva*,

more in-depth interpretation of the wildlife all around, in open jeeps, 2 hrs. Highly recommended. They also run birdwatching trips, adventure tours, tours to Moconá.
Jungle Explorer, T421696, www.iguazu junglexplorer.com. Run a series of boat trips, all highly recommended, eg: **Aventura Náutica** is an exhilarating journey by launch along the lower Río Iguazú, from opposite Isla San Martín right up to the San Martín falls and then into the Garganta del Diablo, completely drenching passengers in the mighty spray. Great fun; not for the faint-hearted, 12 mins. On **Paseo Ecológico** you float silently for 3 km from Estación Garganta to appreciate the wildlife on the river banks, 30 mins.

Puerto Iguazú *p80, maps p78 and p80*
Agencies arrange day tours to the Brazilian side (lunch in Foz), Itaipú and Ciudad del Este. Some include the Duty Free mall on the Argentine side. Tours to the Jesuit ruins at San Ignacio Miní also visit a gem mine at Wanda (you don't see as much of the ruins as you do if staying overnight).
Aguas Grandes, Mariano Moreno 58, T425500, www.aguasgrandes.com. Tours to both sides of the falls and further afield, activities in the forest, abseiling down waterfalls, good fun.
Cabalgatas por la Selva, Ruta 12, just after the Rotonda for the road to the international bridge, T155-42180. For horse riding, 3-hr trips.
Cabalgatas Ecológicas, T155 09942, www. cabalgatasecologicas.com. Personalized horse-riding tours around Iguazu.

⊙ Transport

Iguazú Falls *p77, map p78*
Bus
A public *Cataratas* bus runs every 30 mins from Hito Tres Fronteras every 30 mins, 0700-1930. It stops at Puerto Iguazú bus terminal 10 mins after departure, at the park entrance for the purchase of entry

tickets, then continues to the Visitor Centre, US$3. Journey time 45 mins; return buses from the park: 0745-2015. You can get on or off the bus at any point en route. **Cars** are not allowed beyond visitor centre.

Puerto Iguazú *p80, maps p78 and p80*
Air
Airport is 20 km southeast of Puerto Iguazú near the Falls, T422013. **Four Tourist Travel** bus service between airport and bus terminal, US$3.55, will also drop off/collect you from your hotel. Taxi US$14. **AR/Austral** and **LAN** fly direct to **Buenos Aires**, 1½ hrs.

Bus
The bus terminal, at Av Córdoba y Av Misiones, T423006, has a phone office, restaurant, various tour company desks and bus offices. To **Buenos Aires**, 16-18 hrs, **Tigre Iguazú**, **Via Bariloche** and others, daily, US$114-150. To **Posadas**, stopping at San Ignacio Miní, frequent, 5-6 hrs, US$16.75-18; to **San Ignacio Miní**, US$15. **Agencia de Pasajes Noelia**, local 3, T422722, can book tickets beyond Posadas for other destinations in Argentina, ISIC discounts available.

Taxi
T420973/421707. Fares in town US$2.50-3.

Border with Brazil
Crossing via the Puente Tancredo Neves is straightforward. When leaving Argentina, Argentine immigration is at the Brazilian end of the bridge. Border open 0700-2300. **Brazilian consulate**, Av Córdoba 278, T420192.

Bus
Leave Puerto Iguazú terminal for Foz do Iguaçu every 15 mins, 0730-1830, US$3. The bus stops at the Argentine border post, but not the Brazilian. Both Argentine and Brazilian officials stamp you in and out, even if only for a day visit. Whether you are entering Brazil for the first time, or leaving

and returning after a day in Argentina, you must insist on getting off the bus to get the required stamp and entry card. Buses also stop at the Duty Free mall. The bus does not wait for those who need stamps, just catch the next one, of whatever company.

Taxis Between the border and Puerto Iguazú US$25.

Border with Paraguay

Crossing to Paraguay is via Puente Tancredo Neves to Brazil and then via the Puente de la Amistad to Ciudad del Este. Brazilian entry and exit stamps are not required unless you are stopping in Brazil. The **Paraguayan consulate** is at Puerto Moreno 236, T424230, 0800-1600.

Bus

Direct buses (non-stop in Brazil), leave Puerto Iguazú terminal every 40 mins, US$3.50, 45 mins, liable to delays especially in crossing the bridge to Ciudad del Este. Only one bus on Sun, no schedule, better to go to Foz and change buses there.

⊙ Directory

Puerto Iguazú *p80, maps p78 and p80*
Airline offices Aerolíneas Argentinas, Brasil y Aguirre, T420168. **LAN** T0810-999 9526. **Banks** ATMs at **Macro**, Misiones y Bonpland, and **Banco de la Nación**, Av Aguirre 179. *Sheraton* has an ATM. TCs can only be changed at **Libres Cambio** in the Hito Tres Fronteras, 0800-2200. Good exchange rates at the Brazilian border.

Contents

Uruguay

ARGENTINA

BRAZIL

Bella Unión ○ ─ *Río Quaraí* ─ ○ Artigas

○ Termas del Arapey

Rivera

Salto ○

Termas de Daymán

Minas de Corrales ○

Aceguá ○

Termas de Guaviyú ○

Tacuarembó ○

Tambores ○

Ansina ○

Paysandú ○ Guichón ○

Curtina ○

Las Toscas ○

Melo ○

Río Uruguay

Paso de los Toros ○

Rincón del Bonete (Lago Artificial)

Quebrada de los Cuervos ○

Tres Bocas ○

Río Negro

Carlos Reyes ○

Cerro Chato ○

Fray Bentos ○

Mercedes ○

Treinta y Tres ○

Soriano ○

Durazno ○

Sarandí del Yí ○

José R Varela ○

Palmitas ○

Trinidad ○

Sarandí Grande ○

Pirajá ○

Lascano ○

Dolores ○

Cardona ○

Nueva Palmira ○

Calera de las Huérfanas ○

Florida ○

Cerro Colorado ○

Velásquez ○

Carmelo ○

Rosario ○

Nueva Helvecia ○

San José de Mayo ○

Aiguá ○

Castillo ○

Conchillas ○

Colonia del Sacramento ○

Colonia Valdense ○

Canelones ○ Sta Rosa ○

Minas ○

San Carlos ○

La Paloma ○

Libertad ○

Solís ○

Río de la Plata

Atlántida ○

MONTEVIDEO

Piriápolis ○

Punta del Este

Maldonado ○

Atlantic Ocean

N

20 km
20 miles

Uruguay is a land of rolling hills, best explored on horseback, or by staying at the many estancias that have opened their doors to visitors. It also has its feet in the Atlantic Ocean and one of the best ways to arrive is by ferry across the shipping lanes of the Río de la Plata. Montevideo, the capital and main port, is refurbishing its historical centre to match the smart seaside neighbourhoods, but its atmosphere is far removed from the cattle ranches of the interior.

West of Montevideo is Colonia del Sacramento, a former smuggling town turned gambling centre, and a colonial gem where race horses take their exercise in the sea. Up the Río Uruguay there are pleasant towns, some with bridges to Argentina, some with thermal springs. Also by the river is Fray Bentos, a town that lent its name to corned beef for generations, which is now an industrial museum.

Each summer, millions of holidaymakers flock to Punta del Este, one of the most famous resorts on the continent, but if crowds are not your cup of mate (the universal beverage), go out of season. Alternatively, venture up the Atlantic coast towards Brazil for empty beaches and fishing villages, sea lions, penguins and the occasional old fortress. And anywhere you go, take your binoculars because the birdwatching is excellent.

Planning your trip

Where to go

Montevideo, the capital, is the business heart of the country and has an interesting Ciudad Vieja (old city). The highlights are Mercado del Puerto, the former dockside market, which has become an emporium for traditional food and drink, and the magnificently restored Teatro Solís and the pedestrian Calle Sarandí. Within the city's limits are a number of beaches, which continue along the north shore of the Río de la Plata and on to the Atlantic seaboard. The most famous resort is **Punta del Este** which, in season (December-February), is packed with Argentines, Brazilians and locals taking their summer break. Beyond Punta del Este, there are quieter beaches with less infrastructure, but with sand dunes and other natural features. Along the coast, impressive villas and condominiums blend with their surroundings, a sort of museum of contemporary South American architecture under the open sky.

West of the capital is **Colonia del Sacramento**, a unique remnant of colonial building in this part of the continent. It is well preserved, standing on a small peninsula, and has one of the principal ferry ports for passenger traffic from Buenos Aires. Consequently it is a popular but costly place, but well worth a visit. Continuing west you come to the confluence of the Río Uruguay with the Plata estuary. Up river are the last vestiges of the meat canning industry at **Fray Bentos**, which has a museum commemorating what used to be one of Uruguay's main businesses. Further upstream are towns such as **Paysandú** and the historic **Salto**, from which you can cross to Argentina, and the hot springs which have been developed into resorts.

The centre of the country is mainly agricultural land, used for livestock and crops. Many estancias (farms) accept visitors. Daytrips out of Montevideo, Punta del Este, or Colonia, for instance, to an estancia, usually involve a meal, handicraft shopping and an educational element. Those ranches which offer lodging let you take part in the daily tasks, as these are working farms; you can do as much or as little as you like. Horse riding is the main activity and is suitable for all. Fishing and hunting are also offered at some.

Best time to visit Uruguay

The climate is temperate, often windy, with summer heat tempered by Atlantic breezes. Winter (June-September) is damp; temperatures average 10-16°C, but can sometimes fall to freezing. Summer (December-March) temperatures average 21-27°C. There is always some wind and the nights are relatively cool. The rainfall, with prolonged wet periods in July/August, averages about 1200 mm at Montevideo and some 250 more in the north.

Most tourists visit during the summer, which is also high season, when prices rise and hotels and transport need advance bookings. In the low season on the coast many places close.

Transport in Uruguay

Flight connections
If flying from Uruguay to make an international connection in Buenos Aires, make sure your flight goes to Ezeiza International Airport (eg American Airlines or TAM), not Aeroparque (almost all Aerolíneas Argentinas or Pluna flights). Luggage is not transferred automatically to Ezeiza and you'll have to travel one hour between the airports by taxi or bus. If you need

Price codes

Where to stay

$$$$ over US$150   **$$$** US$66-150

$$ US$30-65   **$** under US$30

Prices include taxes and service charge, but not meals. They are based on a double room, except in the **$** range, where prices are almost always per person.

Restaurants

$$$ over US$20   **$$** US$8-20   **$** under US$8

Prices refer to the cost of a two-course meal, not including drinks.

a visa to enter Argentina, you must get a transit visa (takes up to four weeks to process in Montevideo), just to transfer between airports. See also airport taxes, page 92.

Bus and road

All main cities and towns are served by good companies originating from the Tres Cruces Terminal in Montevideo (www.trescruces.com.uy, purchase must be made in person and early if travelling to popular destinations at peak holiday time). There are good services to neighbouring countries. Driving your own or a rented vehicle is a viable way to explore Uruguay, as it allows flexibility and access to further destinations. **Hitching** is not easy.

Train

The passenger services are slow commuter services from Montevideo to Progreso, Canelones, Santa Lucía, 25 de Agosto and San José de Mayo; and from Montevideo to Pando and Sudriers. Since 2011 a weekly train service connects Paso de los Toros with the Buenos Aires suburb of Pilar, passing by Paysandú and Salto.

Maps

Automóvil Club del Uruguay publishes road maps of the city and country, as do **Esso** and **Ancap**. **ITMB** of Vancouver also publish a country map (1:800,000). Official maps are issued by **Servicio Geográfico Militar**, Av 8 de Octubre 3255, T2487 1810, www.ejercito.mil.uy/cal/sgm/.

Where to stay in Uruguay

There is a range of hotel accommodation in Uruguay. There are hostels in addition to the Hostelling International places mentioned below, mid- and upper-range tourist and business hotels and, particularly around the resorts on the Atlantic coast, luxury and boutique hotels for the international jetset. Many places close out of holiday season, but at the height of beach season prices rise steeply and some places only offer full board. The other main type of lodging is in estancias, as mentioned above in Where to go. Always book in advance from mid-December to mid-March. Check whether 23% VAT is included in the price.

Camping

There are lots of sites. Most towns have municipal sites (quality varies). Many sites along the Ruta Interbalnearia, but most of these close off season. The Tourist Office in Montevideo issues a good guide to campsites and youth hostels; see references in main text.

Youth hostels

Many good quality hostels can be found in Montevideo and other cities and towns (see recommendations in Where to stay sections). **Hostelling International** ① *Paraguay 1212 (y Canelones), Montevideo, www.hosteluruguay.org*, has 16 member hostels.

Food and drink in Uruguay

Restaurants

Dinner hours are generally 2000-0100. Restaurants usually charge *cubierto* (bread and place setting), costing US$1-3, and more in Punta del Este. Lunch is generally served from 1300-1500, when service often stops until dinner. A *confitería* is an informal place which serves meals at any time, as opposed to a *restaurante*, which serves meals at set times. Uruguay doesn't have a great selection of international restaurants. Vegetarians may have to stick to salads or pasta, as even the "meatless" dishes are served with ham or bacon.

Food

In general, you have two choices: meat or Italian food. Beef is eaten at almost all meals. Most restaurants are *parrilladas* (grills) where the main cuts are *asado* (ribs); *pulpa* (no bones), *lomo* (fillet steak) and entrecote. Steak prices normally indicate the quality of the cut. Also very popular are *chorizos* and *salchichas*, both types of sausage. More exotic Uruguayan favorites include *morcilla* (blood sausage, salty or sweet), *chinchulines* or *chotos* (small or large intestines), *riñones* (kidneys) and *molleja* (sweetbreads). *Cordero* (lamb) and *brochettes* (skewers/kebabs) are also common. Grilled *provolone*, *morrones* (red peppers), *boniatos* (sweet potatos), and *chimichurri* sauce are also omnipresent. *Chivitos* (large, fully loaded steak burgers) and *milanesa* (fried breaded chicken or beef) are also popular; usually eaten with mixed salad (lettuce, tomato, onion), or chips. All Italian dishes are delicious, from bread to pastas to raviolis to desserts. Pizza is very common and good. Seafood includes squid, mussels, shrimp, salmon, and *lenguado* (sole). For snacks, *medialunas* (croissants) are often filled with ham and/or cheese, either hot or cold; toasted sandwiches and quiche are readily available; *frankfurters* are hot dogs; *picada* (crackers or breads, cheese, olives, coldcuts) is a common afternoon favourite. Desserts, mostly of Italian origin, are excellent. *Dulce de leche* (similar to caramel) and *dulce de membrillo* (quince cheese) are ubiquitous. As in Argentina, *alfajores* are a favourite sweet snack. Ice cream is excellent everywhere.

Drink

The beers are good (**Patricia** has been recommended). Local wines vary, but tannat is the regional speciality (eg **Don Pascual**, **Pisano**) and several bodegas offer tours. See www. bodegasdeluruguay.com.uy and www.uruguaywinetours.com. Whisky is the favourite spirit, normally Johnny Walker. Local spirits include *uvita*, *caña* and *grappamiel* (honey liquor). In the Mercado del Puerto, Montevideo, a *medio medio* is half still white wine, half sparkling white (elsewhere a *medio medio* is half *caña* and half whisky). *Espillinar* is a cross between whisky and rum. Try the *clericó*, a mixture of wine and fruit juices. Very good fresh fruit juices and mineral water are common. *Mate* is the drink of choice between meal hours. Coffee is good, normally served espresso-style after a meal. Milk, sold in plastic containers, is excellent, skimmed to whole (*descremada* to *entera*).

Essentials A-Z

Accident and emergency
Emergency T911. Ambulance T105 or 911. Fire service T104. Road police T108. Road information: T1954. Tourist Police in Montevideo, at Uruguay y Minas, T0800-8226.

Electricity
220 volts 50 cycles AC. Various plugs used: round 2-pin or flat 2-pin (most common), oblique 2-pin with earth, 3 round pins in a line.

Embassies and consulates
For all Uruguayan embassies and consulates abroad and for all foreign embassies and consulates in Uruguay, see http://embassy.goabroad.com.

Festivals in Uruguay
Public holidays
1 Jan, 6 Jan; Carnival; Easter week; 19 Apr; 1 and 18 May, 19 Jun; 18 Jul; 25 Aug (the night before is Noche de la Nostalgia, when people gather in *boliches* to dance to old songs); 12 Oct; 2 Nov; 25 Dec.

Carnival begins in late Jan/early Feb and lasts for some 40 days until Carnival week, officially Mon and Tue before Ash Wed (many firms close for the whole week). The most prominent elements in Carnival are Candombe, representing the rituals of the African slaves brought to the Río de la Plata in colonial times through drumming and dance. The complex polyrhythms produced by the mass of drummers advancing down the street in the 'Llamadas' parades is very impressive. The other main element is Murga, a form of street theatre with parody, satire, singing and dancing by elaborately made-up and costumed performers.

Business also comes to a standstill during Holy Week (or Semana del Turismo), which coincides with La Semana Criolla del Prado (horse-breaking, stunt riding by gauchos, dances and song). Department stores close only from Good Fri. Banks and offices close Thu-Sun. Easter Mon is not a holiday. A weekend of Sep or Oct is chosen annually for celebrating the Día del Patrimonio (Heritage Day) throughout the country: hundreds of buildings, both public or private, including embassies, are open to the public for that day only. Also special train services run. Mid-Dec there is a Fireworks night at Pocitos beach.

Money → *US$1 = 19.8 pesos (May 2012)*
The currency is the *peso uruguayo*. Bank notes: 20, 50, 100, 200, 500, 1,000 and 2,000 pesos uruguayos. Coins: 1, 2, 5 and 10 pesos. Any amount of currency can be taken in or out. Rates change often.

There's no restriction on foreign exchange transactions (so it is a good place to stock up with US$ bills, though AmEx and some banks refuse to do this for credit cards; most places charge 3% commission for such transactions).

Dollars cash can be purchased when leaving the country. Changing Argentine pesos into Uruguayan pesos is usually a marginally worse rate than for dollars. Brazilian *reais* get a much worse rate. US$ notes are accepted for some services, including most hotels and some restaurants.

Cost of travelling
Prices vary considerably between summer and winter in tourist destinations, Punta del Este being one of the most expensive summer resorts in Latin America. In Montevideo, allow US$70 daily for a cheap hotel, eating the *menú del día* and travelling by bus. Internet price varies around US$1 per hr at Antel *telecentros*.

Credit cards

In some places there is a 10% charge to use Visa and MasterCard. **Banred**, www.banred.com.uy, is the largest ATM network from where you can withdraw US$ or pesos with a Visa or MasterCard. **HSBC, Lloyds TSB, BBVA, Citibank** all have Banred ATMs. **Banco de la República** (BROU) branches have Banred, Link and Cirrus ATMs. ATMs can also be found in supermarkets. MasterCard emergency line call collect to USA, T1-636-722 7111, or 2902 5555. Visa emergency line, call collect T00-0411-940-7915. Most cheaper hotels outside major cities do not accept credit cards.

Opening hours

Shops: Mon-Fri 1000-1900; Sat 1000-1300; **shopping malls**: daily 1000-2200. In small towns or non-tourist areas, there is a break for lunch and siesta, between 1300 and 1600. **Businesses**: 0830-1200, 1430-1830 or 1900. **Banks**: Mon-Fri 1300-1700 (some till 1800). **Government offices**: Mon-Fri 1200-1800 in summer; Mon-Fri 1000-1700 (rest of the year).

Postal services

The main post office in Montevideo is at Misiones 1328 y Buenos Aires; 0800-1800 Mon-Fri, 0800-1300 Sat and holidays. **Poste restante** at main post office will keep mail for 1 month. Other branches in the capital: next to Pluna office on Av Libertador, next to Montevideo Shopping Center, 0800-1300, and under the Intendencia at corner of Av 18 de Julio and Ejido, Mon-Fri 1000-2000, Sat 1700-2200.

Safety

Personal security offers few problems in most of Uruguay. Petty theft does occur in Montevideo, most likely in tourist areas or markets. Beggars are often seen trying to sell small items or simply asking for money. They are not dangerous. The Policía Turística patrol the streets of the capital.

Tax

Airport tax US$17 on all air travellers leaving Uruguay for Buenos Aires, Aeroparque, but US$36 to Ezeiza and all other countries (payable in US$, local currency or by credit card), and a tax of 3% on all tickets issued and paid for in Uruguay. Domestic airport tax is US$2.
VAT/IVA 22%, 10% on certain basic items.

Telephone → *Country code +598.*

Ringing: long equal tones, long pauses. Engaged: short tones, short pauses. In 2010 all phone numbers in Uruguay changed with fixed line numbers becoming 8 digits. Area codes were eliminated by replacing the initial zero with, usually, 4 and the remaining digits being incorporated into the number. In Montevideo calls within the city are 8-digit, starting with 2; in the Maldonado phone code area, previously 042, only the zero is deleted (no extra 4 added). Mobile phone numbers are prefixed by 9. **Antel** *telecentros* in cities are good places to find phone, internet and other means of communication.

Time

GMT -3 (Oct-Mar -2).

Tipping

Restaurant and cafés usually include service, but an additional 10% is expected. Porters at the airport: US$1 per piece of luggage. Taxis: 5-10% of fare.

Tourist information

Ministry of Tourism Rambla 25 de Agosto de 1825 y Yacaré, T2188 5100/5111, www.mintur.gub.uy and www.uruguaynatural.com. It has information on birdwatching and the best places to see birds. Contact also: **Avesuruguay/Gupeca** Canelones 1164, Montevideo, T2902 8642, www.avesuruguay.org.uy. Uruguay is creating a system of national parks under the heading **Sistema Nacional de Areas Protegidas** (SNA), see www.snap.gub.uy.

Useful websites

www.welcomeuruguay.com Excellent bilingual regional guide to all tourist related businesses and events.

www.turismodeluruguay.com A tourism portal in English, Spanish and Portuguese.

www.brecha.com.uy *Brecha*, a progressive weekly listing films, theatres and concerts in Montevideo and provinces, US$2 (special editions sometimes free). Recommended.

Visas and immigration

A passport is necessary for entry except for nationals of most Latin American countries and citizens of the USA, who can get in with national identity documents for stays of up to 90 days. Nationals of the following countries need a visa for a tourist visit of less than 3 months: Albania, Armenia, China, Egypt, Guyana, India, Morrocco and the majority of Caribbean, African, Middle Eastern, Central Asian and Asian states. Visas cost US$40, and you need a passport photo, hotel reservations or letter of invitation and a ticket out of Uruguay. Visa processing may take 2-4 weeks. Visas are valid for 90 days and usually multiple entry. Tourist cards (obligatory for all tourists, obtainable on entry) are valid for 3 months, extendable for a similar period at the **Migraciones office** C Misiones 1513, T2916 0471, www.dnm.minterior.gub.uy. If entering and leaving Uruguay overland (bus or ferry), you may on departure be asked to show the ticket with which you arrived in the country.

Weights and measures

Metric.

Montevideo

Montevideo is a modern city that feels like a town. Barrios retain their personality while the city gels into one. The main areas, from west to east are: the shipping port, downtown, several riverside and central neighbourhoods (Palermo, Punta Carretas, Pocitos), the suburbs and Carrasco International airport, all connected by the Rambla. Everything blends together – architecture, markets, restaurants, stores, malls, stadiums, parks and beaches – and you can find what you need in a short walk.

Montevideo, the capital, was officially founded in 1726 on a promontory between the Río de la Plata and an inner bay, though the fortifications have been destroyed. Spanish and Italian architecture, French and Art Deco styles can be seen, especially in Ciudad Vieja. The city not only dominates the country's commerce and culture: it accounts for 70% of industrial production and handles almost 90% of imports and exports. In January and February many locals leave for the string of seaside resorts to the east. The first football World Cup was held in Centenario Stadium and won by Uruguay in 1930.

Arriving in Montevideo → *Population: 1,292,347.*

Getting there

Carrasco International **airport** is east of the centre, with easy connections by bus or taxi (20-30 minutes to downtown). Many visitors arrive at the port by boat from Buenos Aires, or by boat to Colonia and then bus to the Tres Cruces bus terminal just north of downtown. Both port and terminal have good facilities and tourist information. ▸▸ *See also Transport, page 106.*

Getting around

The Ciudad Vieja can be explored on foot. From Plaza de la Independencia buses are plentiful along Avenida 18 de Julio, connecting all parts of the city. Taxis are also plentiful, affordable and generally trustworthy, although compact. *Remises* (private driver and car) can be rented by the hour. Full details are given in Local Transport, see below. **Note** Street names are located on buildings, not street signs. Some plazas and streets are known by two names: for instance, Plaza de la Constitución is also called Plaza Matriz. It's a good idea to point out to a driver the location you want on a map and follow your route as you go. Also, seemingly direct routes rarely exist owing to the many one-way streets and, outside the centre, non-grid layout.

Tourist offices

Tourist information for the whole country is at the **Tres Cruces bus terminal** ⓘ *T1885801, trescruces@mintur.gub.uy, Mon-Fri 0800-2200, Sat-Sun 0900-2200* ; at the **Ministry of Tourism** ⓘ *Rambla 25 de Agosto de 1825 y Yacaré (next to the port), T21885, ext111*; and at **Carrasco international airport** ⓘ *T2604 0386, carrasco@mintur.gub.uy, 0800-2000*; which has good maps. For information on Montevideo, at **Mercado del Puerto** ⓘ Rambla 25 de Agosto de 1825 y Maciel, T2916 1513, at Pérez Castellano 1424, T2916 5287, and Plaza de los 33 Orientales, Av 18 de Julio entre Minas y Magallanes, all helpful. Pick up a copy of Descubrí Montevideo, useful city guide with an English version, downloadable from the municipal website. Check also at the municipal website for weekend tours, www.

montevideo.gub.uy. For the **Tourist Police** ① *Uruguay 1667 y Minas, T0800-8226*. See also www.montevideo.com.uy and www.cartelera.com.uy.

Maps
Best street maps of Montevideo are at the beginning of the *Guía Telefónica* (both white and yellow page volumes). Free maps in all tourist offices and some museums. Downloadable map at www.montevideo.gub.uy. *Eureka Guía De Montevideo* is recommended for streets, with index and bus routes (US$9 from bookshops and newspaper kiosks).

Places in Montevideo

City centre
In the **Ciudad Vieja** is the oldest square in Montevideo: the **Plaza de la Constitución** or **Matriz**. On one side is the **Catedral** (1790-1804), with the historic **Cabildo** (1804) ① *JC Gómez 1362, T2915 9685, Tue-Fri 1230-1730, Sat 1130-1630, Sun1230-1730, free*, opposite. It contains the **Museo y Archivo Histórico Municipal**. The Cabildo has several exhibition halls. On the south side is the **Club Uruguay** (built in 1888), which is worth a look inside. See also the unusual fountain (1881), surrounded by art and antique vendors under the sycamore trees.

West along Calle Rincón is the small **Plaza Zabala**, with a monument to Bruno Mauricio de Zabala, founder of the city. North of this Plaza are: the **Banco de la República** ① *Cerrito y Zabala* and the **Aduana** ① *Rambla 25 de Agosto*. Several historic houses belong to the Museo Histórico Nacional (see www.mec.gub.uy, or www.mhn.gub.uy): **Casa de Antonio Montero, Museo Romántico** ① *25 de Mayo 428, T2915 5361, Tue-Fri 1100-1700, free*, first built in 1728, rebuilt by Antonio Montero in 1831, contains late 19th, early 20th century furniture, furnishings and portraits. **Museo Casa de Rivera** ① *Rincón 437, T2915 1051, Mon-Fri 1100-1700, Sat 1000-1500, free*, is an early 19th-century mansion of the first president of the republic. Its rooms are dedicated to various stages of Uruguayan history. **Palacio Taranco, Museo de Artes Decorativas** ① *25 de Mayo y 1 de Mayo, T2915 6060, Mon-Fri 1230-1730, free,* whose garden overlooks Plaza Zabala, a palatial mansion in turn-of-the-20th-century French style, with sumptuously decorated rooms, and a museum of Islamic and Classical pottery and glass. It was first built as a theatre in 1793 and rebuilt in 1908 after it was bought by the Ortiz de Taranco family. Also in the Ciudad Vieja is the **MAPI, Museo de Arte Precolombino e Indígena** ① *25 de Mayo 279, T2916 9360, www.mapi.org.uy, Mon-Fri 1300-1830, Sat 1000-1600*, in a 19th-century mansion, bringing together public and private collections of local and non-Uruguayan artefacts.

The main port is near the Ciudad Vieja, with the docks three blocks north of Plaza Zabala. Three blocks south of the Plaza is the Río de la Plata. Cross the Rambla from the docks to visit the **Mercado del Puerto** (see Eating, page 102) and the adjacent **Museo del Carnaval** ① *Rambla 25 de Agosto 1825, T2915 0807, www.museodelcarnavaldeluruguay. blogspot.com, Tue-Sun 1100-1700, US$3.25*, a small exhibition with colourful pictures and costumes from the February celebrations. Proceed south one block to Cerrito, east two blocks to the **Banco de la República** and church of **San Francisco** (1864) ① *Solís 1469*, south across Plaza Zabala to Peatonal Sarandí (pedestrian street) and east to Plaza de la Independencia (see next paragraph), stopping at the aforementioned historical sites as desired. Restoration efforts are slow but steady. Although safe by day, with many tourist police, common sense, even avoidance, at night is recommended.

Between the Ciudad Vieja and the new city is the largest of Montevideo's squares, **Plaza de la Independencia**, a short distance east of Plaza de la Constitución. Numerous cafés, shops and boutiques line Peatonal Sarandí. Two small pedestrian zones full of cafés, live music (mostly after 2300) and restaurants, Peatonal Bacacay and Policia Vieja, lead off Sarandí. Below his statue (1923) in the middle of Plaza de la Independencia is the subterranean marble mausoleum of Artigas. Just west of the plaza is **Museo Torres García** ① *Sarandí 683, T2916 2663, www.torresgarcia. org.uy, Mon-Fri 0930-1930, Sat 1000-1800, US$3, free Wed, bookshop.* It has an exhibition of the paintings of Joaquín Torres García (1874-1949), one of Uruguay's foremost contributors to the modern art movements of the 20th century, and five floors dedicated to temporary exhibitions of contemporary Uruguayan and international artists. At the eastern end is the **Palacio Salvo** ① *Plaza Independencia 846-848,* built 1923- 1928. The first skyscraper in Uruguay and the tallest South American structure of its time, opinions are divided on its architectural merit. Currently it houses a mixture of businesses and residences. The famous tango, *La Cumparsita*, was written in a former café at its base. On the southern side is the **Museo de la Casa de Gobierno** ① *Palacio Estévez, Mon-Fri 1100-1600,* with an exhibition of

Montevideo Ciudad Vieja & Centre

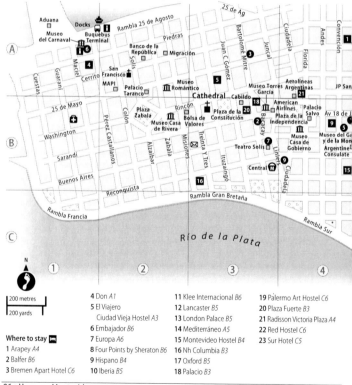

200 metres
200 yards

Where to stay ▭
1 Arapey A4
2 Balfer B6
3 Bremen Apart Hotel C6

4 Don A1
5 El Viajero
   Ciudad Vieja Hostel A3
6 Embajador B6
7 Europa A6
8 Four Points by Sheraton B6
9 Hispano B4
10 Iberia B5

11 Klee Internacional B6
12 Lancaster B5
13 London Palace B5
14 Mediterráneo A5
15 Montevideo Hostel B4
16 Nh Columbia B3
17 Oxford B5
18 Palacio B3

19 Palermo Art Hostel C6
20 Plaza Fuerte B3
21 Radisson Victoria Plaza A4
22 Red Hostel C6
23 Sur Hotel C5

Uruguay's presidential history. Just off the plaza to the west is the splendid **Teatro Solís** (1842-69) ① *Reconquista y Bartolomé Mitre, T2-1950 3323, www.teatrosolis.org.uy. Guided visits on Tue-Sun 1100, 1200, 1200, 1700 (Sat also at 1300), Wed free, otherwise US$2 for tours in English (US$1 in Spanish).* It has been entirely restored to perfection, with added elevators, access for disabled people, marble flooring and impressive attention to detail. Built as an opera house, Teatro Solís is now used for many cultural events, including ballet, classical music, even tango performances. Check press for listings. Tickets sold Tuesday-Saturday 1100-2000, Sunday-Monday 1500-2000 (in summer open 1700, Monday closed).

Avenida 18 de Julio runs east from Plaza de la Independencia. The **Museo de Arte Contemporaneo** ① *18 de Julio 965, 2nd floor, T2900 6662, Tue-Sun 1400-2000, Mon 1400-1830,* holds temporary exhibitions. In the **Museo del Gaucho y de la Moneda** ① *Av 18 de Julio 998, Palacio Heber Jackson, T2900 8764, www.bancorepublica.com.uy, Mon-Fri 1000-1600, free,* the Museo de la Moneda has a survey of Uruguayan currency and a collection of Roman coins. Museo del Gaucho is a fascinating history of the Uruguayan gaucho and is highly recommended. Between Julio Herrera and Río Negro is the **Plaza Fabini**, or **del Entrevero**, with a statue of *gauchos* engaged in battle, the last big piece of work by sculptor José Belloni. Beneath the plaza is the **Centro Municipal de Exposiciones – Subte** ① *www.subte.org.uy, Tue-Sun 1200-2100, free,* temporary exhibitions of contemporary art, photography, etc. In the **Plaza Cagancha** (or Plaza Libertad) is a statue of Peace. The restored **Mercado de la Abundancia** ① *San Jose 1312,* is an attractive old market with handicrafts, meat restaurants and tango dancing by Joventango. The **Palacio Municipal** (La Intendencia) is on the south side of Avenida 18 de Julio, just before it bends north, at the statue of **El Gaucho**. It often has interesting art and photo exhibitions and there is a huge satellite image of the city displayed on the main hall's floor. The road which forks south from the Gaucho is Constituyente, and leads to the beach at Pocitos. **Museo de Historia del Arte** ① *Ejido 1326, T1950 2191, Tue-Sun 1200-1730* is also in the Palacio Municipal. **Centro de Fotografía** ① *Palacio Municipal (San José 1360, T1950 1219, www.montevideo.gub.uy/fotografia), Mon-Fri 1000-1900, Sat 0930-1400,* has photography exhibitions.

The immense **Palacio Legislativo** ① *from Plaza Fabini head along Av del Libertador Brig Gen Juan Lavalleja (known as Av Libertador), 5 blocks east of Plaza de la Independencia (buses 173, 175 from C Mercedes), guided visits hourly Mon-Fri 0900-1800 (3 a day in summer), US$3,* was built 1908-1925 from local marble: there

staurants ⑦

8 Subte Pizzería *B6*
9 Tras Bambalinas *B4*
10 Viejo Sancho *B6*

lbahaca y Nuez *B4*
afé Bacacay & Panini's *B3*
orchos *A3*
l Fogón *B5*
os Leños Uruguayos *B5*
ercado del Puerto *A1*
ara Avis Bar & Restaurant *B3*

are 52 colours of Uruguayan marble in the Salón de los Pasos Perdidos, 12 types of wood in the library. Other rooms are beautiful. Not far, and dramatically changing the city skyline, is the 160-m high **Antel building** ① *Paraguay y Guatemala, Aguada, T2928 0000, free guided visits Mon, Wed, Fri 1530-1700; Tue, Thu 1030-1200*, with a public terrace on the 26th floor for panoramic bay views.

Outside the centre

Museo Nacional de Antropología ① *Av de las Instrucciones 948, Prado, T2355 1480, www. mna.gub.uy, Mon-Fri 1300-1800, Sat, Sun and holidays 1000-1800, free, take bus 149 from Ejido*, has a small, well-presented anthropological collection in the hall of a superb, late 19th-century mansion, the ex-Quinta de Mendilaharzu (see particularly the huge Chinese silk tapestry in the Music Room). On the same street, **Centro Cultural y Museo de la Memoria** ① *Av de las Instrucciones 1057, Prado, T2355 5891 museodelamemoria@imm.gub. uy, Tue-Sun 1200-1800, free*, is a fascinating space dedicated to remembering the horrors of Uruguay's 1970s-80s dictatorship. **Museo Municipal de Bellas Artes Juan Manuel Blanes** ① *Millán 4015, Prado, T2336 2248, www.museoblanes.org.uy, Tue-Sun 1300-1745, free, take buses 148 or 149 from Mercedes*, in the ex-Quinta Raffo (a late 19th-century mansion) is dedicated to the work of the artist Blanes (1830-1901). It also has a room of the works of Pedro Figari (1861-1938), a lawyer who painted strange, naive pictures of peasant life and negro ceremonies, also other Uruguayan artists' work. **Museo Zoológico** ① *Rambla República de Chile 4215, Buceo, T2622 0258, Tue-Sun 1000-1545, free, take bus 104 from 18 de Julio*, is well displayed and arranged, recommended, great for children.

In the **Puerto del Buceo**, following the coast eastwards away from the centre, the ship's bell of *HMS Ajax* and rangefinder of the German pocket-battleship, *Graf Spee*, can be seen at the **Naval Museum** ① *Rambla Costanera y Luis A de Herrera, Buceo, T2622 1084, 0800-1200, 1400-1800, closed Thu, free*. Both ships were involved in the Battle of the River Plate (13 December 1939) after which *Graf Spee* was scuttled off Montevideo. The museum also has displays of documentation from this battle, naval history from the War of Independence onwards and on the sailing ship *Capitán Miranda*, which circumnavigated the globe in 1937-1938.

In **Parque Batlle y Ordóñez** (reached eastwards of Avenida 18 de Julio), are statues: the most interesting group is the well-known **La Carreta** monument, by José Belloni, showing three yoke of oxen drawing a wagon. In the grounds is the **Estadio Centenario**, the national 65,000-seater football stadium and a football museum, an athletics field and a bicycle race-track (bus 107). The **Planetarium** ① *next to the Jardín Zoológico, at Av Rivera 3275, T2622 9109, take bus 60 from Av 18 de Julio, or buses 141, 142 or 144 from San José*, gives good, 40-minute shows on Saturday and Sunday (also Tuesday-Friday on holidays), free.

From the Palacio Legislativo, Avenida Agraciada runs northwest to **Parque Prado**, the oldest of the city's many parks, about 5 km from Avenida 18 de Julio (bus 125 and others). Among fine lawns, trees and lakes is a rose garden planted with 850 varieties, the monument of **La Diligencia** (the stage coach), the Círculo de Tenis and the Sociedad Rural premises. Part of the park is the adjacent **Jardín Botánico** ① *daily summer 0700-1830, winter 0700-1700, guided tours, T2336 4005. It is reached via Av 19 de Abril (bus 522 from Ejido next to Palacio Municipal), or via Av Dr LA de Herrera (bus 147 from Paysandú)*. The most popular park is **Parque Rodó**, on Rambla Presidente Wilson. Here are an open-air theatre, an amusement park, and a boating lake studded with islands. At the eastern end is the **Museo Nacional de Artes Visuales** ① *Tomás Giribaldi 2283, T2711 6054, www.mnav.gub.*

uy, Tue-Sun 1400-1845, free, a collection of contemporary plastic arts, plus a room devoted to Blanes. Recommended.

Within the city limits, the **Punta Carretas**, **Pocitos** and **Buceo** neighbourhoods are the nicest, with a mix of classical homes, tall condos, wonderful stores, services, restaurants, active beaches, parks, and two major malls. Outside the city along Rambla Sur, the affluent **Carrasco** suburb has large homes, quieter beaches, parks and services. **Parque Roosevelt**, a green belt stretching north, and the international airport are nearby. The express bus D1 (US$1.25) runs every 20 to 30 minutes Monday to Saturday (about every hour Sunday and holidays) along Avenida 18 de Julio and the Rambla and is about 30 minutes quicker to Carrasco.

At the western end of the bay is the **Cerro**, or hill ① *getting there: bus from centre to Cerro: 125 'Cerro' from Mercedes,* 139 m high (from which Montevideo gets its name), with the Fortaleza General Artigas, an old fort, on the top. It is now the **Museo Militar** ① *T2313 7716, Wed-Sun 1000-1700, free (fort visit US$0.85).* It houses historical mementos, documentation of the War of Independence and has one of the only panoramic views of Montevideo. The Cerro is surmounted by the oldest lighthouse in the country (1804).

Bathing **beaches** stretch along Montevideo's water front, from Playa Ramírez in the west to Playa Carrasco in the east. The waterfront boulevard, Rambla Naciones Unidas, is named along its several stretches in honour of various nations. Bus 104 from Aduana, which goes along Avenida 18 de Julio, gives a pleasant ride (further inland in winter) past Pocitos, Punta Gorda and all the beaches to Playa Miramar, beyond Carrasco, total journey time from Pocitos to Carrasco, 35 minutes. The seawater, despite its muddy colour (sediment stirred up by the Río de la Plata), is safe to bathe in and the beaches are clean. Lifeguards are on duty during the summer months.

Montevideo listings

For hotel and restaurant price codes and other relevant information, see pages 89-90.

🛏 Where to stay

Non-residents are exempt from paying 22% IVA tax, which is usually listed separately in upper category hotels, but may be included in cheaper and mid-range options; check when booking. High season is 15 Dec-15 Mar, book ahead; many beach hotels only offer full board during this time. After 1 Apr prices are reduced and some hotel dining rooms shut down. During Carnival, prices go up by 20%. The city is visited by Argentines at weekends: many hotels increase prices. Midweek prices may be lower than those posted.

The tourist office has information on the more expensive hotels. The **Holiday Inn**,

reservas@holidayinn.com.uy, and **Ibis** groups are represented. For more information and reservations contact **Asociación de Hoteles y Restaurantes del Uruguay**, Gutiérrez Ruiz 1215, T2908 0141, www.ahru.com.uy.

City centre *p95, map p96*
$$$$ Don, Piedras 234, T2915 9999, www.donhotel.com.uy. Boutique hotel in 1930s building opposite Mercado del Puerto. With breakfast, 3 standards of room, all modern services including Wi-Fi, safe in room, restaurant.
$$$$ Radisson Victoria Plaza, Plaza Independencia 759, T2902 0111, www. radisson.com/montevideouy. A/c, excellent restaurant (rooftop, fine views), less formal restaurant in lobby, luxurious casino in basement, with 5-star wing, art gallery, business centre (guests only), pool, spa, Wi-Fi.

$$$$-$$$ Four Points by Sheraton, Ejido 1275, T2901 7000, www.fourpoints. com/montevideo. Spacious with all contemporary business facilities in the city's financial district.

$$$ Balfer, Z Michelini 1328, T2902 0073, www.hotelbalfer.com. Good, TV, safe deposit, excellent breakfast.

$$$ Bremen Apart Hotel, Dr Aquiles Lanza 1168, T2900 9641, www. bremenmontevideo.com. Recommended for short term rentals, check for discounts.

$$$ Embajador, San José 1212, T2902 0012, www.hotelembajador.com. Sauna, swimming pool in the summer, TV with BBC World, Wi-Fi, excellent. Recommended.

$$$ Europa, Colonia 1341, T2902 0045, www.hoteleuropa.com.uy. Comfortable, spacious rooms, good choice in this price range, buffet breakfast, restaurant, parking.

$$$ Hispano, Convención 1317, T2900 3816, www.hispanohotel.com. A/c, with breakfast, comfortable, Wi-Fi, laundry, parking.

SSS Klee Internacional, San José 1303, T2902 0606, www.klee.com.uy. Very comfortable, good value in standard rooms, spacious, includes internet use, buffet breakfast, a/c, heater, minibar, good view, satellite TV. Highly recommended.

$$$ Lancaster, Plaza Cagancha 1334, T2902 1054, www.lancasterhotel.com.uy. Recently renovated rooms have minibar, a/c, fridge, and some with nice views over Plaza Cagancha. With buffet breakfast and Wi-Fi.

$$$ London Palace, Río Negro 1278, T2902 0024, www.lphotel.com. Restaurant, excellent breakfast, internet. Parking.

$$$ Mediterráneo, Paraguay 1486, T2900 5090, www.hotelmediterraneo.com.uy. With buffet breakfast, TV, comfortable, boxy but clean rooms, a/c, Wi-Fi.

$$$ NH Columbia, Rambla Gran Bretaña 473, T2916 0001, www.nh-hotels.com. 1st class, overlooking the river in Ciudad Vieja. Rooms have minibar and TV. Restaurant, sauna, music show, fitness room, Wi-Fi.

$$$ Oxford, Paraguay 1286, T2902 0046, www.hoteloxford.com.uy. Good breakfast, safes, laundry service, parking. Recommended.

$$$ Plaza Fuerte, Bartolomé Mitre 1361, T2915 6651, www.plazafuerte. com. Restored 1913 building, historical monument, a/c, safe, internet, restaurant, pub.

$$$-$$ Iberia, Maldonado 1097, T2901 3633, www.internet.com.uy/hoiberia. Very helpful staff, 1400 check-out, free bike rental, parking, Wi-Fi, stereos, minibar and cable in rooms. US$5.50 for breakfast. Modern, recently refurbished. Highly recommended.

$$$-$$ Sur Hotel, Maldonado 1098, T2908 2025, www.surhotel.com. Colourful, recently refurbished, welcoming, some rooms with balconies. Good continental breakfast for extra US$5, 24-hr room service, Wi-Fi, and jacuzzi in most expensive rooms.

$$ Red Hostel, San José 1406, T2908 8514, www.redhostel.com. By the Intendencia, hostel with double rooms and dorms (**$**), all with shared bath, cheerful, cable TV, internet connection in rooms, computers, Wi-Fi, safe, breakfast, roof terrace and kitchen.

$$ El Viajero Ciudad Vieja Hostel, Ituzaingó 1436, T2915 6192, www. ciudadviejahostel.com. HI affiliate, hostel with lots of services (Spanish lessons, bike hire, city tours, laundry, theatre tickets, football), double rooms and shared bedrooms (**$**), free internet/Wi-Fi, safes, kitchen, airport transport, helpful staff. Recommended.

$$ Arapey, Av Uruguay 925, near Convención, T2900 7032, www.arapey. com.uy. Slightly run down old building, but has character and central location. Variety of rooms with bath, TV, fan, heating, Wi-Fi, no breakfast.

$$ Palacio, Bartolomé Mitre 1364, T2916 3612, www.hotelpalacio.com.uy. Old hotel, a bit run down, superior rooms with balconies, laundry service, stores luggage, no breakfast, frequently booked, good value. Recommended.

$ pp **Montevideo Hostel**, Canelones 935, T2908 1324, www.monte videohostel.com.uy. HI affiliate. Open all year, 24 hrs (seasonal variations, breakfast and internet included), dormitory style, kitchen, lots of hot water, but shortage of bathrooms and noisy, bicycle hire US$2 per hr.

Outside the centre *p98*
Tres Cruces, Palermo
$$$ Days Inn, Acevedo Díaz 1821-23, T2400 4840, www.daysinn.com.uy. A/c, buffet breakfast, safe, coffee shop and health club, Wi-Fi, look for promotional offers.
$$$ Tres Cruces, Miguelete 2356 esq Acevedo Díaz, T2402 3474, www.hoteltrescruces.com.uy. A/c, TV, safe, café, decent buffet breakfast. Disabled access.
$$$-$$ Palermo Art Hostel, Gaboto 1010, T2410 6519, www.palermoarthostel.com. HI affiliated. Cosy and colourful, with breakfast, bar and live music, private and shared rooms (**$**), bike rental, Wi-Fi, near beach and US Embassy. Highly recommended.

East of the centre (Punta Carretas, Pocitos)
$$$$ Sheraton, Victor Solino 349, T2710 2121, www.sheraton.com. Beside Shopping Punta Carretas, all facilities, good views, access to golf club. Recommended.
$$$$-$$$ Ermitage, Juan Benito Blanco 783, T2710 4021, www.ermitagemontevideo.com. Near Pocitos beach, remodelled 1945 building, rooms, apartments and suites, some with great views, Wi-Fi, buffet breakfast.
$$$$-$$$ Pocitos Plaza, Juan Benito Blanco 640, Pocitos, T2712 3939, www.pocitosplazahotel. com.uy. Modern building in pleasant residential district, next to the river, with large functional rooms, buffet breakfast, Wi-Fi, gym and sauna.
$ pp **Pocitos Hostel**, Av Sarmiento 2641 y Aguilar, T2711 8780, www.pocitos-hostel.com. Rooms for 2 to 6 (mixed and women

only), includes breakfast, use of kitchen, *parrilla*, towels extra, internet, Spanish classes.

Carrasco
$$$$ Belmont House, Av Rivera 6512, T2600 0430, www.belmonthouse.com.uy. 5-star, includes buffet breakfast, 28 beautifully furnished rooms, top quality, excellent restaurant Allegro, pub/bar Memories, pool, 3 blocks from beach. Recommended.
$$$$ Cottage, Miraflores 1360, T2600 1111, www.hotelcottage.com.uy. In a prime location next to wide beaches and in quiet residential surroundings, very comfortable, simply furnished rooms with minibar and a/c, Wi-Fi, restaurant, pool in a lovely garden, excellent.
$$$$ Regency Suites, Gabriel Otero 6428, T2600 1383, www.regencysuites.com.uy. Good boutique-style hotel with all services, free internet, safety deposit, fitness centre, pool, Wi-Fi, restaurant *Cava* and pub/wine bar, a couple of blocks from the beach.

🍴 Restaurants

There is a 22% tax on restaurant bills that is usually included, plus a charge for bread and service (*cubierto*) that varies between US$1-3 pp.

City centre *p95, map p96*
$$$ Albahaca y Nuez, W F Aldunate 1311, T2900 6189. Great lunchtime specials at this healthy, mostly-vegetarian café, very popular. Open 0800-2000, closed Sun. Recommended.
$$$ Café Bacacay, Bacacay 1310 y Buenos Aires, T2916 6074. Good music and atmosphere, food served, try the specials, closed Sun. Recommended.
$$$ Corchos, 25 de Mayo 651, T2917 2051, www.corchos.com.uy. Wine bar and bistro, executive menu US$14.50, open 1100-180 Mon-Thu, Fri 1100-1800, 2000-2400, specializes in Uruguayan wines and gourmet dishes to accompany them.

$$$ Crocus, San Salvador y Minas (Palermo), T2411 0039. Closed Sun. Excellent meals with French and Mediterranean touches.

$$$ El Fogón, San José 1080. Good value, very friendly, always full.

$$$ Los Leños Uruguayos, San José 909, T2900 2285. www.parrilla.com.uy. Good and smart *parrilla*, and also fish.

$$$ El Mercado del Puerto, opposite the Aduana, Calle Piedras, between Maciel and Pérez Castellanos (take 'Aduana' bus), www.mercadodelpuerto. com.uy. Don't miss eating at this 19th-century market building, open late on Sun, delicious grills cooked on huge charcoal grates (menus are limited to beef, chicken and fish, including swordfish). Best to go at lunchtime, especially Sat; the atmosphere's great. Inside the Mercado del Puerto, those recommended are: **Roldós**, sandwiches, most people start with a *medio medio* (half still, half sparkling white wine). **El Palenque**, famed as the finest restaurant. **La Estancia del Puerto**, **Cabaña Verónica**, **La Chacra del Puerto**. **Don Tiburón** has a bar inside and a more expensive and smart restaurant, **La Posada**, with tables outside.

$$$ Panini's, Bacacay 1341 (also at 26 de Marzo 3586, Pocitos). Good Italian pasta. Large and lively.

$$$ Rara Avis Bar & Restaurant, Buenos Aires 652, T2915 0330. Closed Sat lunchtime and Sun. At the Teatro Solís, quite a formal setting, varied, Mediterranean-inspired menu. Expensive.

$$$ Tras Bambalinas, Ciudadela 1250 y Soriano, T2903 2090, www.trasbambalinas. com.uy. Colourful carnival-themed *parrilla*, also featuring pizzas, *picadas* and salads. Live music and stand-up often programmed. Very popular.

$$$ Viejo Sancho, San José 1229. Excellent, popular, complimentary sherry or vermouth to early arrivals; set menus for US$18 pp.

$$ Subte Pizzería, Ejido 1327, T2902 3050. Cheap and good. Recommended.

$$ Restaurant on 6th floor of YMCA building, Colonia 1870. Reasonable for lunch, with good views, ask for Asociación Cristiana de Jóvenes.

Centro Cultural Mercado de la Abundancia, San Jose 1312 (see Sights, above) has good authentic local eateries, with lunch specials. Highly recommended.

Outside the centre *p98*
In and around Pocitos

$$$ Da Pentella, Luis de la Torre 598, esq Francisco Ros, T2712 0981. Amazing Italian and seafood, artistic ambience, great wines. Recommended.

$$$ La Otra, Tomás Diago y Juan Pérez, 2 blocks northeast of 21 de Septiembre in Punta Carretas, T2711 3006. Specialises in meat, lively. Highly recommended.

$$$ Spaghetteria 32, Franzini y Carlos Berg, T2710 9769. Very good Italian choice, serving excellent homemade pasta inspired by a place now closed. Closed Mon.

$$$ Tabaré, Zorrilla de San Martín 152/54, T2712 3242. Wonderful restaurant in a converted old *almacén* (grocery shop). Great wines and entrées.

$$$ El Viejo y el Mar, Rambla Gandhi 400 block (on the coast), Punta Carretas, T2710 5704. Fishing community atmosphere with a great location by the river.

$$ Pizza Trouville, 21 de Septiembre y Francisco Vidal (also at Pereira y 26 de Marzo). A traditional pizza place with tables outside, next to the beach.

$$ Tranquilo Bar, 21 de Septiembre 3104. Popular restaurant/bar, great lunch menu.

Carrasco/Punta Gorda
Several restaurants on Av Arocena close to the beach, packed Sun middle day.

$$$ Café Misterio, Costa Rica 1700, esq Av Rivera, T2600 5999. Lots of choice on menu, sushi, cocktails. Completely new decor and menu every 6 months. Recommended.

$$$ Hemingway, Rambla Méjico on west side of Punta Gorda, T2600 0121. Decent food, worth going for amazing sunset views.

$$$ Nuevo García's, Arocena 1587, T2600 2703. Spacious, indoor and outdoor seating, large wine selection, rack of lamb is a speciality.

Confiterías Café Brasilero, Ituzaingó 1447, half a block from Plaza Matriz towards the port. Small entrance; easy to miss. A must, one of the oldest cafés in Montevideo and a permanent hangout of one of the greatest Latin American writers, Eduardo Galeano. Others include: **Amaretto**, 21 de Septiembre y Roque Graseras, Punta Carretas. Excellent Italian coffee and pastries. **Bar Iberia**, Uruguay esq Florida. Locals' bar. **Conaprole Pocitos**, Rambla Gandhi y Solano Antuña. Ideal at sunset for riverviews, it serves very good strong coffee and quality Conaprole dairy products. A *completo* includes toasts, butter, jam, cheese, a slice of cake, biscuits, juice and coffee or tea, all for US$15. **Manchester Bar**, 18 de Julio 899. Good for breakfasts. **Oro del Rhin**, Convención 1403 (also at Pocitos riverfront, on Plaza Cagancha and at shopping malls). Mon-Fri 0830-2000 (Sat till 1400), open since 1927 it retains the feel of an elegant *confitería* serving good cakes and sandwiches or vegetable pies for lunch. **Café de la Pausa**, Sarandí 493, upstairs. Closed Sun.

Options with multiple locations Several good restaurants and establishments have locations in many neighbourhoods and serve typical Uruguayan fare. Among these are family restaurants: **La Pasiva**, **Don Pepperone** and **Il Mondo della Pizza**. A popular bakery chain is **Medialunas Calentitas**, great for coffee and croissants. Popular *heladerías* are **La Cigale** and **Las Delicias**.

🎵 Bars and clubs

Montevideo *p94, map p96*
Boliches
Head to Sarandí, Bacacay or Bartolomé Mitre in Ciudad Vieja, or to Pocitos and Punta Carretas. Discos charge US$5-10. Bars/discos/pubs offering local nightlife:
503 Bar, Aguilar 832, just north of Ellauri. Pool tables, only steel tip dart bar in town, small wood frame entrance, no sign, open all day 1930-0400.
Baar Fun-Fun, Ciudadela 1229, Ciudad Vieja, T2915 8005. Hangout of local artists, founded in 1895, used to be frequented by Carlos Gardel, where *uvita*, the drink, was born. Great music Fri and Sat. Recommended.
Clyde's, Costa Rica y Rivera, Carrasco. Live music from 2000.
Groove, Rambla República de Mexico 5521, Punta Gorda. Electronic music, Thu-Sat from 2400.
El Lobizón, Zelmar Michelini 1264. Popular restaurant open till very late with rock and fusion live performances.
El Pony Pisador, Bartolomé Mitre 1326, Ciudad Vieja. Popular with the young crowd. Live music. Also at LA de Herrera e Iturriaga, Pocitos.
The Shannon, Bartolomé Mitre 1318. Pub with almost daily live shows and DJs on Thu.
Viejo Mitre, Bartolomé Mitre 1321, Ciudad Vieja. Mixed music, outside tables, open till late all week.

Outside the centre *p98*
Playa Ramírez (near Parque Rodó)
'W' Lounge, Rambla Wilson y Requena García. Fashionable place for young people, Fri-Sat 2300, live music on Sat, rock, electronica, Latin.

🎬 Entertainment

Montevideo *p94, map p96*
Cinema
See http://cultura.montevideo.gub.uy for listings. Blockbusters often appear soon after release in US, most others arrive weeks or months later. Most films are in English (except non- English and animated features). Modern malls (Montevideo

Shopping, Punta Carretas, Portones) house several cine-theatre companies each (Grupocine, MovieCenter, Hoyts, and others), including 3D halls. Independent art theatres: **Cine Universitario**, 2 halls: Lumière and Chaplin, Canelones 1280, also for classic and serious films. **Cinemateca** film club, www.cinemateca,org.uy, has 4 cinemas: Cinemateca 18, 18 de Julio 1280, T2900 9056; Sala Cinemateca y Sala 2, Dr L. Carnelli 1311, T2419 5795; and Sala Pocitos, A Chucarro 1036, T2707 4718. The Cinemateca shows great films from all over the world and has an extended archive. It organizes film festivals. Membership for 6 months, US$64 pp (with discounts if two people together).

Tanguerías

El Milongón, Gaboto 1810, T2929 0594, www.elmilongon.com.uy. A show that may include dinner beforehand, Mon-Sat. For tango, milonga, candombe and local folk music. Recommended. **Joventango**, at Mercado de la Abundancia, Aquiles Lanza y San José, T2901 5561, www.joventango.org. Cheap and atmospheric venue, Sun 2000. **Tango a Cielo Abierto**, Tango Under the Open Sky, in front of Café Facal, Paseo Yi and 18 de Julio, T2908 7741 for information. Free and very good Uruguayan tango shows every day at noon on a wooden stage. Highly recommended. **Sala Zitarrosa**, 18 de Julio 1012 T2901 7303, www.salazitarrosa.com.uy is a very popular music venue.
Museo del Vino, Maldonado 1150, www.tango-club.com/museodelvino. Wine bar and tango lessons and dancing on Thu.

Theatres

Montevideo has a vibrant theatre scene. Most performances are only on Fri, Sat and Sun, others also on Thu. Apart from **Teatro Solís** (see Sights, above), recommended are **Teatro del Centro Carlos E Sheck**, Plaza Cagancha 1168, T2902 8915, and **Teatro Victoria**, Río Negro y Uruguay, T2901 9971.

See listings in the daily press and *La Brecha*. Prices are around US$15; performances are almost exclusively in Spanish starting around 2100 or earlier on Sun. **Teatro Millington-Drake** at the Anglo (see Cultural centres) puts on occasional productions, as do the theatres of the Alianza Cultural Uruguay-Estados Unidos and the Alliance Française (addresses below). Many theatres close Jan-Feb.

O Shopping

Montevideo *p94, map p96*
The main commercial street is Av 18 de Julio, although malls elsewhere have captivated most local shoppers. Many international newspapers can be bought on the east side of Plaza Independencia.

Bookshops

The Sun market on Tristán Narvaja and nearby streets is good for second-hand books. Every December daily in the evening is **Feria IDEAS +**, a book, photography and crafts fair, at Plaza Florencio Sánchez (Parque Rodó), with readings and concerts. The following have a few English and American books, but selection in Montevideo is poor: **Bookshop SRL**, JE Rodó 1671 (at Minas y Constituyente), T2401 1010, www.bookshop. com.uy. With English stock, very friendly staff, also at Ellauri 363 and at both Montevideo and Portones Shopping Centers; specializes in travel. **Ibana**, International Book and News Agency, Convención 1485. Specializes in foreign publications. **El Libro Inglés**, Cerrito 483, Ciudad Vieja. **Librería Papacito**, 18 de Julio 1409, T2908 7250, www.libreriapapacito.com. Good selection of magazines and books, wide range of subjects from celebrity autobiographies to art. **Puro Verso**, 18 de Julio 1199, T2901 6429. Very good selection in Spanish, small secondhand section in English, excellent café, chess tables. It has another branch on Sarandí 675, **Más Puro Verso**. Others include: **Librería El Aleph**, Bartolomé Mitre 1358. Used and rare books in Spanish. **Linardi y Risso**, Juan Carlos Gómez 1435, Ciudad Vieja, www.linardiyrisso.com. **Purpúrea**, Plaza Fabini, www.purpurea.com. uy. For books, magazines and music.

Galleries
There are many good art galleries. **Galería Latina**, Sarandí 671, T2916 3737, www. galerialatina.com.uy, is one of the best, with its own art publishing house. Several art galleries and shops lie along C Pérez Castellanos, near Mercado del Puerto.

Handicrafts
Suede and leather are good buys. There are several shops and workshops around Plaza Independencia. Amethysts, topazes, agate and quartz are mined and polished in Uruguay and are also good buys. For authentic, fairly- priced crafts there is **Mercado de los Artesanos**, www. mercadodelosartesanos.com.uy, on Plaza Cagancha (No 1365), at Espacio Cultural R Barradas, Pérez Castellano 1542, and at Mercado de la Abundancia, San José 1312, T2901 0550, all branches closed Sun. For leather goods, walk around C San José y W Ferreira Aldunate. **Montevideo Leather Factory**, Plaza Independencia 832, www.montevideoleather factory.com. Recommended. **Manos del Uruguay**, San José 1111, and at Shopping Centres, www. manos.com.uy. A non-profit organization that sells very good quality, handwoven woollen clothing and a great range of crafts, made by independent craftsmen and women from all over Uruguay.

Markets
Calle Tristán Narvaja (and nearby streets), opposite Facultad de Derecho on 18 de Julio. On Sun, 0800-1400, there is a large, crowded street market here, good for silver and copper, and all sorts of collectibles. **Plaza de la Constitución**, a small Sat morning market and a Sun antique fair

are held here. **Villa Biarritz**, on Vásquez Ledesma near Parque Rodó, Punta Carretas. A big market selling fruit, vegetables, clothes and shoes (Tue and Sat 0900-1500, and Sun in Parque Rodó, 0800-1400).

Shopping malls
The Montevideo Shopping Center, on the east edge of Pocitos (Herrera 1290 y Laguna, 1 block south of Rivera, www. montevideoshopping.com.uy), bus 141 or 142 from San José. **Punta Carretas Shopping**, Ellauri 350, close to Playa Pocitos in the former prison, www. puntascarretasweb.com.uy, bus 117 or 121 from Calle San José. Other shopping centres at the Tres Cruces bus station, www.trescruces.com.uy, and in Carrasco, Portones, www.portones.com.uy, and Plaza Arocena Shopping Mall.

⚙ What to do

Montevideo *p94, map p96*
Sports
Football (soccer) is the most popular sport. Seeing a game in **Centenario Stadium** is a must, located in Parque Batlle. If possible, attend a game with Uruguay's most popular teams, **Nacional** or **Peñarol**, or an international match. General admission tickets (US$5-20) can be bought outside before kickoff for sections Amsterdam, América, Colombes, Tribuna Olímpica. Crowds in Uruguay are much safer than other countries, but it's best to avoid the *plateas*, the end zones where the rowdiest fans chant and cheer. Sit in Tribuna Olímpica under or opposite the tower, at midfield. **Parque Central**, just north of Tres Cruces, **Nacional**'s home field, is the next best venue. Other stadiums are quieter, safer and also fun. For information try www. tenfieldigital.com.uy, but asking a local is also advisable. **Basketball** is increasingly popular; games can be seen at any sports club (**Biguá** or **Trouville**, both in Punta Carretas/Pocitos neighbourhoods). See

www.fubb.org.uy for schedules. Rugby, volleyball, tennis, cycling, surfing (www.olasyvientos.com), windsurfing and kite surfing, lawn bowling, running, and walking are also popular. **Golf**: Uruguay has seven 18-hole and two 9-hole courses, between Fray Bentos and Punta del Este. Apart from Jan-Feb, Jul-Aug, you should have no problem getting onto the course, see www.aug.com.uy.

Tours

The Asociación de Guías de Turismo de Montevideo, T2915 4857, agtmguias@adinet.com.uy, runs historical and architecture tours. Check times and availability in English. Tours of the city are organized by the Municipalidad, see www.montevideo.gub.uy (go to Paseos) for details.

For visiting the several wineries around Montevideo, see www.loscaminosdelvino.com.uy.

Day tours of Punta del Este are run by many travel agents and hotels, US$50-100 with meals.

Estancia tourism Information on estancias can be found at **Lares** (see below), which represents many estancias and *posadas*; at the tourist offices in Montevideo; or general travel agencies and those that specialize in this field: **Estancias Gauchas**, Cecilia Regules Viajes, agent for an organization of 280 estancias offering lunch and/or lodging, English, French and Portuguese spoken. Full list of estancias (Establecimientos Rurales) at www.turismo.gub.uy. Ask at these organizations about **horse riding**, too.

Cecilia Regules Viajes, Bacacay 1334, T2916 3012, T9968 3608, www.ceciliaregulesviajes.com, very good, knowledgeable, specialist in estancia, tango and bike tours in Uruguay, and skiing in Argentina.

Jetmar, Plaza de la Independencia 725, T2902 0793, www.jetmar.com.uy. A helpful tour operator.

JP Santos, Colonia 951, T2902 0300, www.jpsantos.com.uy. Helpful agency.

Lares, Wilson Ferreira Aldunate 1341, T2901 9120, www.lares.com.uy. Specializes in birdwatching and other nature tours, cultural tours, trekking, horse riding and estancia tourism.

Odile Beer Viajes, Plaza Independencia 723 of 102, T2902 3736, www.odiletravel.com. ISO-certified agency offering personalized service in a variety of fields, including sports (marathons, too), city cycling tours, gourmet and wine, bird and whale watching.

Simply, Colonia 971, T2900 8880, www.simply.com.uy. Adventure and nature tourism specialists, plus many other national and international packages.

Rumbos, Galería del Libertador, Rio Branco 1377, p 7, T2900 2407, www.rumbosturismo.com. Caters specifically for independent travellers, very helpful.

TransHotel, Acevedo Díaz 1671, T2402 9935, www.transhotel.com.uy. Accommodation, eco-tourism, sightseeing and tailor-made itineraries.

Turisport Ltda, San José 930, T2902 0829, www.turisport.com.uy. American Express for travel and mail services, good; sells Amex dollar TCs on Amex card.

🚍 Transport

Montevideo *p94, map p96*
Air

The main airport is at Carrasco, 21 km outside the city, T2604 0329, www.aic.com.uy; 24-hr exchange facilities. If making a hotel reservation, ask them to send a taxi to meet you; it's cheaper than taking an airport taxi. To Montevideo 30 mins by taxi or *remise* (official fares US$241-55, depending on destination in the city, by van US$10 (payable in Uruguayan or Argentine pesos, reais, US$ or euros), T2604 0323, www.taxisaeropuerto.com; about 50 mins by bus. Buses, Nos 700, 701, 704, 710 and 711, from Terminal Brum, Río Branco y

Galicia, go to the airport US$1.30 (crowded before and after school hours); dark brown 'Copsa' bus terminates at the airport. COT buses connect city and airport, US$5.50, and Punta del Este, US$9.

Air services to **Argentina**: for the Puente Aéreo to Buenos Aires, check in at Montevideo airport, pay departure tax and go to immigration to fill in an Argentine entry form before going through Uruguayan immigration. Get your stamp out of Uruguay, surrender the tourist card you received on entry and get your stamp into Argentina. There are no immigration checks on arrival at Aeroparque, Buenos Aires.

Bus

Local City buses are comfortable and convenient, see Sistema de Transporte Metro-politano (STM) pages on www.montevideo.gub.uy and www.cutcsa.com.uy. A single fare, US$0.90, may be paid on the bus, otherwise you can buy a rechargeable smart card for multiple journeys at designated places throughout the city. Buses D1 (see Sights Carrasco, above), D2, D3, 5, 8, 9, 10 and 11 charge US$1.30. There are many buses to all parts from 18 de Julio; from other parts to the centre or old city, look for those marked 'Aduana'. For Punta Carretas from city centre take bus No 121 from Calle San José. **Remises**: fares from US$20 from airport to city; **Remises Carrasco**, T2606 1412, www.remisescarrasco.com.uy; **Remises Elite**, T9918 3802; **Remises Urbana**, T2400 8665, www.urbanaremises.com.

Long distance During summer holidays buses are often full; it is advisable to book in advance (also for Fri and weekend travel all year round).
Buses within Uruguay: excellent terminal, Tres Cruces, Bulevar Artigas y Av Italia, T2401 8998 (10-15 mins by bus from the centre, Nos CA1, 64, 180, 187, 188 – in Ciudad Vieja from in front of Teatro Solís); it

has a shopping mall, tourist office, internet café, restaurants, left luggage (free for 2 hrs at a time, if you have a ticket for that day, then US$2 up to 4 hrs, 12-24 hrs US$4.75), post and phone offices, toilets, good medical centre, **Banco de Montevideo** and **Indumex** cambio (accepts MasterCard). Visit www.trescruces.com.uy for bus schedules. Fares and journey times from the capital are given under destinations.

To Argentina (ferries and buses) You need a passport when buying international tickets. Direct to **Buenos Aires**: Buquebus, at the docks, in old customs hall, Terminal Fluvio- Marítima; Terminal Tres Cruces, Local 28/29, Hotel Radisson, and Punta Carretas Shopping, local Miranda; in all cases T130. 1-3 daily, 3 hrs, US$185 tourist class, return; departure tax included in the price of tickets. At Montevideo dock, go to Preembarque 30 mins before departure, present ticket, then go to Migración for Uruguayan exit and Argentine entry formalities. The terminal is like an airport and the seats on the ferries are airplane seats. On board there is duty-free shopping, video and poor value food and drinks.
Services via Colonia: bus/ ferry and catamaran services by **Buquebus**: from 5 crossings daily from 1 to 3 hrs from Colonia, depending on vessel, fares: US$78 tourist class return on slower vessel, US$108 tourist class return on faster vessel. All have 2½-hr bus connection Montevideo-Colonia from Tres Cruces. There are also bus connections to **Punta del Este**, 2 hrs, and La Paloma, 5 hrs, to/from Montevideo. Cars and motorcycles are carried on either route. Schedules and fares can be checked on www.buquebus.com, who also have flights between Uruguay and Argentina. Fares increase in high season, Dec-Jan, when there are more sailings. Check the website for promotional discounts that may offer up to almost half the price. If you want to break your journey in Colonia, you will have to buy your own bus ticket on

another company to complete the trip to/from Montevideo. **Colonia Express**, at Tres Cruces bus terminal, T2400 3939, and at the dock in Colonia, www.colonia express.com, makes 2-3 crossings a day between Colonia and Buenos Aires in fast boats (no vehicles) with bus connections to/from Montevideo, Punta del Este and other Uruguayan towns. Fares range from US$43 to US$68 return, depending on type of service and where bought, or US$47-68 with bus connections to Montevideo. **Seacat**, www. seacatcolonia.com, 2-3 fast ferries to Colonia, 1 hr, US$41-84 return, with bus to Montevideo US$46-114, and to Punta del Este US$82-126. Offices: Río Negro 1400, at Tres Cruces, T2915 0202, and in Colonia. **Bus de la Carrera** (T2402 1313), **Belgrano** (T2401 4764) and **Cauvi** (T2401 9196) run road services to Buenos Aires for US$45-50, 7½-9½ hrs.

Services to **Carmelo** and **Tigre** (interesting trip): bus/ motor launch service by **Cacciola**, 2 a day, Uruguay 1218, T2908 2244, at Tres Cruces, local 32, T2401 9350, www.cacciolaviajes.com, US$45, US$87 return (Montevideo to Buenos Aires via Carmelo and Tigre). Advanced booking is advisable on all services at busy periods. On through buses to Brazil and Argentina, you can expect full luggage checks both by day and night.

Taxi

The meter starts at about US$1.30 in *fichas*, which determine fares as shown on a table in taxi. Tipping is not expected but welcomed, usually by rounding up the fare. Do not expect change for large peso notes. Prices go up on Sat, Sun, holidays and late at night.

Train

Uruguayan railways, **AFE**, use outdated trains, but interesting rides for enthusiasts. The old train station has been abandoned, replaced by a nice new terminus next to the Antel skyscraper, known as **Nueva Estación Central** at Paraguay y Nicaragua (Aguada), T2924 8080, www.afe.com.uy. Passenger trains run Mon-Sat only along 2 lines, called 25 de Agosto and Sudriers. Most commuter trains run north between Montevideo and Progreso (about 5 a day), passing some of the country's poorest areas. Fewer services go beyond Progreso. Once a day, a service goes as far as San José de Mayo on the same line and once a day as far as Florida. Another commuter line runs northeast from Montevideo to Sudriers, passing Pando. To Progreso (50 min, US$1), to Canelones (1 hr 20 min, US$1.25), to Santa Lucía (1 hr 35 min, US$1.80), to 25 de Agosto (1 hr 40 min, US$1.80), to San José de Mayo (2½ hrs, US$2.50), to Pando (1 hr, US$1). Occasionally, long distance services and a steam-engine run for special events, such as the 48-hr celebration of the Día del Patrimonio (Heritage Day) in Oct. More information, T2924 3924.

Directory

Montevideo *p94, map p96*
Banks Don't trust the few black market money changers offering temptingly good rates. Many are experienced confidence tricksters. **Casas de cambio and** banks only open 1300-1700 (some till 1800). Airport bank daily 0700-2200. Find most banks along 25 de Mayo, Cerrito or Zabala, and on Plaza Matriz, in Ciudad Vieja, and in the centre along Av 18 de Julio. Exchange houses along 18 de Julio, eg **Bacacay**, at 853, **La Favorita** (Amex agents) at 1497, **Suizo** at 1190, **Regul**, at 1126, or **Globus**, 25 de Mayo 466 in Ciudad Vieja, but shop around for best rates (rates for cash are better than for TCs, but both are often better than in banks, and quicker service). **Delta**, Río Negro 1341, has been recommended. **Car hire** It is wise to hire a small car (1.3 litre engine) as Uruguay is relatively flat and gas prices are high.

A small car can be negotiated for about US$90 per day, free mileage, including insurance and collision damage waiver, if you are hiring a car for at least 3 days (rates are lower out of season). Cheaper weekly rates available. Best to make reservations before arrival. **Autocar**, Mercedes 863, T2908 5153, autocaruruguay@hotmail.com. Economical, helpful. **Punta Car**, Cerro Largo 1383, T2900 2772, www.puntacar.com. uy, also at Aeropuerto Carrasco. **Snappy**, Andes 1363, T2900 7728, www.snappy.com. uy.**Sudancar**, Av Italia 2665, T2480 3855, www.sudancar.com.uy. Most car companies don't allow their cars to be taken abroad. To travel to Argentina or Brazil, you can use **Maxicar** rentals in Salto, see page 124.

Cultural centres Alianza Cultural Uruguay-Estados Unidos, Paraguay 1217, T2902 5160, www.alianza.edu.uy, library Tue-Fri, 0930-2000, US publications (excellent selection), theatre, art gallery. **Instituto Cultural Anglo-Uruguayo** (known as the 'Anglo'), San José 1426, T2902 3773, www. anglo.edu.uy (theatre, recommended, library Mon- Thu 0930-1930, Fri 1500-1900, Sat 0900-1300); café at No 1227. **Alliance Française**, Blvr Artigas 1271, T2400 0505, www.alianzafrancesa.edu.uy (theatre, concerts, library, excellent bookshop). **Goethe Institut**, Santiago de Chile 874, T2908 0234, www.goethe.de/montevideo. **Instituto Italiano di Cultura**, Paraguay 1177, T2900 3354, www.iicmontevideo. esteri.it. **Centro Cultural de España**, Rincón 629, Ciudad Vieja, T2915 2250, www.cce. org.uy, has art exhibitions and a café.

Embassies and consulates For all foreign embassies and consulates in Montevideo, see http://embassy.goabroad.com. **Internet and telephones** At Antel *telecentros*.

Language schools Academia Uruguay, Juan Carlos Gómez 1408, T2915 2496, www.academia uruguay.com. **Medical services** Hospital Británico, Av Italia 2420, T2487 1020, www.hospitalbritanico.com.uy. Recommended.

Western Uruguay

West of Montevideo, Route 1, part of the Pan-American Highway, heads to the UNESCO World Heritage Site of Colonia del Sacramento and the tranquil town of Carmelo. Off the road are the old British mining town of Conchillas and the Jesuit mission at Calera de las Huérfanas. Other roads lead to the Río Uruguay, Route 2 from Rosario to Fray Bentos, and Route 3 via San José de Mayo and Trinidad to the historic towns of Paysandú and Salto. The latter passes farms, man-made lakes and the river itself. There are also many hot-spring resorts .

Colonias Valdense and Suiza

Route 1 to Colonia de Sacramento is a four-lane highway. At Km 121 from Montevideo the road passes Colonia Valdense, a colony of Waldensians who still cling to some of the old customs of the Piedmontese Alps. For tourist information, T455-88412. A road branches off north here to Colonia Suiza, a Swiss settlement also known as **Nueva Helvecia** (*population: 10,000*), with lovely parks, gardens and countryside. In the town is the Santuario de Nuestra Señora De Schönstatt, all walls are covered by plants, and the first steam mill in Uruguay (1875).The Swiss national day is celebrated with great enthusiasm.

The highway skirts **Rosario** (130 km from Montevideo, 50 km before Colonia del Sacramento), called 'the first Uruguayan Museum of Mural Art'. Dozens of impressive murals are dotted around the city, some with bullfights, some abstract designs.

Colonia del Sacramento → *Population: 26,000. See map, over page.*

ⓘ *All museums Fri-Mon 1115-1645, closed either Tue, Wed or Thu, except Museo Archivo Regional (shut Sat-Sun) and Museo Naval (shut Mon-Wed), combined tickets US$2.50. See http://museoscolonia.blogspot.com.*

Founded by Portuguese settlers from Brazil in 1680, Colonia del Sacramento was a centre for smuggling British goods across the Río de la Plata into the Spanish colonies during the 18th century. The small historic section juts into the Río de la Plata, while the modern town extends around a bay. It is a lively place with streets lined with plane trees, a pleasant Plaza 25 de Agosto and a grand Intendencia Municipal (Méndez y Avenida Gen Flores, the main street). The town is kept very trim. The best beach is Playa Ferrando, 1.5 km to the east, easily accessible by foot or hired vehicle. There are regular connections by boat with Buenos Aires and a free port.

The **Barrio Histórico**, with its narrow streets (see Calle de los Suspiros), colonial buildings and reconstructed city walls, is charming because there are few such examples in this part of the continent. It has been declared Patrimonio Cultural de la Humanidad by UNESCO. The old town can be easily seen on foot in a day (wear comfortable shoes on the uneven cobbles), but spend one night there to experience the illuminations by nostalgic replica street lamps. The **Plaza Mayor** is especially picturesque and has parakeets in the palm trees. Grouped around it are the **Museo Municipal**, in a late-18th-century residence, rebuilt in 1835 (with indigenous archaeology, historical items, natural history, palaeontology), the **Casa Nacarello** next door (18th century; depicting colonial life), the **Casa del Virrey** (in ruins), the **Museo Portugués** (1717) with, downstairs, an exhibition of beautiful old maps, the ruins of the Convento de San Francisco, to which is attached the **Faro** (lighthouse, entry US$0.80, daily 1300-sunset, from 1100 at weekends, on a clear day you can see

Buenos Aires), and the **Museo Naval** ① *Calle Enríquez de la Peña y San Francisco, T4522 5609*, opened in the historic Casa de Lavalleja in 2009. At the Plaza's eastern end is the **Portón del Campo**, the restored city gate and drawbridge. Just north of the Plaza Mayor is the **Museo Archivo Regional** (1750), collection of maps, police records 1876-1898 and 19th-century watercolours. The **Iglesia Matriz**, on Calle Vasconcellos (beside the Plaza de Armas/Manuel Lobo), is the oldest church in Uruguay. Free concerts are held occasionally. At the end of Calle Misiones de los Tapes, the tiny **Museo del Azulejo** (1740-1760, rebuilt 1986), houses a collection of Portuguese, French and Catalan tiles, plus the first Uruguayan tile from 1840. At Calles de San José y España, the **Museo Español** (1720, rebuilt 1840), displays Spanish colonial items plus modern paintings by Uruguayan Jorge Paéz Vilaró. At the north edge, the fortifications of the **Bastión del Carmen** can be seen; nearby is the Centro Cultural Bastión del Carmen, Rivadavia 223, in a 19th-century glue and soap factory, with frequent theatre productions. In the third week of January, festivities mark the founding of Colonia. The **Feria de la Ciudad** ① *Campus Municipal, Fosalba y Suárez*, is a crafts fair worth a visit. Kids will love the **Acuario** in the Barrio Histórico ① *Calle Virrey Cevallos 236, esq Rivadavia, www.acuario.com.uy, open Wed-Mon 1400-1800, 1600-2000 in summer, US$1.80*.

Around the bay is **Real de San Carlos** ① *5 km, take 'Cotuc' or 'ABC' buses from Av Gral Flores, leaving Barrio Histórico, US$0.75*, an unusual, once grand but now sad tourist complex, built by Nicolás Mihanovic 1903-1912. The elegant bull-ring, in use for just two years, is falling apart (closed to visitors, bullfighting is banned in Uruguay). The casino, the nearest to Buenos Aires then (where gambling was prohibited), failed when a tax was imposed on Mihanovic's excursions; also disused is the huge Frontón court. Only the racecourse (Hipódromo) is still operational (free, except three annual races) and you can see the horses exercising on the beach.

Tourist offices ① *Flores y Rivera, T4522 6141, daily 0900-1900 (closes at 2000 in peak summer and 1800 in winter), turismo@ colonia.gub.uy and www.coloniaturismo.com*, good maps of the Barrio Histórico and the region. Beside the **Old Gate** ① *Manuel Lobo e Ituzaingó, T4522 8506, daily 0800-2000 (0900- 1900 in winter)*. Also an information desk at bus terminal. There is a **Ministry of Tourism** office at the passenger terminal at the dock, T4522 4897. **Centro BIT** ① *Calle Odriozola 434 (next to the port), www.bitcolonia.com*, is a large building complex with an official tourist information centre (daily 1000-1900), restaurant, terrace, gift shop and a permanent exhibition on the country and region (show entry US$3.50). Visit www.guiacolonia.com.uy, www.colonianet.com.

Conchillas, 50 km from Colonia and 40 km from Carmelo, is a former British mining town from the late 19th century. It preserves dozens of buildings constructed by C H Walker and Co Ltd. Tourist information is available at the **Casa de la Cultura** (daily 0800-1400) on Calle David Evans. The police station is also a good source of information. Direct buses from Colonia; road well marked on Route 21.

Carmelo → *Population: 18,000.*

From Colonia, Route 21 heads northwest to Carmelo (77 km) on the banks of Arroyo Las Vacas. A fine avenue of trees leads to the river, crossed by the first swing bridge built 1912. Across the bridge is the Rambla de los Constituyentes and the Fuente de las Tentaciones. The church, museum and archive of El Carmen is on Plaza Artigas (named after the city's founder). In the Casa de la Cultura Ignacio Barrios (IMC), 19 de Abril 246, T4542 2001, is a tourist office. Historically a mining centre, it is said that many luxurious buildings in

Buenos Aires were made from the grey granite of Cerro Carmelo (mines flooded and used for watersports). It is one of the most important yachting centres on Río de la Plata and its microclimate produces much wine.

Calera de Las Huérfanas (Estancia Belén or de las Vacas) is the remains of one of the area's main Jesuit missions. Vines were introduced and lime was exported for the construction of Buenos Aires. After the expulsion of the Jesuits, its production sustained an

Colonia del Sacramento

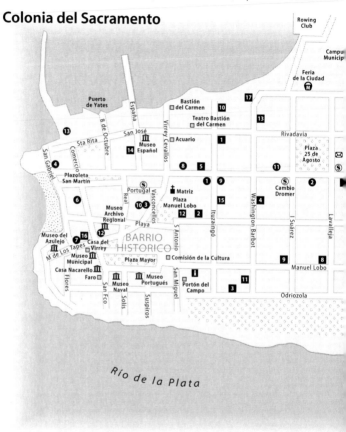

Where to stay 🛏
1 Don Antonio Posada
2 El Capullo Posada
3 El Viajero B&B
4 El Viajero Hostel
5 Esperanza & Artemisa Spa
6 Hostal de los Poetas
7 Hostel Colonial
8 Hostel El Español
9 Italiano
10 Posada de la Flor
11 Posada del Angel
12 Posada del Gobernador
13 Posada del Río
14 Posada del Virrey
15 Posada Manuel de Lobo
16 Posada Plaza Mayor
17 Radisson Colonia de
  Sacramento &
  Restaurant Del Carmen
18 Romi

200 metres
200 yards

orphanage in Buenos Aires. It's in relatively good state and is best reached by car (exit from Route 21 clearly marked, some 10 km before Carmelo, see www.caleradelashuerfanas.org).

Between Carmelo and Nueva Palmira, another river port, is the colonial monument, **Capilla de Narbona** (Route 21, Km 263), built in the early 18th century. At **Granja y Bodega Narbona** (T4540 4160, www.narbona.com.uy), wine, cheese and other produce are available, as well as a fine restaurant and exclusive hotel rooms. Nearby, at Km 262, is the luxurious **Four Seasons Resort**, www.fourseasons.com/carmelo.

Mercedes → *Population: 42,000.*

This livestock centre is best reached by Route 2 from the main Colonia-Montevideo highway. Founded in 1788, it is pleasant town on the Río Negro, a yachting and fishing centre during the season. Its charm (it is known as 'the city of flowers') derives from its Spanish-colonial appearance, though it is not as old as the older parts of Colonia. There is an attractive *costanera* (riverside drive) and a jazz festival in January.

West of town 4 km is the **Parque y Castillo Barón de Mauá** ① *T4532 3005*, dating from 1857. It has a mansion which contains the **Museum of Palaeontology** ① *T4532 3290, museoberro@gmail.com, daily 1100-1700, free,* on the ground floor. The building is worth wandering around to see the exterior, upper apartments and stable block. Cheese, wine and olive oil are produced. It takes 45 minutes to walk to the park, a pleasant route passing Calera Real on the riverbank, dating back to 1722, the oldest industrial ruins in the country (lime kilns hewn out of the sandstone). At the **tourist office** ① *Detomasi 415, T4532 2733, turismo@soriano.gub.uy*, maps and hotel lists are available.

Fray Bentos → *Population: 24,000.*

Route 2 continues westwards (34 km) to Fray Bentos, the main port on the east bank of Río Uruguay. Here in 1865 the Liebig company built its first factory producing meat extract. The original plant, much extended and known as **El Anglo**, has

Restaurants 🍴
1 Blanco y Negro Bar & Arte
2 Club Colonia
3 El Drugstore & Viejo Barrio
4 El Torreón
5 La Amistad
6 La Bodeguita
7 La Casa de Jorge Páez Vilaró
8 Lo de Renata
9 Mercosur
10 Mesón de la Plaza
11 Parrillada El Portón
12 Pulpería de los Faroles
13 Yacht Club

been restored as the **Museo de la Revolución Industrial** ① *T4562 2918/3690, Mon-Fri 0900-2000, Sat-Sun 0900-1300, 1600-2000, US$1.50 (or US$2.50 including a 1½-hr guided tour 1000 and 1800 in Spanish, leaflet in English).* The office block in the factory has been preserved complete with its original fittings. Many machines can be seen. Within the complex is the Barrio Inglés, where workers were housed, and La Casa Grande, where the director lived. There are **beaches** to the northeast and southwest. **Tourist office** ① *25 de Mayo 3400, T4562 2233, turismo@rionegro.gub.uy.*

Crossing to Argentina
About 9 km upriver from Fray Bentos is the San Martín International Bridge (vehicles US$6; pedestrians and cyclists may cross only on vehicles, officials may arrange lifts).

Paysandú → *Population: 76,000.*

North of Fray Bentos, 110 km, is this undulating, historic city on the east bank of the Río Uruguay. Along Route 3, it's 380 km from Montevideo. Summer temperatures can be up to 42°C. There is a 19th-century **basilica** ① *daily 0700-1145, 1600-2100.* The **Museo Histórico Municipal** ① *Zorrilla de San Martín y Leandro Gómez, Mon-Sat 0800-1300,* has good collection of guns and furniture from the time of the Brazilian siege of 1864-1865. **Museo de la Tradición** ① *north of town at the Balneario Municipal, 0900-1745 daily, reached by bus*

Paysandú · To 3 · To Train station

C Gardel · Florida · Plaza Constitución · Cathedral · Av España · 18 de Julio · Rincón · Gral Leandro Gómez · Museo Histórico Municipal · Sarandí · Setembrino Pereda · 33 Orientales · Luis A de Herrera · Av Zorrilla de San Martín · Montecaseros · Guayabos · Ituzaingó · Plaza José P Varela · 25 de Mayo · 19 de Abril · 25 de Mayo · V de Mauá · José P Varela · Cerrito · Juncal · 6 de Abril · Montevideo · Colón · Colón · Artigas · Río Negro · Solís · To 6 · To 1 · To Football Stadium

N
100 metres
100 yards

Where to stay 🛏
1 Bulevar
2 Casagrande
3 El Jardín
4 La Posada
5 Lobato
6 Mykonos
7 Plaza

Restaurants 🍴
1 Artemio
2 Los Tres Pinos

to Zona Industrial, gaucho articles, is also worth a visit. **Tourist office** ① *Plaza Constitución, 18 de Julio 1226, T4722 6220, www.paysandu.gub.uy, Mon-Fri 0800-1900, Sat-Sun 0900-1900 (2000 in summer), and at Puente Gen Artigas, T4722 7574, paysandu@mintur.gub.uy.*

Around Paysandú

The **Central Termal Guaviyú** ① *Ruta 3 Km 431.5, T4755 2049, guaviyu@paysandu.gub.uy, US$3.75-4.50, getting there: 50 mins by bus, US$3, 6 a day*, thermal springs 60 km north, with four pools, restaurant, three motels (**$$$-$$** for 3 to 5 people) and private hotel with own thermal pools (**$$$**, **Villagio**) and excellent cheap camping facilities. Along Route 90, 85 km east, is the **Centro Termal Almirón** ① *Ruta 90 Km 85.5, T4740 2203, termas.almiron@ paysandu.gub.uy, or visit www.guichon.com.uy*, six pools, with camping, apartments and motels. The **Meseta de Artigas** ① *110 km north of Paysandú, 15 km off the highway to Salto, no public transport, free*, is 45 m above the Río Uruguay, which here narrows and at low water forms whirlpools at the rapids of El Hervidero. It was used as a base by General Artigas during the struggle for independence. The terrace has a fine view, but the rapids are not visible from the Meseta. The statue topped by Artigas' head is very original.

Crossing to Argentina

The José Artigas international bridge connects with Colón, Argentina (US$6 per car, return), 8 km away. Immigration for both countries is on the Uruguayan side in the same office. If travelling by bus, the driver gets off the bus with everyone's documents and a list of passengers to be checked by immigration officials.

Salto → *Population: 103,000.*

A centre for cultivating and processing oranges and other citrus fruit, Salto is a beautifully kept town 120 km by paved road north of Paysandú. The town's commercial area is on Calle Uruguay, between Plazas Artigas and Treinta y Tres. There are lovely historic streets and walks along the river. See the beautiful **Parque Solari** (northeast of the centre) and the **Parque Harriague** (south of the centre) with an open-air theatre. The **Museo María Irene Olarreaga Gallino de Bellas Artes y Artes Decorativas** ① *Uruguay 1067, T4732 9898 ext 148, Tue-Sun 1500-2000 (Tue-Sun 1400-1900 in winter), free*, in the French-style mansion of a rich *estanciero* (Palacio Gallino), is well worth a visit. **Museo del Hombre y La Tecnología** ① *Brasil 511, T4732 9898, ext 151, Tue-Sun 1400-1900 (Tue-Sun 1300-1800 in winter), free entry and free guided tours in Spanish*, is very interesting, with a small archaeological museum. There is a Shrove Tuesday carnival. **Tourist office** ① *Uruguay 1052, T4733 4096, www.salto .gub.uy, Mon-Sat 0800-1930, free map*; and at the international bridge, T4732 8933, salto@mintur.gub.uy.

The most popular tourist site in the area is the large **Presa de Salto Grande dam** and hydroelectric plant 13 km from Salto, built jointly by Argentina and Uruguay ① *taxi to dam US$20.50; guided tours 0700-1600 arranged by Relaciones Públicas office, T4732 6131, rrppmi@saltogrande.org*; small visitors centre at the plant. A road runs along the top of the dam to Argentina. By launch to the **Salto Chico** beach, fishing, camping.

Near the dam (2 km north on ex-Route 3) is **Parque Acuático Termas de Salto Grande** ① *open all year 1000-2000 (Jan and Feb 1000-2300), US$7.50, T4732 0902/4733 4411, www. hotel horacioquiroga.com*, 4 ha, in a natural setting. There are several pools, slides, hydro massages, water jets and a man-made waterfall.

Crossing to Argentina

North of the town, at the Salto Grande dam, there is an international bridge to Concordia, Argentina, open 24 hours a day, all year. Passengers have to get off the bus to go through immigration procedures. Buses don't go on Sundays. Both Argentine and Uruguayan immigration offices are on the Argentine side.

Termas del Daymán and other springs

About 10 km south of Salto on Route 3, served by bus marked 'Termas' which leave from Calle Brasil every hour, are **Termas del Daymán**, a small town built around curative hot springs. It is a nice place to spend a night, though it is crowded in the daytime; few restaurants around the beautifully laid out pools. **Complejo Médico Hidrotermal Daymán** ① *T4736 9090, www.viatermal.com/spatermaldayman, therapeutical massage US$14 for 20 mins, US$23 for 40 mins, 3-day antistress treatment from US$44*, has a spa and many specialized treatments in separate pools (external and internal), showers and jacuzzis. There is also Acuamania, a theme park, nearby.

The road to **Termas del Arapey** branches off Route 3 to Bella Unión, at 61 km north of Salto, and then runs 19 km east and then south. Pampa birds, rheas and metre-long lizards in evidence. Termas del Arapey is on the Arapey river south of Isla Cabellos (Baltasar Brum). The waters at these famous thermal baths contain bicarbonated salts, calcium and magnesium.

To the Brazilian border: Bella Unión

Route 3 goes north to the small town of Bella Unión, from where an international bridge 5 km away crosses to the Brazilian town of Barra de Quaraí. This village lies next to a unspoilt area of densely wooded islands and beautiful sandbanks on the Río Uruguay, at the triple frontier point. About 80 km northwest is Uruguaiana which takes the main international bus traffic between Brazil and Argentina.

To the Brazilian border: Artigas

From near Bella Unión Route 30 runs east to Artigas, a frontier town in a cattle raising and agricultural area (excellent swimming upstream from the bridge). The town (*population: 40,000*) is known for its good quality amethysts. There is a bridge across the Río Cuareim to the Brazilian town of Quaraí. The Brazilian consul is at Lecueder 432, T4772 5414, vcartigas@mre.gov.br.

Western Uruguay listings

For hotel and restaurant price codes and other relevant information, see pages 89-90.

🛏 Where to stay

Nueva Helvecia (Colonia Suiza) *p110*
$$$$ Nirvana, Av Batlle y Ordóñez, T4554 4081, www.hotelnirvana.com. Restaurant (Swiss and traditional cuisine), half- and full board available, see website for promotions, Wi-Fi, sports facilities, 25 ha of park and gardens. Recommended.
$$ Del Prado, Av G Imhoff, T4554 4169, www.hoteldelprado.info. Open all year, huge buffet breakfast, TV, Wi-Fi, pool, hostel accommodation **$**.

Camping

Several campsites south of Route 1 on Río de la Plata. A good one at Blancarena is

Camping Enrique Davyt (access from La Paz village east of Colonia Valdense), T4587 2110, campinged@adinet.com.uy, US$3 pp.

Tourism farms

$$$$ pp Finca Piedra, Ruta 23, Km 125, Mal Abrigo, northwest of San José de Mayo (convenient for Montevideo or Colonia), T4340 3118, www.fincapiedra.com. Price is full board, various rooms in different parts of this 1930s estancia and vineyard, lots of outdoor activities including riding, tours of the vines, winetasting, pool, caters for children, Wi-Fi.

$$$$ La Vigna, T4558 9234, Km 120 Ruta 51 to Playa Fomento, www.lavigna.com. uy. Wonderful boutique eco-hotel, solar-powered and recycled furniture. Offers horse-riding and art lessons. Good food, all farm reared and organic. Owner is a cheese farmer, excellent produce. Highly recommended.

$$$ El Galope, Cno Concordia, Colonia Suiza, T9910 5985, www.elgalope.com. uy. Access on Route 1 Km 114.5. Discounts for HI members, limited to 10 guests, 6 km from Nueva Helvecia, **$** in bunk bed, use of kitchen, sauna US$10, 2-hr riding US$30, bicycles US$1, walking, English, French, German and Spanish spoken.

$$$ El Terruño, Paraje Minuano, Ruta 1, Km 140, 35 km before Colonia, T4550 6004, www.estanciaelterrunio.com. Price includes breakfast, horse-rides and activities.

$$$ pp Estancia Don Miguel, 6 km from Pueblo Cufré, access from Ruta 1 Km 121 y Ruta 52, T4550 2041, www.estancia donmiguel.com. Rustic, working farm, full board, good activities, little English spoken.

Colonia del Sacramento *p110, map p112*
Choice is good including several recently renovated 19th-century posada hotels.

Barrio Histórico

$$$$-$$$ El Capullo Posada, 18 de Julio 219, T4523 0135, www.elcapullo.com.

Spacious living area, English and American owners, stylish boutique-style rooms, Wi-Fi, outdoor pool and parrilla.

$$$$-$$$ Posada Plaza Mayor, Del Comercio 111, T4522 3193, www. posadaplazamayor.com. In a 19th- century house, beautiful internal patio with lemon trees and Spanish fountain, lovely rooms with a/c or heating, English spoken.

Centre

$$$$-$$$ Don Antonio Posada, Ituzaingó 232, T4522 5344, www. posadadonantonio.com. 1850 building, buffet breakfast, a/c, TV, garden, pool, internet, Wi-Fi, excellent.

$$$$-$$$ Hotel Esperanza & Artemisa Spa, Gral Flores 237, T4522 2922, www. hotelesperanzaspa.com. Charming, with buffet breakfast, Wi-Fi, sauna, heated pool and treatments.

$$$$ Radisson Colonia del Sacramento, Washington Barbot 283, T4523 0460, www.radisson colonia.com. Great location overlooking the jetty, contemporary architecture, casino attached. 2 pools, Jacuzzi, Wi-Fi, restaurant **Del Carmen**, very good.

$$$ Italiano, Intendente Suárez 105, T4522 7878, www.hotelitaliano.com.uy. Open since 1928, it has been renovated with comfortable rooms, cheaper rates Mon-Thu. Large outdoor and indoor pools, gym, sauna, good restaurant. Recommended.

$$$ Posada del Angel, Washington Barbot 59, T4522 4602, www.posadadelangel.net. Early 20th-century house, pleasant, warm welcome, Wi-Fi, gym, sauna, pool.

$$$ Posada del Virrey, España 217, T4522 2223, www.posadadelvirrey.com. Large rooms, some with view over bay (cheaper with small bathroom and no balcony), with buffet breakfast, Wi-Fi. Recommended.

$$$ Posada de la Flor, Ituzaingó 268, T4523 0794, www.hotelescolonia.com/ posadadelaflor. At the quiet end of C Ituzaingó, next to the river and to the

Barrio Histórico, simply decorated rooms on a charming patio and roof terrace with river views.

$$$ Posada Manuel de Lobo, Ituzaingó 160, T4522 2463, www. posadamanueldelobo.com. Built in 1850. Large rooms, huge baths, parking, some smaller rooms, nice breakfast area inside and out.

$$$ Posada del Gobernador, 18 de Julio 205, T4522 2918, www.delgobernador.com. Charming, with open air pool, garden and tea room open 1600-2000.

$$$ Posada del Río, Washington Barbot 258, T4522 3002, www.posadadelrio. uy. A/c, small breakfast included, Wi-Fi, terrace overlooking bay.

$$$ El Viajero B&B, Odriozola 269, T4522 8645, www.elviajerobb.com. Very well located modern building with river views, bike rental, Wi-Fi.

$$$ El Viajero Hostel (HI affiliate), Washington Barbot 164, T4522 2683, www.elviajerocolonia.com. Small hostel with a/c and Wi-Fi, helpful, **$** in dorm, breakfast included.

$$$-$$ Romi, Rivera 236, T4523 0456, www.hotelromicolonia.com. 19th-century posada-style downstairs, with lovely tiles at entrance. Airy modernist upstairs and simple rooms. Recommended.

$$ Hostal de los Poetas, Mangarelli 677, T4523 1643, www.guiacolonia.com.uy/ hostaldelospoetas. Some distance from the Barrio Histórico but one of the cheapest. Friendly owners, few simple bedrooms and a lovely breakfast room, tiny exuberant garden.

$$ Hostel El Español, Manuel Lobo 377, T4523 0759, www.hostelelespaniol.com. Good value, **$** pp with shared bath in dorms, breakfast US$4, internet, kitchen. Recommended.

$$ Hostel Colonial, Flores 440, T4523 0347. HI affiliated. Pretty patio and quirky touches, such as barber's chair in reception. **$** in dorm, breakfast included. Kitchen, bar with set meals, free internet access and use

of bikes (all ancient), run down and noisy, but popular.

Carmelo *p111*

$$ Timabe, 19 de Abril y Solís, T4542 5401, www.ciudad carmelo.com/timabe. Near the swing bridge, with a/c or fan, TV, dining room, parking, good.

Camping

At Playa Seré, hot showers.

Mercedes *p113*

$$$ Rambla Hotel, Av Asencio 728, T4533 0696, www.mercedesramblahotel.com. uy. Riverside 3-star hotel with quite good rooms and Wi-Fi.

$$ Ito, Eduardo V Haedo 184, T4532 4919, www.sorianototal.com/hotelito/mercedes. htm. Basic though decent rooms with cable TV in an old house.

Tourism farm

$$$$ pp La Sirena Marinas del Río Negro, Ruta 14, Km 4, T4530 2271, www. lasirena.com.uy. Estancia dating from 1830, picturesque, on the river, birdwatching, fishing, waterskiing, accommodation, meals, full board (**$$$** double room with breakfast) friendly owners Rodney, Lucia and Patricia Bruce. Warmly recommended.

Fray Bentos *p113*

$$ Colonial, 25 de Mayo 3293, T4562 2260, www.hotelcolonial.com.uy. A/c and breakfast extra, **$** without bath.

$$ El Entorno, 8 km south at Balneario Las Cañas, T4562 4970, www.elentorno.net. Hotel and motel rooms, restaurant.

$$ Plaza, 18 de Julio y 25 de Mayo, T4562 2363, www.grupocarminatti.com/hot1ha. html. Comfortable, a/c, TV, internet, with breakfast, on the Plaza Constitución.

Camping

At the **Club Remeros**, on Rambla Costanera (opposite Parque Roosevelt), T4562 2236.

Paysandú *p114, map p114*

Book hotels in advance during Holy Week.

$$$ Bulevar, Bulevar Artigas 960, T4722 8835, www.hotelbulevar.com.uy. Bar, garage, internet, cable TV.

$$$ Casagrande, Florida 1221, Plaza Constitución, T4722 4994, www. hotelcasagrande.com.uy. A/c, welcoming, buffet breakfast, restaurant, Wi-Fi, parking, very good.

$$$ El Jardín, Montevideo 1085, T4722 3745, www.hoteljardon.com. Comfortable family-run residence with a/c, parking, and a neat garden.

$$$ Mykonos, 18 de Julio 768, T4722 0255, www.hotelmykonos.com.uy. Buffet breakfast, meeting room, cable TV.

$$$ Plaza, Leandro Gómez 1211, T4722 2022, www.hotel plaza.com.uy. A/c, buffet breakfast, parking.

$$ Lobato, Leandro Gómez 1415, T4722 2241, hotellobato@adinet.com.uy. With buffet breakfast, a/c, Wi-Fi, modern, good.

$$ La Posada, José Pedro Varela 566, T4722 7879, laposada@adinet.com.uy. Wi-Fi, patio with BBQ, a/c, restaurant and bar.

Camping

Camping Club de Pescadores, Rambla Costanera Norte, T4722 2885, clubpescadorespaysandu@gmail.com. US$3.50 pp per day plus US$6 per tent, electricity, hot showers after 1800.

Tourism farms

$$$$-$$$ Hostería y Estancia La Paz, Colonia La Paz, 15 km south of Paysandú, T4720 2272, www.estancialapaz.com.uy. Excellent rustic rooms, pool, customized gaucho experiences, horseriding, birdwatching. Half- and full board available. Highly recommended.

$$$ pp Estancia Resort La Calera, 60 km from Guichón, 150 km east of Paysandú, T2601 0340, www.lacalera. com. 40 luxurious suites with fireplace and kitchenette, pool, riding, rodeo,

conference facilities. Self-catering. Highly recommended.

Salto *p115*

$$$$ Hotel Horacio Quiroga, at Parque del Lago, T4733 4411, www. hotelhoracioquiroga.com. Best in town although some distance from centre, at the Termas complex, sports facilities, spa treatments, staffed by nearby catering school, special packages in season.

$$$ Los Cedros, Uruguay 657, T4733 3984, www.loscedros.com.uy. In centre, comfortable 3-star hotel, Wi-Fi, buffet breakfast, conference room.

$$ pp Concordia, Uruguay 749, T4733 2735, www.granhotelconcordia.com.uy. Oldest hotel in Uruguay, founded 1860, Carlos Gardel stayed here, fine courtyard, pleasant breakfast room.

$$ Español, Brasil 826, T4733 4048, www.hotelespanolsalto.com. Central and functional, with Wi-Fi, TV, breakfast, a/c, minibar and parking.

Termas del Daymán *p116*

$$$ Termas de San Nicanor, 12 km from Termas de Daymán, Km 485, Route 3, T4730 2209, www.termassannicanor. com. Estancia and gaucho experience, excellent nature watching, private pool. Recommended. Also camping (US$10 pp), good facilities.

$$$-$$ Del Pasaje, near Ruta 3, T4736 9661, www.hoteldelpasaje.com. Hotel rooms, apartments for 2, 4, 6 or 7 people and cabañas. Situated in front of the Parque Acuático Acuamania.

$$ Bungalows El Puente, near the bridge over Río Dayman, T4736 9876, includes discount to thermal baths. For 2 to 7 people, cheaper without a/c, kitchen, cable TV.

$$ Hostal Canela, Los Sauces entre Los Molles y Calle 1, T4736 9121, www. hostalcanela.com.uy. HI affiliated. Good value, with kitchenette, pool, Wi-Fi, gardens.

$$ Estancia La Casona del Daymán, Ruta 3 Km 483, 3 km east of the bridge at Daymán, T4733 2735, www.granhotelconcordia/dayman. Well-preserved farm, horse riding.

$$ pp La Posta del Daymán, Ruta 3, Km 487, T4736 9801, www.lapostadeldayman.com. A/c, half- and full board or breakfast only (cheaper, but still **$$**, in hostel), thermal water in more expensive rooms, thermal pool, good restaurant, long-stay discounts, camping. Recommended. Also hydrothermal complex.

Camping See Termas de San Nicanor, above.

Termas del Arapey

$$$ Hotel Termas del Arapey, T4768 2441, www.hoteltermasdelarapey.com. Open all year, a/c, TV, safe, indoor/outdoor pool, restaurant, Wi-Fi, spa, half-board available.

Camping US$5 pp, good facilities.

Artigas p116

There are a few hotels in town and the **Club Deportivo Artigas**, Pte Berreta and LA de Herrera, 4 km from city, T4772 2532, open all year, rooms (**$**) and camping (US$2.50 pp plus US$1.50 per tent), restaurant, no cooking facilities.

Camping

At Club Zorrilla, T4772 4341.

❼ Restaurants

Nueva Helvecia (Colonia Suiza) p110
$$$-$$ Don Juan, main plaza. Snack bar/restaurant excellent food, pastries and bread.

Colonia del Sacramento p110, map p112
$$$ Blanco y Negro Bar & Arte, Ituzaingó y Gen Flores 248, T4522 2236. Closed Wed. Set in a stone building, smart, great range of meat dishes, live music Fri and Sat. Cellar of local wines.

$$$ Del Carmen, Washington Barbot 283, T4522 0575. Open from breakfast to dinner in **Radisson Hotel**, fantastic views, great for evening drink. Recommended.

$$$ La Casa de Jorge Páez Vilaró, Misiones de los Tapes 65, T4522 9211. Attractively set at an artist's former residence, it offers a short though varied and fine menu, only 8 tables. Closed Wed.

$$$ Lo de Renata, Flores 227, T4523 1061, www.loderenata.com. Open daily. Popular for its lunchtime buffet of meats and salads.

$$$ Mesón de la Plaza, Vasconcellos 153, T4522 4807, www.mesondelaplaza.com. 140-year old house with a leafy courtyard, elegant dining, good traditional food.

$$$ Viejo Barrio (VB), Vasconcellos 169, T4522 5399. Closed Wed. Very good for home-made pastas and fish, renowned live shows.

$$$ Yacht Club (Puerto de Yates), T9100 4427. Ideal at sunset with wonderful view of the bay. Good fish.

$$$ La Amistad, 18 de Julio 448, T4520 6808. Good local grill.

$$$ La Bodeguita, Del Comercio 167, T4522 5329. Tue-Sun evenings and Sat-Sun lunch. Its terrace on the river is the main attraction of this lively pizza place that serves also good *chivitos* and pasta.

$$$ Club Colonia, Gen Flores 382, T4522 2189. Good value, frequented by locals, live music Thu-Sun.

$$$ El Drugstore, Portugal 174, T4522 5241. Hip, fusion food: Latin American, European, Japanese, good, creative varied menu, good salads and fresh vegetables. Music and show.

$$$ Parrillada El Portón, Gral Flores 333, T4522 5318. Best parrillada in town. Small, relatively smart, good atmosphere. House speciality is offal.

$$$ Pulpería de los Faroles, Misiones de los Tapes 101, T4523 0271. Very inviting tables (candlelit at night) on the cobbled streets for a varied menú that includes tasty salads, seafood and local wines.

$$$-$$ El Torreón, end of Av Gen Flores, T4523 1524. One of the best places to enjoy a sunset meal with views of the river. Also a café serving toasties and cakes.

$$$-$$ Mercosur, Flores y Ituzaingó, T4522 4200. Popular, varied dishes. Also café serving homemade cakes.

Arcoíris, Av Gral Flores at Plaza 25 de Agosto. Very good ice cream.

Mercedes *p113*

$$$ Casa Bordó, Paysandú 654, T4532 9817. French-owned and an unmissable stopover on the routes of Uruguay.

$$$-$$ Parador Rambla, Rivera y 18 de Julio, T4532 7337. For good Spanish-influenced meals on the riverside.

Fray Bentos *p113*

$$$ Wolves, at Barrio Anglo, T4562 3604. Produces good homemade pastas next to the museum.

$$$-$$ Juventud Unida, 18 de Julio 1130, T4562 3365. The restaurant of a local football club is a popular place for varied meals.

Several other cafés and pizzerías on 18 de Julio near Plaza Constitución.

Paysandú *p114, map p114*

$$$ Artemio, 18 de Julio 1248. Simple, reputation for serving "best food in town"

$$$ Los Tres Pinos, Av España 1474, T4724 1211. *Parrillada*, very good, as well as its pastas and fish.

Salto *p115*

$$$ La Caldera, Uruguay 221, T4732 4648. Good *parrillada* and local wines, also seafood, closed Mon lunchtime.

$$$ La Casa de Lamas, Chiazzaro 20, T4732 9376. Fish and homemade pasta.

$$$ La Trattoria (at Club de Uruguay), Uruguay 754, T4733 6660. Breakfast and good-value meals, especially excellent pasta.

$$ Trouville, Uruguay 702, T4732 9331, www.pizzeriatrouville.com. Pizzería.

○ Shopping

Colonia del Sacramento *p110, map p112*
There's a large artist community, Uruguayan and international, with good galleries across town. **El Almacén**, Real 150, creative gifts. **Paseo del Sol**, Del Comercio 158, is a small commercial centre selling local gifts. **Oveja Negra**, De la Playa 114, recommended for woollen clothes. Leather shops on C Santa Rita, next to Yacht Club. At **Arteco**, Rambla de las Américas y Av Mihanovich (Real de San Carlos) and **Gadec**, on C San Miguel (opposite Puerta de la Ciudadela) local artisans sell their produce. **Colonia Shopping**, Av Roosevelt 458, www.coloniashopping.com.uy, shopping mall on main road out of town (east) selling international fashion brands.

○ What to do

Nueva Helvecia (Colonia Suiza) *p110*
Finca La Rosada, Federico Fisher s/n, Nueva Helvecia, T4554 7026, www.larosada.com.uy. A soft-fruit farm, famous for its blueberries, pick-your-own in season, offers tours with lunch or tea, plus local sites.

Colonia del Sacramento *p110, map p112*
City tours available with **Destino Viajes**, General Flores 341, T4522 5343, destinoviajes@adinet.com.uy. **Asociación Guías de Turismo de Colonia**, T4522 2309, www.asociacionguiascolonia.blogspot.com, organizes walking tours (1 hr, in Spanish, US$5) in the Barrio Histórico, daily 1100 and 1500 from tourist office next to Old Gate. Booking required for tours in English (US$7.50).

Paysandú *p114, map p114*
Bodega Leonardo Falcone, Av Wilson Ferreira Aldunate y Young, T4722 7718, www.bodegaleonardo falcone.com.uy. Winery tours at one of Uruguay's finest wine makers.

⊖ Transport

Nueva Helvecia (Colonia Suiza) p110
Bus
Montevideo-Colonia Suiza, frequent, with COT, 2-2½ hrs, US$7.50; **Turil**, goes to Colonia Suiza and Valdense; to **Colonia del Sacramento**, frequent, 1 hr, US$4. Local services between Colonia Valdense and Nueva Helvecia connect with Montevideo/Colonia del Sacramento buses.

Colonia del Sacramento p110, map p112
Road
There are plenty of filling stations between Colonia and the capital. If driving north to Paysandú and Salto, especially on Route 3, fill up with fuel and drinking water at every opportunity, stations are few and far between. From Colonia to Punta del Este by-passing Montevideo: take Ruta 11 at Ecilda Paullier, passing through San José de Mayo, Santa Lucía and Canelones, joining the Interbalnearia at Km 46.

Bus
All leave from bus terminal on Av Roosevelt, 7 blocks east of the Barrio Histórico, between the ferry port and the petrol station (free luggage lockers, ATM, exchange, café and internet). To **Montevideo**, several services daily, 2¼-2¾ hrs, COT, T4522 3121, Chadre, T4522 4734, and **Turil**, T4522 5246, US$10.50. Turil to Col Valdense, 1 hr, US$4. Chadre to Conchillas, US$2.50. To **Carmelo**, 1½ hrs, Chadre and Berrutti, T4522 5301, US$4.70. Chadre to Mercedes, 3½ hrs, US$10.50, Fray Bentos, 4 hrs, US$12, Paysandú, 6 hrs, US$18.50 and Salto, 8 hrs, US$25. **Nossar**, T4522 2934, to Durazno, 3 hrs, US$13.

Ferry
Book in advance for all sailings in summer. Fares and schedules given under Montevideo, Transport. To **Buenos Aires**: from 5 crossings daily, with **Buquebus** (T130), cars carried. **Colonia Express**, office at the port, T4522 9676, www.colonia express.com, makes 2-3 crossings a day between Colonia and **Buenos Aires** (50 min) in fast boats (no vehicles carried) with bus connections to/from Montevideo, Punta del Este and Uruguayan towns. **Seacat**, www.seacatcolonia.com, 2-3 fast ferries to Buenos Aires, 1 hr, office in Colonia T4522 2919. **Note** Passports must be stamped and Argentine departure tax paid even if only visiting Colonia for 1 day.

Taxi
A Méndez y Gral Flores, T4522 2920.

Carmelo p111
Bus
To **Montevideo**, US$14, Intertur, Chadre and Sabelín. To **Fray Bentos**, **Salto**, with Chadre from main plaza 0655, 1540. To **Colonia**, see above. To **Buenos Aires**: via Tigre, across the Paraná delta, an interesting bus/boat ride past innumerable islands: **Cacciola** 2 a day; T2908 2244, www.cacciolaviajes.com, see Montevideo page 106.

Mercedes p 113
Bus
To **Paysandú**, with Sabelín, in bus terminal, 1½ hrs, US$6.50; also **Chadre** on the Montevideo-Bella Unión route. To **Montevideo**, US$16, 3½ hrs, CUT, Agencia Central and Sabelín. To **Gualeguaychú**, 2 hrs, US$9, ETA CUT, Ciudad de Gualeguay (not Sun).

Fray Bentos p113
Bus
Terminal at 18 de Julio y Blanes. To/from **Montevideo**, CUT, 4-5 hrs, US$18, also Chadre and Agencia Central. To **Mercedes**, ETA, US$1.80, 5 daily (not Sun).

Crossing to Argentina: Fray Bentos p114
Bus
To **Buenos Aires**, 4 hrs, US$34, CITA, COT. To **Gualeguaychú**, 1½ hrs, US$7, ETA CUT (not Sun).

Paysandú *p114, map p114*
Bus
Can be hard to get a seat on buses going north. Terminal at Zorrilla y Artigas, T4722 3225. To/from **Montevideo**, US$22 (Núñez, Copay, T4722 5234, 4 a day), 5-6 hrs, also Chadre and Agencia Central. To **Salto**, Agencia Central, Alonso, T7722 4318, 1½-2 hrs, US$7. To **Rivera**, US$21, Copay, 0400, 1700 Mon-Sat (Sun 1700 only). To **Fray Bentos**, 2 a day, 2 hrs direct, US$6.50. To **Colonia** by Chadre, 0750, 1750, 6 hrs, US$18.50.

Crossing to Argentina: Paysandú *p115*
Bus
To **Colón**, Copay, Río Uruguay, 45 min-1 hr, US$4.

Train
Station at Cerrito y Lucas Piriz, www. trenbinacional.com, 1 service on Mon to **Salto**, 3 hrs, US$8, **Concordia**, 4 ½ hrs, US$11, and **Pilar** with a bus connection to **Buenos Aires** downtown, US$32, 15 hrs. On Thu 1 service to **Paso de los Toros**, US$13, 6 hrs.

Salto *p115*
Bus
Terminal 15 blocks east of centre at Batlle y Blandengues, café, shopping centre, *casa de cambio*. Take taxi to centre. To/ from **Montevideo**, 5½ -7½ hrs, US$28 (Norteño, Núñez, Agencia Central and Chadre). Chadre , Cotabu and Hernández to **Termas del Arapey**, 1½ hrs, daily, US$5. Also Agentur, 1 to 2 a day, US$6, via C Treinta y Tres. **Paysandú** US$7, 1½ -2 hrs, 6 a day. To **Bella Unión**, 2 hrs, US$10, 2 a day. To **Colonia**, 0555, 1555, 8 hrs, US$25; to **Fray Bentos**, same times, US$14.

Crossing to Argentina: Salto *p116*
Bus
To **Concordia**, Chadre and Flecha Bus, 2 a day each, not Sun, US$4, 1¼ -1½ hrs. To **Buenos Aires**, US$38, Flecha Bus.

Launch To **Concordia**, US$4, 15 mins, 4 a day (not Sun), depart port on C Brasil; immigration either side of river, quick and easy.

Train
Tickets at Larrañaga 86, T4734 1529, www. trenbinacional.com, 1 service on Mon to **Concordia**, 1 ½ hrs, US$4, and **Pilar** with a bus connection to **Buenos Aires** downtown, US$30, 12 hrs. On Thu 1 train to **Paysandú**, US$8, 4 hrs, to **Paso de los Toros**, US$19, 10 hrs.

Artigas *p116*
Bus
To **Salto**, COA, T4772 2268, US$13. Turil and COT from **Montevideo** 7-7½ hrs, US$36 via Durazno, Paso de los Toros and Tacuarembó.

⊙ Directory

Colonia del Sacramento *p110, map p112*
Banks Banks open afternoon only. Most museums and restaurants accept Argentine pesos or US$, but rarely euros. **HSBC**, De Portugal 183 (Barrio Histórico), Mon-Fri 1300- 1700. **Cambio Dromer**, Flores 350, T4522 2070, Mon-Fri 1000-1800, Sat 1000-1700 (branch at **Casino Radisson** daily 1400-0400). **Cambio Colonia** and **Western Union**, Av Flores y Lavalleja, T4522 5032. **Car hire** In bus terminal: **Avis**, T4522 9842, from US$150 per day, **Hertz**, T4522 9851, from US$90 per day. **Thrifty** by port, also at Flores 172, T4522 2939, where there are bicycles too (US$3 per hr), scooters (US$7 per hr) and golf buggies (US$15 per hr) for hire, recommended as traffic is slow and easy to navigate. **Consulates** Argentine Consulate and Cultural Centre, Flores 209, T4522 2086, open weekdays 1300-1800.

Mercedes *p113*
Banks Cambio Fagalde, Giménez 709.

Fray Bentos *p113*

Banks For exchange try **Cambio Nelson**, 18 de Julio y Roberto Young, T4562 0409.

Paysandú *p114, map p114*

Banks *Casas de cambio* on 18 de Julio: **Cambio Fagalde**, No 1004; **Cambio Bacacay**, No 1039; change TCs, Sat 0830-1230. **Consulates** Argentina, Gómez 1034, T4722 2253, Mon-Fri 1300-1800.

Salto *p115*

Banks *Casas de cambio* on Uruguay. **Car hire Maxicar**, Paraguay 764, T4733 5554, 9943 5454, www.maxicarsalto.com. 24 hrs, cars allowed to travel to Argentina and Brazil. **Consulates** Argentina, Artigas 1162, T4733 2931, Mon-Fri 0900- 1400. **Scooter hire** Daniel Irabuena Motos, Errandonea 69, T4732 9967.

Eastern Uruguay

Resorts line the coast from Montevideo to Punta del Este, the ultimate magnet for summer holidaymakers, especially from Argentina. Out of season, it is quieter and you can have the beaches to yourself, which is pretty much the case the closer you get to Brazil year round. Inland are cattle ranches, some of which welcome visitors, and hills with expansive views.

East from Montevideo

This beautiful coast consists of an endless succession of small bays, beaches and promontories, set among hills and woods. The beach season is from December to the end of February. An excellent four-lane highway leads to Punta del Este and Rocha, and a good two-lane highway to Chuy. This route will give you a chance to see the most important Uruguayan beach resorts, as well as Parque Nacional Santa Teresa and other natural attractions. If driving there are four tolls each way (about US$2.50 each), but this route is the easiest and the most comfortable in Uruguay with sufficient service stations along the way.

Piriápolis → *Population: 7579.*

This resort set among hills, 101 km from Montevideo, is laid out with an abundance of shady trees, and the district is rich in pine, eucalyptus and acacia woods. It has a good beach, a yacht harbour, a country club, a motor-racing track (street circuit) and is particularly popular with Argentines. It was, in fact, founded in the 1890s as a bathing resort for residents of Buenos Aires. Next to the marina is a small cable car (with seats for two) to the top of **Cerro San Antonio** ⓘ *US$4, 10 mins ride, free car park and toilets at lower station*. Magnificent views of Piriápolis and beaches, several restaurants. Recommended, but be careful when disembarking. North of the centre, at **Punta de Playa Colorada**, is a **marine rescue centre** ⓘ *sos-faunamarina@ adinet.com.uy*, that looks after injured sea creatures before releasing them to the wild. **Tourist office**, Asociación de Turismo ⓘ *Paseo de la Pasiva, Rambla de los Argentinos, summer 0900-2400, winter 1000-1800, T4432 5055, www.turismopiriapolis.com.*

   About 6 km north on the R37 is **Cerro Pan de Azúcar** (Sugar Loaf Hill) ⓘ *getting there: take bus 'Cerro Pan de Azúcar' and get off after 6 km*, crowned by a tall cross with a circular stairway inside, fine coastal views. There is only a steep path, marked by red arrows, up to the cross. Just north of Piriápolis R 37 passes the **La Cascada** municipal park (open all year) which contains the house of Francisco Piria, the founder of the resort, **Museo Castillo de Piria** ⓘ *open daily in summer, weekends in winter, 1000-2100*. About 4 km beyond Cerro Pan de Azúcar is the village of Pan de Azúcar, which has a **Museo al Aire Libre de Pintura** where the walls of the buildings have been decorated by Uruguayan and Argentine painters, designers and writers with humorous and tango themes (direct bus every hour from Piriápolis).

Portezuelo and Punta Ballena

R93 runs between the coast and the Laguna del Sauce to Portezuelo, which has good beaches. The **Arboreto Lussich** ⓘ *T4257 8077, 0900-1800*, on the west slope of the Sierra de la Ballena (north of R93) contains a unique set of native and exotic trees. There are footpaths, or you can drive through; two *miradores*; worth a visit. From Portezuelo drive north towards the R9 by way of the R12 which then continues, unpaved, to Minas. Just off R12 is **El Tambo**

Lapataia ① *1 km east from Solanas, then 4 km north, T4222 0000,* a dairy farm open to the public, selling cheese, ice cream, *dulce de leche,* homemade pizzas and pastas.

At Punta Ballena there is a wide crescent beach, calm water and very clean sand. The place is a residential resort but is still quiet. At the top of Punta Ballena there is a panoramic road 2.5 km long with remarkable views of the coast. **Casa Pueblo**, the house and gallery of Uruguayan artist Carlos Páez Vilaró, is built in a Spanish-Moroccan style on a cliff over the sea; the gallery can be visited (US$6), there are paintings, collages and ceramics on display, and for sale; open all year. Walk downhill towards the sea for a good view of the house.

Maldonado → *Population: 55,000.*

The capital of Maldonado Department, 140 km east of Montevideo, is a peaceful town, sacked by the British in 1806. It has many colonial remains and the historic centre has been restored. It is also a dormitory suburb of Punta del Este. Worth seeing is the **El Vigia watch tower** ① *Gorriti y Pérez del Puerto;* the Cathedral (started 1801, completed 1895), on Plaza San Fernando; the windmill; the **Cuartel de Dragones exhibition centre** ① *Pérez del Puerto y 18 de Julio, by Plaza San Fernando,* and the **Cachimba del Rey** ① *on the continuation of 3 de Febrero, almost Artigas,* an old well – legend claims that those who drink from it will never leave Maldonado. **Museo Mazzoni** ① *Ituzaingó 687, T4222 1107, Tue1600-2030, Wed-Sat 1030-2130, Sun 1300- 2100,* has regional items, indigenous, Spanish, Portuguese and English. **Museo de Arte Americano** ① *Treinta y Tres 823 y Dodera, T4222 2276, http:// maam-uruguay.blogspot. com, 2000-2200, Dec and Feb Fri-Sun only (closed winter),* a private museum of national and international art, interesting. **Tourist office** ① *Dirección General de Turismo, Edificio Municipal, T4222 3333, www.maldonado.gub.uy.*

Punta del Este

About 7 km from Maldonado and 139 km from Montevideo (a little less by dual carriageway), facing the bay on one side and the open waters of the Atlantic on the other, lies the largest and best known of the resorts, **Punta del Este**, which is particularly popular among Argentines and Brazilians. The narrow peninsula of Punta del Este has been entirely built over. On the land side, the city is flanked by large planted forests of eucalyptus, pine and mimosa. Two blocks from the sea, at the tip of the peninsula, is the historic monument of El Faro (lighthouse); in this part of the city no building may exceed its height. On the ocean side of the peninsula, at the end of Calle 25 (Arrecifes), is a shrine to the first mass said by the Conquistadores on this coast, 2 February 1515. Three blocks from the shrine is Plaza General Artigas, which has a *feria artesanal* (handicraft market); along its side runs Avenida Gorlero, the main street. There are two casinos, a golf course, and many beautiful holiday houses. **Museo Ralli of Contemporary Latin American Art** ① *Curupay y Los Arachanes, Barrio Beverly Hills, T4248 3476, www.museoralli.com.uy, Tue-Sun 1700-2100 in Jan-Feb, Sat-Sun 1400-1800 rest of year, closed Jun-Sep, free.* Worth a visit but a car is needed.

Punta del Este has excellent bathing **beaches**, the calm *playa mansa* on the bay side, the rough *playa brava* on the ocean side. There are some small beaches hemmed in by rocks on this side of the peninsula, but most people go to where the extensive *playa brava* starts. Papa Charlie beach on the Atlantic (Parada 13) is preferred by families with small children as it is safe. Quieter beaches are at La Barra and beyond.

There is an excellent yacht marina, yacht and fishing clubs. There is good fishing both at sea and in three nearby lakes and the Río Maldonado. **Tourist information** ① *Liga de Fomento, Parada 1, T4244 6519, open summer 0900-2400, winter 1000-1800; in bus station*

Punta del Este

Where to stay

1 1949 Hostel
2 Conrad
3 Gaudi
4 Iberia
5 Palace
6 Punta del Este Hostel
7 Remanso
8 Tánger

Restaurants

1 Cantón Chino
2 El Ciclista
3 Gure-etxe
4 Il Barreto
5 Isidora
6 Juana Enea
7 Lo de Charlie
8 Lo de Tere
9 Los Caracoles
10 Viejo Marino
11 Virazón
12 Yatch Club Uruguayo

Isla de Gorriti, visited by explorers including Solís, Magellan and Drake, was heavily fortified by the Spanish in the 1760's to keep the Portuguese out. The island, densely wooded and with superb beaches, is an ideal spot for campers (0800-1830, 0900-1700 in winter, entry US$5; boats from 0900-1700, return 1015-1815, US$15, T4244 6166; *Don Quico*, also does fishing trips, T4244 8945). On **Isla de Lobos**, which is a government reserve within sight of the town, there is a huge sea-lion colony; public boat US$20 per person, tour US$50. Ticket should be booked in advance (T4244 1716, or **Dimartours** T4244 4750, www.isladeloslobos.com.uy).

Beaches east of Punta del Este

Between the Peninsula and the mouth of the Río Maldonado, a road runs along the coast, passing luxurious houses, dunes and pines. Some of the most renowned architects of Uruguay and Argentina design houses here. The river is crossed by a unique undulating bridge, like a shallow M, to **La Barra**, a fashionable place, especially for summer nightlife, with beaches, art galleries, bars and restaurants (take a bus from Punta del Este terminal or taxi US$20). The **Museo del Mar Sirenamis** ⓘ *1 km off the coast road, watch for signs, T4277 1817, www.museodelmar.com.uy, summer daily 1030-2000 winter 1100-1700, US$5,* has an extensive collection on the subject of the sea, its life and history and on the first beach resorts. The coast road climbs a headland here before descending to the beaches further north, Montoya and **Manantiales** (reached by Condesa bus; taxi US$30). Some 30 km from Punta del Este is the fishing village of **Faro José Ignacio** with a **lighthouse** ⓘ *summer daily 1100-2030, winter 1100-1330, 1430-1830, US$0.75,* a beach club and other new developments, now the road is paved. Coastal R10 runs some way east of José Ignacio, but there is no through connection to La Paloma until a bridge across the mouth of the Lago Garzón is opened. A ferry runs 0600-0200; T9976 3816 for details.

La Paloma and around → *Population: 5000.*

Protected by an island and a sandspit, this is a good port for yachts. The surrounding scenery is attractive, with extensive wetlands nearby. You can walk for miles along the beach. The pace is more relaxed than Punta del Este. **Tourist office** ① *in La Paloma bus station, T9995 6662,* very helpful. For the Department of Rocha office at Rutas 9 y 15, open daily 0800-2000, T4472 3100, www.turismorocha.gub.uy. See also www.rochauruguay.com.

Coastal R10 runs to Aguas Dulces (regular bus services along this route). About 10 km from La Paloma is **La Pedrera**, a beautiful village with sandy beaches. Beyond La Pedrera the road runs near pleasant fishing villages which are rapidly being developed with holiday homes, for example **Barra de Valizas**, 50 minutes north. At **Cabo Polonio** (permanent population 80), visits to the islands of Castillos and Wolf can be arranged to see sea lions and penguins. It has two great beaches: the north beach is more rugged, while the south is tamer by comparison. Both have lifeguards on duty (though their zone of protection only covers a tiny portion of the kilometres and kilometres of beach). The village is part of a nature reserve. This limits the number of people who are allowed to stay there since the number of lodgings is limited and camping is strictly forbidden (if you arrive with a tent, it may be confiscated). During January or February (and especially during Carnival), you *have* to reserve a room in one of the few posadas or hotels, or better yet, rent a house (see Sleeping, below). From Km 264 on the main road all-terrain vehicles run 8 km across the dunes to the village (several companies, around US$5; tourist office by the terminal, open 1000-1800, T9996 8747). Day visitors must leave just after sundown (see Transport, below). Ask locally in Valizas about walking there, 3-4 hours via the north beach (very interesting, but hot, unless you go early). There are also pine woods with paths leading to the beach or village.

The **Monte de Ombúes** ① *open in summer months, from Jan, free, basic restaurant with honest prices* is a wood containing a few *ombú* trees (Phytolacca dioica – the national tree), *coronilla* (Scutia buxifolia) and *canelón* (Rapanea laetevirens). It has a small circuit to follow and a good hide for birdwatching. To reach the woods from Km 264, go 2 km north along R10 to the bridge. Here take a boat with guide, 30 minutes along the river (*Monte Grande* recommended as they visit both sides of the river, montegrande@adinet.com.uy). You can also walk from Km 264 across the fields, but it's a long way and the last 150 m are through thick brush. The bridge is 16 km from Castillos on R9 (see next paragraph): turn onto R16 towards Aguas Dulces, just before which you turn southwest onto R10.

From **Aguas Dulces** the road runs inland to the town of **Castillos** (easy bus connections to Chuy), where it rejoins R9. A tourist office at Aguas Dulces/Castillos crossroads on R9 has details on hotels open 1000-1300, 1700-2200, T9981 7068.

Punta del Diablo

At Km 298 there is a turn to a fishing village in dramatic surroundings, again with fine beaches. Punta del Diablo is very rustic, popular with young people in high season, but from April to November the solitude and the dramatically lower prices make it a wonderful getaway for couples or families. Increased popularity has brought more lodging and services year round, although off-season activity is still extremely low compared to summer. **Note** there is no ATM in Punta del Diablo so bring enough cash with you. The nearest ATM is in Chuy. Municipal tourist office, open daily 0800-2200, T4477 2412. See www.portaldeldiablo.com.

Parque Nacional Santa Teresa

ⓘ *100 km from Rocha, 308 km from Montevideo, open 0700-1900 to day visitors (open 24 hrs for campers), T4477 2103 ext 209.*

This park has curving, palm-lined avenues and plantations of many exotic trees. It also contains botanical gardens, fresh-water pools for bathing and beaches which stretch for many kilometres (the surf is too rough for swimming). It is the site of the impressive colonial fortress of Santa Teresa, begun by the Portuguese in 1762 and seized by the Spanish in 1793. The fortress houses a **museum** of artefacts from the wars of independence ⓘ *Tue-Sun 0900-1900 (winter Fri-Sun 1000-1700), US$0.50*; there is a restaurant opposite, *La Posada del Viajero* (recommended). On the inland side of Route 9, the strange and gloomy Laguna Negra and the marshes of the Bañado de Santa Teresa support large numbers of wild birds. A road encircles the fortress; it's possible to drive or walk around even after closing. From there is a good view of Laguna Negra.

There are countless campsites (open all year), and a few cottages to let in the summer (usually snapped up quickly). At the *capatacia*, or administrative headquarters, campers pay US$4 pp per night. Here there are also a small supermarket and food shops, medical clinic, service station, post and telephone offices, and the *Club Santa Teresa*, where drinks and meals are available, but expensive. Practically every amenity is closed off-season. The bathing resort of **La Coronilla** is 10 km north of Santa Teresa, 20 south of Chuy; it has the **Karumbé** marine turtle center ⓘ *Ruta 9, Km 314, T099917811, www.karumbe.org, open Jan-Apr 1000-1900.* There are several hotels and restaurants, most closed in winter (tourist information T9977 7129). Montevideo-Chuy buses stop at La Coronilla.

Chuy → *Population: 10,400.*

At Chuy, 340 km from Montevideo, the Brazilian frontier runs along the main street, Avenida Internacional, which is called Avenida Brasil in Uruguay and Avenida Uruguaí in Brasil. The Uruguayan side has more services, including supermarkets, duty-free shops and a casino. Tourist office on the plaza open 0900-2200, T4474 3627, infochuy@turismorocha. gub.uy. See www.chuynet.com.

On the Uruguayan side, on a promontory overlooking Laguna Merín and the gaúcho landscape of southern Brazil, stands the restored fortress of **San Miguel** ⓘ *US$0.75, bus from Chuy US$1.50, Rutas del Sol buses from Montevideo go here after passing through Chuy,* dating from 1734 and surrounded by a moat. It is set above a 1500-ha wetland park, which is good for birdwatching and is 10 km north of Chuy along Route 19 which is the border. There is a small museum of *criollo* and *indígena* culture, displaying, among other artefacts, old carriages and presses. Not always open in low season. A fine walk from here is 2 km to the Cerro Picudo. The path starts behind the museum, very apparent. Tours (US$10 from Chuy) end for the season after 31 March.

Border with Brazil

Uruguayan passport control is 2.5 km before the border on Ruta 9 into Chuy, US$2 by taxi, 20 minutes' walk, or take a town bus; officials friendly and cooperative. Ministry of Tourism kiosk here is helpful, especially for motorists, T4474 4599. Tourists may freely cross the border in either direction as long as they do not go beyond either country's border post. Taking a car into Brazil is no problem if the car is not registered in Brazil or Uruguay.

(Uruguayan rental cars are not allowed out of the country. Although you can freely drive between Chuy and Chuí, if you break down/have an accident on the Brazilian side, car rental insurance will not cover it: park in Chuy, even if only one metre from Brazil, and walk.) From the border post, Ruta 9 bypasses the town, becoming BR-471 on the Brazilian side, leading to Brazilian immigration, also outside town. The Brazilian consulate is at Tito Fernández 147 esq Samuel Priliac, T4474 2049, Chuy, http://consbraschuy.org, open 0900-1300. For buses to Brazilian destinations, go to the rodoviária in Chuí. The bus companies that run from Chuy into Brazil ask for passports – make sure you get yours back before boarding the bus.

Entering Uruguay You need a Brazilian exit stamp and a Uruguayan entry stamp (unless visiting only Chuí), otherwise you'll be turned back at customs or other official posts. Those requiring a visa will be charged around US$80 depending on the country.

East from Montevideo listings

For hotel and restaurant price codes and other relevant information, see pages 89-90.

⊙ Where to stay

Piriápolis *p125*
Many hotels along the seafront, most close end-Feb to mid-Dec. Book in advance in high season. Many others than those listed.
$$$ pp Argentino, Rambla de los Argentinos y Armenia, T4432 2791, www. argentinohotel.com.uy. A fine hotel and landmark designed by Piria with casino, 2 restaurants, medicinal springs, sauna and good facilities for children.
$$$ Escorial, Rambla de los Argentinos 1290, T4432 2537, www.hotelescorial.com. With breakfast, a/c, minibar, safe in room, pool, parking, laundry service.
$$$ Luján, Sanabria 939, T4432 2216, www.welcomeuruguay.com/piriapolis/alojamientos.html. Simple rooms, family run, some rooms have balconies, internet, homeopathist on top floor. Not great value.
$$$-$$ Rivadavia, Rambla de los Argentinos y Trápani, T4432 2532, www. hotelrivadavia.com. Cable TV, mini-bar, Wi-Fi, restaurant, parking, open all year (much cheaper in winter).
$ pp Hostel Piriápolis, Simón del Pino 1136 y Tucumán, T4432 0394, www. hostelpiriapolis.com. Rooms for 2-4 (open all year), private rooms **$$**, 240 beds, non-HI members pay more, hot showers, cooking facilities, student cards accepted.

Camping
El Toro, Av de Mayo y Fuente de Venus, T4432 3454, doubles in bungalows, and tents. Site at Misiones y Niza, just behind bus station, T4432 3275, piriapolisfc@ adinet.com.uy, US$5.75.

Portezuelo and Punta Ballena *p125*
$$$$ Hotel-Art Las Cumbres, Ruta 12 Km 3.9, 4 km inland, T4257 8689, www. cumbres.com.uy. Themed as an artist's house-studio, on a wooded hill with great views over Laguna del Sauce and the coast, highly regarded, pool, restaurant and tea room (expensive but popular).
$$$$ Casa Pueblo, T4257 8611, www.clubhotelcasapueblo.com. Highly recommended hotel and apartments, restaurant, spa and, lower down the hill, a *parrillada*.

Camping
Punta Ballena, Km 120, Parada 45, T4257 8902, www.campinginternacional puntaballena.com. US$110 pp per night, many facilities, very clean. Also has tents for hire, US$12.50, and cabins for 4-8 people (**$$$**).

Maldonado *p126*

Hotel accommodation is scarce in summer; cheaper than Punta del Este, but you will have to commute to the beach. Basic 1-2 star places (**$$**), open all year, include: **Catedral**, Florida 830 casi 18 de Julio, T4224 2513, hotelcatedral@ adinet.com.uy, central, and **$$$-$$ Colonial**, 18 de Julio 841 y Florida, T4222 3346.
$$ Celta, Ituzaingó 839, T4223 0139. Helpful, Irish owner, No 7 bus stop outside.
$$ Isla de Gorriti, Michelini 884, T4224 5218. Nice courtyard. Recommended.

Camping
Parque El Placer, T4227 0034, free.

Punta del Este *p126, map p127*
Note Streets on the peninsula have names and numbers; lowest numbers at the tip. Hotels are plentiful but expensive: we list recommended ones only. Rates in the few hotels still open after the end of Mar are often halved. Visitors without a car have to take a hotel on the peninsula, unless they want to spend a fortune on taxis.

On the peninsula
$$$$ Conrad Hotel y Casino, Parada 4, Playa Mansa, T4249 1111, www.conrad. com.uy. Luxurious hotel with spa, concerts and events, wonderful views. Book in advance in high season.
$$$$ Remanso, C 20 y 28, T4244 7412, www.hotel remanso.com.uy. Some rooms **$$$** low season, comfortable, businesslike, pool, safe, open all year (also suites in **$$$$** range). Recommended.
$$$ Iberia, C 24, No 685, T4244 0405, www.iberiahotel.com.uy. **$$$$** in high season, breakfast included, open all year, internet and Wi-Fi area, disabled access, garage opposite.
$$$ Palace, Av Gorlero esq 11, T4222 9596, on www.reservas.net click on Punta del Este (closed in winter). 3-star. Breakfast only (expensive restaurant, *La Stampa*, in the hotel), well kept.

$$$-$$ Gaudi, C Risso, parada 1, by bus terminal, T4249 4116, www.hotelgaudi. com.uy. 2-star. Good, a/c, convenient, safe, fridge, Wi-Fi, bar, open all year.
$$$ Tánger, C 31 entre 18 y 20, T4244 1333, www.hoteltanger.com. Open all year, **$$$$** in highest season, a/c, safe, disabled access, 2 pools.
$ pp **1949 Hostel**, C 30 y 18, T4244 0719, www.1949hostel.com. 100 m from bus station. Small, 6, 8 and 10-bed dorms (ensuites available), kitchen, bar, TV and DVD, close to beaches, minimum 2 nights booking Jan-Mar.
$ pp **Punta del Este Hostel**, C 25 No 544 y 24, T4244 1632, www.puntadelestehostel. com. US$17-30 in dorm (price depends on season; no doubles), includes breakfast, lockers, central, basic.

Beaches east of Punta del Este *p127*
San Rafael (Parada 12)
$$$$ La Capilla, Viña del Mar y Valparaíso, behind San Marcos, T4248 4059, www. lacapilla.com.uy. Open all year (**$$$** in low season), includes breakfast, kitchenette in some rooms, safes in rooms, gardens, pool.
$$$$-$$$ San Marcos, Av Mar del Plata 191, T4248 2251, see page on facebook while website www.hotelsanmarcos.com is u/c. Pool (covered in winter), prices fall in mid and low season, restaurant, bicycle hire, free internet, very pleasant.
$$$$-$$$ San Rafael, Lorenzo Batlle y Pacheco, Parada 11 Brava, T4248 2161, www.hotelsan rafael.com.uy. Large hotel, open all year, a/c, heating, safe, TV, spa.

La Barra
$$$$ Hostal de la Barra, Ruta 10, Km 161.300, T4277 1521, www.hostaldelabarra. net. A small hotel, not a hostel, with sea view, forest view and loft rooms, open all year, neat, Christmas, Carnival and Semana Santa require 7 or 4-night minimum stays. In low season prices **$$$**.
$$$$ Kalá, Pedregal s/n, Altos de Montoya, T4277 3500, www.kalahotel.

com. A boutique hotel with 12 rooms, with breakfast, bars, pools and jacuzzi, bicycles and Wi-Fi.

$$$$ La Posta del Cangrejo, hotel/restaurant, Ruta 10 Km 160, T4277 0021, www.lapostadel cangrejo.com. Nice location, smart, prices reduced in low season, Wi-Fi. Recommended.

$$$$ Mantra, Ruta 10, Parada 48, T4277 1000, www.mantraresort.com. Very good and award-winning, but you will need a car to move around. Open all year, great pool, casino, restaurants, concerts, own cinema and wine bar. Recommended.

$$-$ pp Backpacker de La Barra, C 9, No 2306, 0.5 km off main road, T4277 2272, www.backpackerdelabarra.com. Youth hostel style, price depends on dates and class of room (**$$$$** in luxury double, high season), café and restaurant, internet, Wi-Fi, laundry.

Camping Camping San Rafael, Camino Aparicio Saravia, T4248 6715, www.campingsanrafael.com.uy. Good facilities, US$8.50-12.50 for 2, also has *cabañas*, Wi-Fi, bus 5 from Maldonado.

Faro José Ignacio
$$$$ Posada del Faro, C de la Bahía y Timonel, T4486 2110, www.posadadelfaro.com. Exclusive hotel overlooking the sea, 12 rooms in 4 standards, internet, pool, bar, restaurant, often quoted as the best of the new developments.

Manantiales
Resorts include: **$$$$ Las Dunas**, Ruta 10, Km 163, T4277 1211, www.lasdunas.com.uy, 5-star, opulent, and **$$$$ Las Olas**, Ruta 10, Km 162.5, T4277 0466, www.lasolasresort.com.uy, 4-star.

$ pp El Viajero Manantiales, Ruta 10, Km 164, T4277 4427, www.manantialeshostel.com. Price is for dorm; doubles **$$$** (**$$** in Apr), depends on season. HI affiliated. Swimming pool, kitchen, bikes and surfboards for rent, lockers, DVDs, laundry, Wi-Fi, bar, open Nov to Apr.

Luxury
In keeping with Punta del Este's reputation as the most sophisticated resort in the region, the area is attracting a number of luxury hotels and resorts, all **$$$$**. Chief among them are: **Fasano Las Piedras**, La Barra, http://laspiedrasfasano.com. In 480 ha on the banks of the Río Maldonado, hotel with bungalows, restaurant, private beach, golf, equestrian centre, tennis, spa. **Estancia Vik**, www.estanciavikjoseignacio.com, and **Playa Vik**, www.playavik.com, at José Ignacio, T9460 5212, two super-luxury, art-filled properties, the Estancia with a polo field, the Playa in a commanding position overlooking the sea.

La Paloma *p128*
$$$$-$$$ Palma de Mallorca, on Playa La Aguada, in nearby La Aguada, T4479 6739, www.hotelpalmademallorca.com. Right on the ocean. Discounts for longer stays, heated pool, Wi-Fi, parking.

$$$ Bahía, Av del Navío s/n, entre Solari y Del Sol, T4479 6029, www.elbahia.com.uy. Breakfast, rooms for 2-4, clean and simple, quite old-fashioned, TV, Wi-Fi, laundry, half-board available.

$$$ Embeleco, Virgen y Sol, T4479 6108. Breakfast, half price in winter, welcoming. One block from the beach.

Youth hostels $ pp Altena 5000 at Parque Andresito, T4479 6396, www.lapalomahostel.com. 50 beds, HI discounts, clean, friendly, good meals, kitchen, open all year. Also **$ pp Ibirapita**, Av Paloma s/n, 250 m from bus station, 200 m from beach, T4479 9303, www.hostelibirapita.com. Cheaper in mixed dorm and for HI members, doubles **$$**. Buffet breakfast, Wi-Fi, surf boards, bicycles.

Camping In Parque Andresito, T4479 6081, complejoandresito@adinet.com.uy. Overpriced, thatched *cabañas* for rent, from US$33 per day with maid and kitchen facilities, sleep 4-6. *Grill del Camping* for *parrillas*. **La Aguada**, T4479 9293, www.complejolaaguada.com, 1 km east of town,

300 m from beach, camping from US$7.50, also *cabañas* and a hostel. Good, each site with BBQ, tap, sink, water and electricity.

Northeast of La Paloma

At **Cabo Polonio** you cannot camp. There are posadas, some listed below, or you can rent a house; see www.cabopolonio.com or www.portaldelcabo.com.uy for all options. Water is drawn from wells (*cachimba*) and there is no electricity (some houses have generators, some gas lamps, otherwise buy candles). There are 4 shops for supplies, largest is **El Templao**. At **Aguas Dulces** there are various places to stay and lots of cheap cabins for rent.

$$$ Mariemar, Cabo Polonio, T4470 5164, 9987 5260, mariemar@cabopolonio.com. Nice owners, own electricity generator, hot water, with breakfast, restaurant, open all year. Recommended.

$$$ La Perla, Cabo Polonio, T4470 5125, www.laperladelcabo.com. Meals US$8-11. Rooms to rent; no credit cards, horse riding, visits to lighthouse, open all year.

$$-$ pp **Cabo Polonio Hostel**, T9944 5943, www.cabopoloniohostel.com. Small wooden hostel, hot showers, shared rooms, doubles available outside high season, kitchenettes, solar power, bar, good fresh food, can arrange tours and riding.

$$-$ pp **La Cañada**, about 1 km outside Cabo Polonio, T9955 0595, posadalacaniada@cabopolonio.com. Shared rooms and a few doubles, friendly, includes breakfast, small restaurant, fruit and veg from own garden.

$$-$ pp **Reserva Ecológica La Laguna**, 2 km north of Aguas Dulces, T4475 2118/9960 2410. Rustic cabins on the shore a lake, also hostel lodging, day rates for adults and children, full and half-board available, close to beach, horse riding, trekking, sailing, hydrobikes, meditation. Always phone in advance for directions and reservation.

Youth hostels At La Pedrera: **El Viajero**, 500 m from beach, T4479 2252, www.

lapedrera hostel.com. Open mid-Nov to 31 Mar, US$42-65 pp in double with bath, US$18-30 in dorm, kitchen, internet, surf classes, riding.

Camping Camping PP, Ruta 10 Km 226.5, T9715 9899, La Pedrera, www.campingpp.com.uy. US$7.50-11.50 camping, also has cabins for 2 to 6 people.

Punta del Diablo *p128*

In high season you should book in advance; www.portaldeldiablo.com gives a full list of choices.

$$$$ Aquarella, Av No 5, ½ block from beach, T4477 2400, www.hotelaquarella.com. Pool, jacuzzi, great views, a/c, Wi-Fi, gourmet restaurant.

$$$ Posada Rocamar, Calle 5 No 3302, T2477 2047, www.posadarocamar.com.uy. Doubles and family suites, tastefully decorated, outdoor patio, peaceful, excursions to Laguna Negra organized.

$$$-$$ Hostería del Pescador, on road into village, Blv Santa Teresa, T4477 2017, www.portaldel diablo.com. Rooms for 2-5, price vary for season and day of week, with breakfast, restaurant, pool.

$ pp **El Diablo Tranquilo Hostel and Bar**, Av Central, T4477 2519, www.eldiablotranquilo.com. Shared and private rooms, double suites with fireplaces (**$$$-$$**), great internet access, breakfast and cooking facilities, year round. Separate bar that is one of the nightlife hotspots. Highly recommended.

$ pp **Punta del Diablo Hostel**, Km 298, Ruta 9, T4477 2655, www.puntadeldiablohostel.com. Discounts for HI members. With kitchen, camping (US$8-10 pp), bicycles, free internet, open end-Dec to end-Feb.

Chuy *p129*

All hotels are open the year round.

$$$ Parador Fortín de San Miguel, Paraje 18 de Julio, near San Miguel fortress, T4474 6607, www.elfortin.com. Excellent, full and half-board available, colonial- style hotel.

Beautiful rooms, gym, pool, fine food and service. Highly recommended. You don't have to go through Uruguayan formalities to get there from Brazil.

$$$-$$ Nuevo Hotel Plaza, C Artigas y Av Arachanes, T4474 2309, www.hotelplaza. chuynet.com. On plaza, bath, good buffet breakfast, TV, very helpful, good, restaurant El Mesón del Plaza.

$$ Alerces, Laguna de Castillos 578, T4474 2260, alerces@adinet.com.uy. 4 blocks from border. Bath, TV, breakfast, heater, pool.

$$ Vittoria, Numancia 143, T4474 2280. Price includes breakfast, simple and clean, parking.

Camping

From Chuy buses run every 2 hrs to the Barra del Chuy campsite, Ruta 9 Km 331, turn right 13 km, T4474 9425, www.complejoturisticochuy.com. Good bathing, many birds. *Cabañas* and hostal accommodation for 2 people or more start at **$$$**, depending on amenities, camping from US$23.50 pp.

❼ Restaurants

Portezuelo and Punta Ballena *p125*
$$$ Medio y Medio, Cont Camino Lussich s/n, Punta Ballena, T4257 8791, www.medioymedio.com. Jazz club and restaurant, music nightly and good food.
$$$-$$ Las Vertientes, Camino de Los Ceibos, 2 km on the Route 9, T4266 9997. Country restaurant, fresh food which all comes from own farm, also good salads and sweets.

Maldonado *p126*
Best ice cream at **Popy's**.
$$$-$$ Lo de Rubén, Florida y Santa Teresa, T4222 3059. Parrillada, best restaurant in town, open every day.
$$$-$$ Taberna Patxi, Dodera 944, T4223 8393. Very good Basque food with authentic recipes.

Punta del Este *p126, map p127*
Many enticing ice cream parlours on Gorlero.
$$$ La Bourgogne, Pedragosa Sierra y Av del Mar, T4248 2007. Elegant French/South American cuisine, fresh ingredients, chef Jean-Paul Bondoux.
$$$ Bungalow Suizo, Av Roosevelt y Parada 8, T4248 2358. Excellent Swiss, must book.
$$$ Cantón Chino, Calle 28 y Gorlero, T4244 1316. Creative Chinese food, good.
$$$ Los Caracoles, Calle 20 y 28, T4244 0912. Excellent food (international, *parrilla*, seafood) at good prices.
$$$ El Ciclista, Calle 20 y 29, T4244 8371. Long-standing, with international cuisine, Italian, *parrilla* and seafood. Recently moved to new building.
$$$ Gure-etxe (also in La Coronilla), Calle 9 y 12, T4244 6858. Seafood and Basque cuisine.
$$$ Isidora, Rambla del Puerto, esq 21, T4244 9646, www.isidora.com.uy. Smart, by the port, international cuisine that's beautifully presented.
$$$ Juana Enea, Calle 9, No 607, T4244 7236. Restaurant and fishmonger, fresh fish, popular with locals.
$$$ Lo de Charlie, Calle 12 y 9, T4244 4183. Fish, including tuna and octopus, plus pasta and *parrilla* standards.
$$$ Lo de Tere, Rambla Artigas y 21, T4244 0492, www.lode tere.com. Good local food, open all year but closed Wed in winter, 20% discount if eating lunch before 1300 or dinner before 2100. Highly recommended.
$$$ Viejo Marino, Calle 11 entre 14 y 12, Las Palmeras, T4244 3565. Fish restaurant, busy, go early.
$$$ Virazón, Rambla Artigas y C 28, T4244 3924. Good food and great view, but expensive. Recommended.
$$$ Yatch Club Uruguayo, Rambla Artigas y 8, T4244 1056. Very good, fish, seafood, views over the port (not to be confused with the Yacht Club).
$$ Il Barreto, C 9 y 10, T4244 5565. Italian vegetarian, good value, live music some evenings, in low season open weekends only.

Beaches east of Punta del Este p127
La Barra

$$$ Baby Gouda Café, Ruta 10, Km 161, T4277 1874. Alternative food, yoga and Arab dances.

$$$-$$ Restaurant T, Ruta 10, Km 49.5, T4277 1356. Old-style, Italian and French as well as local dishes, good wine selection. Claims to be the only "real" bistro in Punta del Este.

Faro José Ignacio
$$$ La Huella, Los Cisnes on Playa Brava, T4486 2279. Excellent seafood, on beach.
$$$ Marismo, Ruta 10 Km185, T4486 2273. Romantic, outdoor tables around a fire.

Manantiales
$$$ Cactus y Pescados, Primera Bajada a Bikini, T4277 4782. Very good seafood, international menu.

La Paloma p128
$$$ La Marea, Av Solari, near tourist office. Very popular, has outstanding seafood.
$$ Arrecife, Av Principal, T4479 6837. First class, serving pizzas, *parrilla* and a good range of salads.
$$ Da Carlos, Av Solari. Moderate prices, pizzas plus Uruguayan food.

Northeast of La Paloma
In **Cabo Polonio**, there are a few restaurants, some with vegetarian options, so you don't have to bring any food with you. Fish is on the menu when the sea is calm enough for the fishermen to go out. The most expensive and fashionable is **La Puesta**, on the south beach. At weekends during the summer there are DJs, dancing and live music. For self-catering, the stores sell fruit, vegetables, meat, etc. There are several restaurants in **Castillos** including **$$$ La Strada**, 19 de Abril, and several restaurants in **Punta del Diablo**, mostly colourful huts grouped around the sea front serving excellent fish. A couple of pizza places too.

$$ Chivito Veloz, Aguas Dulces. Good, large portions for US$5.

Parque Nacional Santa Teresa p129
$$ La Ruta, La Coronilla. This small round restaurant at the entrance to town may be your only option if you are driving in the evening and off season from Chuy to Punta or Montevideo. Good meat dishes. Off season, other restaurants in Coronilla are closed.

Chuy p129
$$-$ Fusion, Av Brasil 387. Good food, not traditional Uruguayan fare. Recommended
$$-$ Restaurant Jesús, Av Brasil y L Olivera. Good value and quality.

🎵 Bars and clubs

Punta del Este p126, map p127
Hop, Rambla Artigas, T4244 6061, www. hop.com.uy. Bar and restaurant, popular drinking spot.
Moby Dick, Rambla del Puerto, T4244 1240, www.mobydick.com.uy. Mock English-style pub by the port, open until the early hours, very popular.
Ocean Club, Parada 12 de la Brava, T4248 4869, www.oceanclub.com.uy. Very fashionable and smart club playing mostly pop and house. Dress up.

⚙ What to do

Punta del Este p126, map p127
Riding Nueva Escuela de Equitación, at Cantegril Country Club, Av Saravia, T4222 0560, www.cantegrilcountryclub.com.uy. Classes, guided rides for all levels and ages.

🚌 Transport

Piriápolis p125
Road
Piriápolis may be reached either by following the very beautiful R10 from the end of the Interbalnearia, or by taking the

original access road (R37) from Pan de Azúcar, which crosses the R93. The shortest route from Piriápolis to Punta del Este is by the Camino de las Bases which runs parallel to the R37 and joins the R93 some 4 km east of the R37 junction.

Bus

Terminal on Misiones, 2 blocks from Hotel Argentino, T24141. To/from **Montevideo**, US$6, 1½ hrs. To **Punta del Este**, US$5, 50 mins. To **Maldonado**, US$4, 40 mins. For **Rocha**, **La Paloma** and **Chuy**, take bus to Pan de Azúcar and change.

Maldonado *p126*
Bus

Av Roosevelt y Sarandí. To/from **Montevideo**, US$8.65; to **Minas**, 2 hrs, 5 a day, US$5. To **San Carlos** take a local bus 3 blocks from the main bus station, US$2.

Punta del Este *p126, map p127*
Air

Direct daily Boeing 737 flights from Buenos Aires to the new Punta del Este airport during the high season. **Laguna del Sauce**, Capitán Curbelo (T4255 9777), which handles flights to Buenos Aires, 40 mins. Airport tax US$30. Exchange facilities, tax-free shopping. Regular bus service to airport from Punta del Este (will deliver to and collect from private addresses and hotels), US$5, 90 mins before departure, also connects with arriving flights. Taxi US$30-40; *remise* around US$35 depending on destination (T4244 1269). El Jagüel airport is used by private planes.

Bus

Local: Traffic is directed by a one-way system; town bus services start from C 5 (El Faro), near the lighthouse. www.puntaweb. com has details of bus routes.

Long distance: terminal at Av Gorlero, Blvd Artigas and C 32, T4248 6810 (served by local bus No 7); has toilets, newsagent, café

and Casa de Cambio. To/from **Montevideo** via Carrasco airport, COT (T4248 6810) or **Copsa** (T1975 or 2902 1818), US$9, just over 2 hrs, many in the summer; 19 a day in winter. To **Piriápolis**, US$5. To **San Carlos** (US$2) for connections to Porto Alegre, Rocha, La Paloma, Chuy. Direct to **Chuy**, 4 hrs, US$15. Local bus fare about US$0.75. For transport Montevideo-Buenos Aires, **Buquebus** T130, at bus terminal, loc 09, buses connect with ferries. Also Colonia Express.

La Paloma *p128*
Bus

Frequent to and from **Rocha**, US$2, and to and from **the capital** (5 hrs, US$14.50). 4 buses daily to **Chuy**, US$10, 3½ hrs, 2 a day to San Carlos, Pan de Azúcar and Aguas Dulces, all with Rutas del Sol. Northeast of La Paloma, some Montevideo-Chuy buses go into **Punta del Diablo**, 4 km from the main road.

To **Cabo Polonio**, Rutas del Sol from Montevideo, US$13.50, 4-5 hrs, and any of the coastal towns to Km 264, where you catch the truck to the village (see above).

Chuy *p129*
Bus

To **Montevideo** (COT, Cynsa, Rutas del Sol) US$20.65, 4¾-6 hrs, may have to change buses in San Carlos; to **Maldonado** US$9.50. International buses passing through en route from Montevideo to Brazil either stop in Chuy or at the border. Make sure the driver knows you need to stop at Uruguayan immigration. Sometimes everybody must get off for customs check. If looking for onward transport, if there is a free seat, most companies will let you pay on board.

ⓘ Directory

Piriápolis *p125*
Banks Casa de Cambio Monex, Argentinos s/n, T4432 5295.

Maldonado *p126*
Banks Cambio Bacacay, Florida 803, good rates, TCs.

Punta del Este *p126, map p127*
Airline offices Aerolíneas Argentinas, Edif Edmos Dumont, Av Gorlero, T4244 4343. **Pluna**, Av Roosevelt y Parada 9, T4249 2050/4249 0101. **Banks** Best rates of exchange from BROU, which opens earlier and closes later than the other banks and accepts MasterCard, but no TCs. Many ATMs at banks on the peninsula and at Punta Shopping (Roosevelt). Also *casas de cambio*, eg **Indumex**, Av Gorlero y 28, **Brimar**, C 31 No 610. **Car hire** Punta Car, Continuación Gorlero s/n, Hotel Playa, T4248 2112, puntacar@puntacar.com.uy. **Uno**, Gorlero y 21, T4244 5018, unonobat@movinet. com.uy. And others. See Essentials, for international agencies. **Scooter hire** US$51 per day, with drivers licence (US$50 fine if caught without it) and ID documents from

Filibusteros, Av Artigas y Parada 5, T4248 4125. They also rent out bicycles (US$3.50 per hr, US$7.50 per half day, US$10 per day, includes padlocks).

La Paloma *p128*
Useful services Bike rental from El Tobo, T4479 7881, US$3.50 a day. One bank which changes TCs; also internet, a supermarket and post office.

Chuy *p129*
Banks Several *cambios* on Av Brasil, eg **Gales**, Artigas y Brasil, Mon-Fri 0830-1200, 1330-1800, Sat 0830-1200, and in World Trade Center, open 1000-2200; on either side of Gales are Aces and Val. All give similar rates, charging US$1 plus 1% commission on TCs, US$, pesos and reais. On Sun, try the casino, or look for someone on the street outside the *cambios*. No problem spending reais in Chuy or pesos in Chuí.

Montevideo north to Brazil

Two roads run towards Melo, heart of cattle-ranching country: Route 8 and Route 7, the latter running for most of its length through the Cuchilla Grande, a range of hills with fine views. Route 8 via Minas and Treinta y Tres, is the more important of these two roads to the border and it is completely paved.

Minas and around → *Population: 39,000.*
This picturesque small town, 120 km north of Montevideo, is set in wooded hills. Juan Lavalleja, the leader of the Thirty-Three who brought independence to the country, was born here, and there is an equestrian statue to Artigas, said to be the largest such in the world, on the Cerro Artigas just out of town. The church's portico and towers, some caves in the neighbourhood and the countryside are worth seeing. Good confectionery is made in Minas; you can visit the largest firm, opposite Hotel Verdun. Banks are open 1300-1700 Monday-Friday. There is a tourist office at the bus station. See www.lavalleja.gub.uy.

The Parque Salus, on the slopes of Sierras de las Animas, is 8 km to the south and very attractive; take the town bus marked 'Cervecería Salus' from plaza to the Salus brewery, then walk 2 km to the mineral spring and bottling plant (**$$$ Parador Salus**, T4443 1652, paradorsalus@ dedicado.net.uy, good). It is a lovely three-hour walk back to Minas from the springs. The Cascada de Agua del Penitente waterfall, 11 km east off Route 8, is interesting and you may see wild rheas nearby. It's hard to get to off season. The Minas area is popular for mountain biking.

To the Brazilian border

Route 8 continues north via **Treinta y Tres** (*population: 31,000*) to Melo (also reached by Route 7), near Aceguá close to the border. In **Melo** (*population: 51,500*), there are places to stay and exchange rates are usually better than at the frontier. If crossing to Brazil here, Brazilian immigration is at Bagé, not at the border. At 12 km southeast of Melo is the Posta del Chuy (2 km off Route 26). This house, bridge and toll gate (built 1851) was once the only safe crossing place on the main road between Uruguay and Brazil. It displays gaucho paintings and historical artefacts.

Río Branco was founded in 1914, on the Río Yaguarón. The 1 km-long Mauá bridge across the river leads to Jaguarão in Brazil. The Brazilian vice-consulate in Río Branco is at Ismael Velázquez 1239 (T4675 2003, bravcrb@gmail.com, Mon-Fri 0800-1400). For road traffic, the frontier at Chuy is better than Río Branco or Aceguá. There is a toll 68 km north of Montevideo.

An alternative route to Brazil is via Route 5, the 509-km road from Montevideo to the border town of Rivera, which runs almost due north, bypassing Canelones and Florida before passing through Durazno. After crossing the Río Negro, it goes to Tacuarembó. South of the Río Negro is gently rolling cattle country, vineyards, orchards, orange, lemon and olive groves. North is hilly countryside with steep river valleys and cattle ranching. The road is dual carriageway as far as Canelones.

East of Florida, Route 56 traverses the countryside eastwards to **Cerro Colorado**, also known as Alejandro Gallinal, which has an unusual clock tower.

Durazno → Population: 30,700.

On the Río Yí 182 km from Montevideo, Durazno is a friendly provincial town with tree-lined avenues and an airport. There is a good view of the river from the western bridge. See www.imdurazno.com.uy.

Dams on the Río Negro have created an extensive network of lakes near **Paso de los Toros** (population: 15,000; 66 km north of Durazno, bus from Montevideo US$15.50), with camping and sports facilities. Some 43 km north of Paso de los Toros a 55-km road turns east to **San Gregorio de Polanco**, at the eastern end of Lago Rincón del Bonete. The beach by the lake is excellent, with opportunities for boat trips, horse riding and other sports.

Tacuarembó → Population: 51,000.

This is an agro-industrial town and major route centre 390 km north of Montevideo. The nearby Valle Edén has good walking possibilities. Some 23 km west of Tacuarembó, along Route 26, is the **Carlos Gardel Museum** ① *US$1, daily 0900-1800*, a shrine to the great tango singer who was killed in an air crash in Medellín (Colombia). Uruguay, Argentina and France all claim him as a national son. The argument for his birth near here is convincing.

Brazilian border

Rivera (*Population: 64,430*) is divided by a street from the Brazilian town of Santa Ana do Livramento. Points of interest are the park, the Plaza Internacional, and the dam of Cañapirú. Uruguayan immigration is at the end of Calle Sarandí y Presidente Viera, 14 blocks, 2 km, from the border (take bus along Agraciada or taxi from bus terminal for around US$1.50). There is also a tourist office here, T4622 5899. Luggage is inspected when boarding buses out of Rivera; there are also three checkpoints on the road out of town. The Brazilian consulate is at Ceballos 1159, T4622 4470, consbrasrivera@adinet.com.uy. Remember that you must have a Uruguayan exit stamp to enter Brazil and a Brazilian exit stamp to enter Uruguay.

Montevideo north to Brazil listings

For hotel and restaurant price codes and other relevant information, see pages 89-90.

🛏 Where to stay

Minas *p137*
$$ Posada Verdun, W Beltrán 715, T4422 4563, hverdun@adinet.com.uy. Good, breakfast extra (**Confitería Nuevo Sabor** nearby serves good food).
$ Hostel de Villa Serrana, C Molle s/n off Route 8, Km 145, in Villa Serrana, T9922 6911. Oldest hostel in Uruguay. Open all year, 28 km beyond Minas on road to Treinta y Tres. Thatched house, HI affiliated, kitchen for members, horses for hire, basic, take plenty of food and drink (no shop). Direct bus from Montevideo to Treinta y Tres or Melo, ask to be set down at Km 145 and walk 2 km to Villa Serrana. Or take bus to Minas from Montevideo or Punta del Este then **Cosu** bus Tue, Thu 0900, 1730 to Villa Serrana.

Camping
Arequita, Camino Valeriano Magri, T4440 2503, beautiful surroundings, cabañas (for two people with shared bathroom US$17.50), camping US$4.50 each.

Tourism farm
$$$ Posada El Abra, Puntas de Santa Lucía, 25 km from Minas, T4440 2869, elabra@adinet.com.uy. Small estancia in hills at Río Santa Lucía headwaters, full board, includes transport, guides, horses for riding, good walking, swimming in river, expansive views.

To the Brazilian border *p138*
Treinta y Tres
$$-$ La Posada, Manuel Freire 1564, T4452 1107, www.hotellaposada33.com. With breakfast, Wi-Fi, good overnight stop.
$ pp Cañada del Brujo, Km 307.5, Ruta 8, Sierra del Yerbal, 34 km north of Treinta

y Tres, T4452 2837, T9929 7448, www.pleka.com/delbrujo/. Isolated hostel, no electricity, basic but "fantastic", dorm, local food, meals extra, owner Pablo Rado drives you there (US$15), cycling, trekking on foot or horseback, trips to Quebrada de los Cuervos. Recommended.

Melo
$$ Virrey Pedro de Melo, J Muñiz 727, T4642 2673, www.hotelvirreypedrodemelo.com. Better rooms in new part, 3-star, TV, minibar, Wi-Fi, café.

Cerro Colorado
$$$$ San Pedro de Timote, Km 142, R7, 14 km west of Cerro Colorado, T4310 8086, www.sanpedrodetimote.com. A famous colonial-style estancia, working ranch, landscaped park, 3 pools, cinema, gym, horse riding, good restaurant.
$$$ Arteaga, 7 km off R7 north of Cerro Colorado, T2707 4766, arteaga@paradaarteaga.com. Typical European estancia, famous, beautiful interior, pool.

Durazno *p138*
There are a few hotels (**$$-$**).
Camping At 33 Orientales, in park of same name by river, T4362 2806, nice beach, hot showers, toilets, laundry sinks.
Tourism Farm Estancia Albergue El Silencio, Ruta 14 Km 166, 10 km west of Durazno, T4362 2014 (or T4360 2270, HI member), www.estancia elsilencio.net. About 15 mins walk east of bridge over Río Yí where bus stops, clean rooms, friendly, riding, swimming, birdwatching. Recommended.

Paso de los Toros
$$-$ Sayonara, Sarandí y Barreto, T4664 2535/2743. 2 blocks from centre, renovated old residence, rooms with bath, a/c and cable TV. Breakfast extra.

San Gregorio de Polanco
$$ Posada Buena Vista, De Las
Pitangueras 12, T4369 4841. Overlooking
lake, breakfast extra, Wi-Fi, a/c, snack bar,
good, prices rise Dec-Easter.

Tacuarembó *p138*
$$$ Carlos Gardel, Ruta 5 Km 388,500,
T4633 0306, www.hotelcarlosgardel.
com.uy. Internet, pool, restaurant and
meeting room.
$$$ Tacuarembó, 18 de Julio 133, T4632
2105, www.tacuarembohotel.com.uy.
Breakfast, central, TV, Wi-Fi, safe, restaurant,
pool, parking.
$$ Central, Gral Flores 300, T4632 2841.
Cable TV, ensuite bathrooms, rooms with or
without a/c, laundry service.
$$ pp Panagea, 1 hr from Tacuarembó,
T9983 6149, http://panagea-uruguay.
blogspot. com. Estancia and backpackers'
hostel, working cattle and sheep farm,
home cooking, lots of riding, electricity
till 2200 is only concession to modern
amenities, many languages spoken.

Camping
Campsites 1 km out of town in the Parque
Laguna de las Lavanderas, T4632 4761, and
7 km north on R26 at Balneario Iporá.

Brazilian border: Rivera *p138*
$$$ Uruguay Brasil, Sarandí 440, T4622
3068, www.hoteluruguaybrasil.com.uy.
Buffet breakfast, a/c, TV, minibar, Wi-Fi area,
laundry service, restaurant.
$$$-$$ Casablanca, Agraciada 479, T4622
3221, www.casablanca.com.uy. A/c, TV,
breakfast, comfortable, pleasant.
Camping Municipal site near AFE station,
and in the Parque Gran Bretaña 7 km south
along R27.

🍴 Restaurants

Minas *p137*
Restaurants include **Complejo San
Francisco de las Sierras**, Ruta 12 Km
347,500 (4 km from Minas); **Ki-Joia**, Diego
Pérez in front of Plaza Libertad.
Irisarri, C Treinta y Tres 618. Best pastry
shop, *yemas* (egg candy) and *damasquitos*
(apricot sweets).

Tacuarembó *p138*
Parrilla La Rueda, W Beltrán 251. Good.

⊖ Transport

Minas *p137*
Bus
To **Montevideo**, US$8.50, several
companies, 2 hrs. To **Maldonado**, US$5, 7
a day, 1½ hrs (COOM).

To the Brazilian border: Melo *p138*
Bus
To **Montevideo** US$24, 5 hrs (Núñez,
Turismar). Several buses daily to Río Branco.

Durazno *p138*
Bus
To **Montevideo** US$11, 2½ hrs.

Tacuarembó *p138*
Bus
From **Montevideo**, US$23.65, 4-5 hrs.

Brazilian border: Rivera *p138*
Bus
Terminal at Uruguay y Viera (1.5 km from the
terminal in Santa Ana). To/from **Montevideo**,
US$30, 5½-6¾ hrs (**Agencia Central, Turil,
Núñez**). To **Paysandú, Copay**, T4622 3733,
at 0400, 1600, US$20. To **Tacuarembó**, US$6
(**Núñez, Turil**), no connections for Paysandú.
To **Salto**, Mon and Fri 1630, 6 hrs, US$23. For
Artigas, take bus from Livramento to Quaraí,
then cross bridge.

Contents

Footnotes

Index → *Entries in bold refer to maps.*